Crisis
Communication

Crisis

Communication
THEORY AND PRACTICE

Alan Jay Zaremba

M.E.Sharpe
Armonk, New York
London, England

Library of Congress Cataloging-in-Publication Data

Zaremba, Alan Jay.
   Crisis communication : theory and practice / Alan Jay Zaremba.
       p. cm.
   ISBN 978-0-7656-2051-4 (cloth : alk. paper) — ISBN 978-0-7656-2052-1 (pbk. : alk. paper)
   1. Communication in organizations. 2. Crisis management. I. Title.
   HD30.3.Z3694 2009
   658.4'5—dc22   2009019485

Printed in the United States of America

The paper used in this publication meets the minimum requirements of
American National Standard for Information Sciences
Permanence of Paper for Printed Library Materials,
ANSI Z 39.48-1984.

∞

IBT (c)   10   9   8   7   6   5   4   3   2   1
IBT (p)   10   9   8   7   6   5   4

Dedication and Acknowledgments

DEDICATION

A theme in this book is that an organization under duress would be wise to act and communicate responsibly, to do the right thing. Crises can derail organizations and cause them to teeter. In the throes of a skid, organizations sometimes do the wrong thing in a shortsighted attempt to gain firm ground. Such behavior is counterproductive. Not only does it exacerbate the crisis, but the effects of doing the wrong thing bruises the organization and creates impediments for future generations of organizational executives and employees.

When my mother was three, her father perished in a work-related accident. She endured an emotional and financial crisis. She could have assumed a life of victimization or abandoned her moral compass for an enticing expedient one that pointed in the wrong direction. But she did not and never lost her way. It is appropriate then for this book to be dedicated to my mother, Helen Zaremba. I am a direct beneficiary of her strength.

ACKNOWLEDGMENTS

I am grateful to a number of people for their help with this book. Lynn Taylor was my initial contact at M.E. Sharpe. She was encouraging when I proposed the book, supportive as we took the necessary preliminary steps before contracting, and very professional as my developmental editor once the writing process began. Lynn was accessible, kind, and responsive to my inquiries throughout. She made suggestions, provided feedback, and in general helped make this book as good as it could be. Katie Corasaniti worked with me once the manuscript was submitted and was always conscientious, meticulous, and caring as we prepared the manuscript for production.

Also, I am happy to have worked with Stacey Victor who served as production editor for the project. Anyone who has published a book knows that once the manuscript has been submitted, there are several necessary production stages that must be completed before the book goes out for printing and publication. These production steps are time consuming and laborious both for an author and for the production editor. I am grateful to Stacey for her work as we moved toward publication. I am indebted to the many practitioners who gave up their time to be interviewed for the practitioner perspective feature of this book. Specifically I want to thank Ed Klotzbier, Caroline Sapier, Julie Hall, Vincent Loporchio, Joe Lukas, Sue Phillips, Steve Frankel, and Alan Barocas. In addition, a special thanks to Laura Ross, Jim Golden, and Craig Ingraham for putting me in touch with people who would be appropriate for this feature.

I am grateful for the support of friends, colleagues and family who asked me about the project, listened patiently when I discussed it in far more detail, no doubt, than they were especially interested, but nevertheless encouraged me. Specific thanks to friends Patricia Campbell, Ken Turow, Ken Baltin, Margie Glazer, Helen Goodman, Cheryl Chandler, and Marcia and Ken Weiss. At Northeastern thanks to Tom Sheahan, Carl Zangerl, Erica Haagenson, Kristin Mullaney, Mark Gould, Tom Nakayama, Murray Forman, Greg Goodale, Kumi Silva, Susan Picillo, Carey Noland, David Monje, Todd Leach, Nicole Maurantonio, and Craig Robertson who may have forgotten, but at one time or another asked me about the writing of this book, offered their encouragement, and wished me well as I worked on this project.

I have written in the prefaces to my other books that I imagine there is not much that is more difficult than living with an author who has a deadline. That remark is still apt. My dear companion, Donna Glick, has been patient with me when I have been irritable, an editor when I needed another set of eyes, and supportive when it must have been trying to do so. I am grateful as always for her insights, understanding, and love.

I am beyond fortunate to have been born to loving parents, and the brother of a brilliant and compassionate sibling. I have been, am, and always will be aware of these blessings.

There are likely others who have helped me with this book that I've forgotten to name. For all those who have participated either with insights or just emotional support, thank you for contributing to this product.

Contents

Crisis
Communication

1 Foundations for Crisis Communication

Chapter in a Nutshell

Crises happen. Organizations that are exceptionally profitable and well managed can encounter sudden problems that may stagger their enterprise. When crises occur, organizations are compelled to communicate to various audiences. The quality of these communications is crucial for the success of the organization. Sloppy communication during crises can plague an organization right out of existence. Effective communication during these times can transform potential disasters into positive situations for a company. There are a number of foundational planks upon which an understanding of crisis communication rests. This chapter discusses these foundations. In addition, the chapter explains the structure of the book and the features of each chapter.

Specifically, at the end of this chapter, readers will be able to

- Identify *five* fundamental principles for effective crisis communications.
- Explain the relevance of these principles to organizations and organizational health.

SWEET SIXTEEN

- On March 10, 2008, the *New York Times* published an article that rocked Albany, New York. Soon the rest of the country was similarly stunned. Elliot Spitzer the governor of the state of New York had run for office on a reform platform dedicated to ethical accountability and pledged to purge scandal from government and elsewhere. When Spitzer served as attorney general of New York in the 1990s he had vowed similarly to bring an end to corruption. On this March day in 2008, however, news stories suggested that Spitzer had been involved in activities that many people would consider very corrupt. Spitzer, it seemed, had spent thousands of dollars visiting a brothel in Washington D.C. It was not clear on this March day whether the moneys spent on these indulgences were from taxpayer dollars.

- On July 1, 2002, officials at America West were dumbfounded and dazed by the news that two of their pilots were detained at the Miami airport. The pilots had been scheduled to fly 124 passengers across the country to Phoenix, Arizona. However, security personnel thought these pilots might be inebriated. The aircraft was taxiing on the runway, when it was called back. The pilots were pulled off the plane and examined. Both failed Breathalyzer tests. America West's image, of course, was damaged. The company was embarrassed. Subsequently, the airline was humiliated further when it was revealed that at least one of the pilots had a history of alcohol abuse.

- Virginia Tech University and all of its students, staff, alumni, and faculty were devastated on April 16, 2006, when a lunatic maniacally and indiscriminately killed students and professors on the Blacksburg, Virginia campus. In the early hours of that horrible day the deranged killer, a student himself, had shot students in a dormitory. The killer then returned to his own room. Two hours later he burst into several classrooms murdering professors, more students, and then himself. Subsequently, the university was chastised by a review board for "failing to take action that might have reduced the number of casualties, failing to take note of certain 'red flags.'" [1] The shooter had a history of psychological problems and had previously been asked to leave a class because of inappropriate behavior.

- On January 19, 2004, Howard Dean, a presidential aspirant, reacted wildly, almost maniacally, to his loss in the Iowa caucuses. Dean appeared to be just a notch short of crazed as he asserted how he would fight on, sounding less like a resilient campaigner and more like a distraught, dispirited, if not demented loser. Dean's rant was captured on television and played regularly on news reports. The videotape portrayed the candidate as someone who had less than the requisite equanimity to lead a nation. Once the front-runner in the primaries, Dean subsequently had to battle a tarnished image because of what became known as the "Dean Scream." Eventually, Dean's candidacy lost traction, and John Kerry became the Democratic candidate for president.

- Reebok, a company that prides itself on innovation and cutting-edge chic, named a new brand of sneaker the *Incubus.* This was a bewildering name choice. The word "incubus" has sexual connotations with which Reebok, one assumes, would prefer not to be associated. An incubus, by definition, is a ghost that has unsolicited intimate relations with a woman while she is asleep. Reebok claimed to be unaware of the meaning of the word when it was chosen as the name for the shoe. This claim made audiences wonder about the intelligence, internal communication structure, and/or credibility of the company.

- Hurricane Katrina blasted into New Orleans, Louisiana on August 29, 2005, nearly destroying the city. Residents were forced either to race away from nearly everything they owned or stay and risk their lives as the deluge literally swamped their homes and neighborhoods. Property was destroyed, families separated, children went hungry, and complaints were earsplitting as leaders in New Orleans became incensed at what was perceived to be a slow response from the federal government. Close to 2,000 people perished because of Katrina-related damage.

- Kobe Bryant, a basketball player for the Los Angeles Lakers, was accused of raping a woman he met while attending a conference in Aspen, Colorado. Bryant contended that the 2004 encounter was consensual and pleaded not guilty to the charges, but the accusations lingered and the idea that Bryant had behaved inappropriately gained international attention. Eventually the case ended with a settlement, but Bryant's image was affected well beyond the monetary damage resulting from a loss in endorsements from McDonald's and other companies. There were those who contended that the National Basketball Association and the Los Angeles Lakers had also taken a hit in terms of prestige.

- On December 5, 2002, at the hundredth birthday celebration for retiring Senator Strom Thurmond, Senator Trent Lott of Mississippi made a comment that created a firestorm. In 1948, Thurmond had been the presidential nominee of the Dixiecrat party. In 1948, the Dixiecrats had broken away from the Democrats to run on a segregation platform. At the ceremony for Thurmond, Lott reminded all that the state of Mississippi had voted for the Dixiecrat candidate in 1948. Lott commented, "We're proud of it. And if the rest of the country had followed our lead, we wouldn't have had all these problems over all these years, either."[2] After the ceremony, Lott was chastised for what appeared to be a clearly racist remark. Ironically, six months later when Thurmond passed away, a woman named Essie Mae Washington-Williams surfaced. Soon it was revealed that Washington-Williams was Thurmond's illegitimate African-American daughter. Thurmond, a staunch segregationist during his political career, never acknowledged Washington-Williams when he was alive, but supported her financially throughout his life.

• On Valentine's Day 2008, JetBlue, an airline that had become the darling of the low-cost flight industry, experienced disaster when a snowstorm forced excruciating delays. As planes sat on the runway for several hours, passengers awaiting takeoff were trapped unable to use toilet facilities as they stewed on board, essentially imprisoned on the stuck vessel. The national press that reported the incident was excoriating in its criticism. JetBlue employees began to refer to the event as 2/14 in the same way that Americans would refer to the bin Laden attacks as 9/11. For JetBlue the experience was, as the CEO subsequently said, "pretty humiliating."[3]

• The five-week period beginning on Monday September 15, 2008, is one that investment giants such as Fidelity Investments in Boston are unlikely to forget. Rumors had started the weekend before that two venerable financial institutions, Lehman Brothers and Merrill Lynch, would soon declare bankruptcy. When these fears were realized on that Monday and concomitant concerns rocked Wall Street, the stock market plummeted 500 points. On Tuesday September 16, the market went down another 400. On September 29, the market went down a record 777 points. Throughout the first three weeks in October the stock market bobbed up and plunged down creating enormous anxiety. Investors in companies like Fidelity became worried about the security of their funds. Fidelity was NOT a company in jeopardy like Lehman, but many customers were nervous nonetheless. Would Fidelity go down too? Were investments safe? Billions of dollars were withdrawn from companies like Fidelity to be placed in banks where, ostensibly, money would be more secure.

• Food Lion, a grocery-store chain, was mortified after an ABC segment on *Primetime Live* suggested that the company employed unsanitary practices in its preparation of products. The program that aired on November 5, 1992, suggested that the company not only sold products that had been tainted, it deliberately attempted to mask the flaws in the foods to be able to sell the products as if they were not damaged. Not only was Food Lion's image tarnished, but the ABC network's behavior was also called into question. The network was accused of employing unethical journalistic techniques to gather information about Food Lion. Both the object of the investigation, Food Lion, and the journalists/network describing the offense were tainted by the allegations.

• Procter and Gamble, a company located in Cincinnati, Ohio, was hounded for years by rumors that it was somehow engaged in devil worship. A logo on the bottom of its products was misinterpreted as suggesting a relationship between the company and Satan. This defamatory (and wholly inaccurate) information was nevertheless promulgated, which forced the company to react to the rumor.

- Shortly after the 2008 summer Olympics, Michael Phelps, a swimming champion, was pictured on the cover of *Sports Illustrated* magazine with his record-breaking eight Olympic gold medals draped around his neck. By February 2009, Phelps had secured endorsement contracts from several companies to help peddle their products and sweeten the swimmer's personal treasury. It was therefore calamitous for both Phelps and these companies when a British tabloid, *News of the World,* published a photograph of Phelps at a party. The photo captured the eight-time gold medalist smoking marijuana from a bong pipe. The picture, which appeared in early 2009, was taken in November 2008, a few months after the Olympics and Olympian achievements.[4] Phelps was able to retain his endorsement contract with Subway, the sandwich chain, but lost contracts with other organizations.

- John Lakian, a candidate for the Republican nomination for governor in Massachusetts, was stunned on August 18, 1982, when the *Boston Globe* ran a story exposing dozens of falsehoods that apparently appeared in Lakian's campaign literature. Among other things, the candidate was accused of lying about his educational background, military experience, and parents' history. His literature, for example, claimed that he studied at Harvard University located in Cambridge, Massachusetts. The *Boston Globe* article reported that Lakian actually only took a few classes at the Cambridge Adult Education Center. Lakian had been clearly ahead in the primary race when the article appeared. His nomination hopes plummeted after August 18. Eventually, he did not receive his party's nomination.

- Rupert Murdoch, the media mogul, who owns among other newspapers the *New York Post,* issued an apology on February 24, 2009. In that day's issue of the paper Murdoch wrote that he wanted to "personally apologize to any reader who felt offended and even insulted." The issue in question was a cartoon that appeared in the *Post* on February 18, which, allegedly, was intended to criticize President Barack Obama's economic stimulus package. The cartoon drew outraged responses from readers because it compared the author of the legislation to a chimpanzee—an age-old disparaging reference to African-Americans. A few days earlier a chimpanzee that had mauled a woman in Connecticut had been put to death.

- The city of Boston and the state of Massachusetts were already embarrassed by the failure of what was called "The Big Dig" to stay within its budget. The overexpenditures were enormous. Tales of poor management, frivolous spending, and shoddy work had become part of the urban legend not only in Boston but throughout the world. The Big Dig had become grist for monologue ridicule on the Letterman and Leno programs. Everyone seemed to have a Big Dig story. So the horrible news on July 10, 2006, created an even greater headache than it otherwise would have. On that night a large part of a tunnel's ceiling dropped and crushed a car traveling through the tunnel. Milena Del Valle, a mother of three, was crushed to death.

These events have three things in common.

1. They represented a crisis for an organization or an individual representing an organization.

2. The events negatively affected the image the organizations and the individuals had enjoyed with their various publics.
3. The incidents compelled organizations to communicate effectively with their various audiences in order to restore the images damaged by the crises.

This book is about communicating during such crises. Crisis communication involves planning for crises and responding to various audiences under what sometimes can be severe pressure. The chapters that follow describe the underlying theories that pertain to crisis communication and the practices that can be utilized by those who are compelled to communicate during times of crisis.

PRACTICE AND SIMULATIONS

Studying relevant theories and principles is a necessary step for those preparing to be crisis communicators. However, effective crisis communication also requires practice and simulation. Like many activities, knowing *how to do* something is not sufficient even for those who have the requisite skills. Crisis communicators and students of crisis communication should be able to demonstrate that they can actually do what it is that they describe how to do.

Therefore, simulating events and practicing communicating during pressured situations is an important dimension of crisis communication preparation. Throughout the book you will find exercises that challenge you to consider how you would communicate during crises and challenge you to demonstrate your skill in these simulated situations.

The first of these exercises appears below.

Apply the Principles

You have just read brief descriptions of several crises. Assume you represent the organization or person/s affected by these crises. How would you proceed? For each of the scenarios take the following steps.

1. Identify the two most important audiences. In other words, whom must you contact because of the crisis that has occurred? Which two groups are most significant?

   For example, consider the initial scenario regarding former New York State governor Elliot Spitzer. Beyond his immediate family, who are Spitzer's most important audiences? Would they be:

   - The citizens of the state of New York?
   - Members of the Democratic National Committee?
   - The other forty-nine governors in the United States?
   - Members of his staff?
   - Albany news media?
   - The author of the *New York Times* article?
   - The national networks?
   - The people who control the Web site for the State of New York?
   - His lieutenant governor?
   - Some other group?

   Which of these would be Elliot Spitzer's two most significant audiences?

2. Write down the single most important message you would need to communicate to each of these audiences.

    Again, consider the Spitzer case. Review the audiences you identified in (1). What is the most important message Spitzer needs to relay to each of the audiences? Should it be:

- An apology?
- A statement regarding his devotion to his family despite this incident?
- An expression of embarrassment?
- A minimization of the offense?
- An enumeration of his accomplishments while governor?
- A distinction between his offense and more egregious errors of other public officials?
- A request for forgiveness?
- A denial of the charges?
- An implicit or explicit threat to any person or media source that discredits him?
- A claim that like all Americans he is innocent until proven guilty?
- Some other message?
- Some combination of messages?

3. Determine what method or methods you would employ to relay these messages.

    In the previous two parts you have determined with *whom* you need to communicate and *what* you wish to communicate. Now consider *how* you will communicate the messages. For each message you have identified in Step 2 that you desire to relay to each audience you identified in Step 1 determine whether Spitzer should:

- Post the message on a Web site?
- Make personal phone calls?
- Express the message in a blog?
- Send a letter to each member of a particular audience?
- Call a press conference and make a statement?
- Take out an advertisement in the *New York Times?*
- Ask *60 Minutes* for an interview?
- Hold "town meetings" each day for a week in New York, Buffalo, Syracuse, Rochester, and Albany?
- Have a spokesperson deliver the message in a televised address?
- Make a speech before the New York State Assembly?
- Some other method?
- Some combination of approaches?

After you have completed the Spitzer case, perform the same three steps for each of the minicases in the sweet sixteen. When you have completed this exercise you will begin to have an understanding of what crisis communicators do—and some of the challenges of effective crisis communication.

FOUNDATIONAL PLANKS

Robert Fulghum published a very popular collection of essays in the mid-1980s, which he titled *All I Really Need to Know I Learned in Kindergarten.* It was an engaging read, so much so that the book is still in print, over twenty years after its initial publication. It has sold over 6 million copies, as much, I believe, for the way the title resonated with consumers as for any specific nuggets found in the essays.

Fulghum's implicit argument is as simple as any of the kindergarten lessons. The basics and basis for life's challenges and complexities are explained to us as children when we learn fundamental truths about how to behave and interact with others. If these truths become embedded in our consciousness, then when confronted, if not overwhelmed, with what appear to be complex problems, we can use these kindergarten lessons as a compass that will guide our behavior and decision making.

One might argue that all you need to know about crisis communication can be similarly distilled. At the conclusion of this book you will be familiar with cases, research studies, and recommendations from scholars and practitioners who work in the area of crisis communication. It is important to examine these cases, studies, and counsel because crises *are* multifaceted. Appropriate communications in preparation for and response to crises *do* require a nuanced understanding of principles. However, this nuanced awareness is founded on incontrovertible and essential tenets. Fulghum argues that all we need to know is what we learn when we are children, not because there isn't more sophisticated knowledge to process, but because without fundamental understandings we can never really be in a position—or sufficiently "grounded" to use the contemporary metaphor—to process additional information and act appropriately. Internalizing fundamental principles creates the foundation that facilitates the defaulting to effective decision making.

While I hope you will read the rest of the book to gain an informed and comprehensive understanding of crisis communication, one could make an argument that the fundamental principles described below—just like our kindergarten lessons—are all that an intelligent person really needs to know in order to address crises. We will return to some of these principles throughout the text for emphasis and elaboration, and as they relate to case analyses. But as a foundation appropriate for an introductory chapter, and as a stepping-off point, consider these five immutable truths about crisis communication activity.

1. CRISES ARE INEVITABLE. CRISIS COMMUNICATORS CAN AND MUST ACKNOWLEDGE THE INEVITABILITY OF CRISES AND PLAN FOR THEM BEFORE THEY OCCUR

It is surprising to me how often I meet MBA students who tell me that their company does not have a crisis communication plan because the nature of their work renders crisis planning unnecessary. Regardless of the nature of your work, at some point your organization or you will face a crisis. In some industries the chances of facing a crisis might be greater than in others. However, all organizations can and will experience a crisis.

Some people think of crises as events that affect large organizations such as fuel companies, airlines, or large nonprofits. But every organization no matter how large or small will face crises and has to plan for that eventuality. A grocery store may sell tainted goods, a stationery franchisee may be faced with screaming protestors because the paper is not "green" enough, a local sportscaster may inadvertently utter a word that is considered offensive to a large number of listeners, a mild-mannered educator may be accused of plagiarizing an article, a chain of hairstyling companies may be exposed for hiring illegal immigrants. Any organization one might consider can have a crisis that requires planning.

In his book, *You'd Better Have a Hose If You Want to Put Out the Fire,* Rene Henry writes, "Any CEO who believes he or she is immune from a crisis is most vulnerable. . . . Even the church and Mickey Mouse have been under attack."[5] Steve Wilson, another practitioner, titles the first chapter of his crisis communication book "Never Say Never."[6] Dr. Alan Friedman is quoted making the same point in the introduction to the book *Crisis in Organizations:* "We need to get people to understand that in our society, it's not a question of if a crisis will occur during your career, it's when."[7]

Given this reality, all organizations need to take proactive steps to prepare for these inevitabilities. In Chapter 4, we discuss what proactive steps an organization should take, but as a sturdy foundational plank, organizational women and men must internalize the reality that all companies are susceptible and need to plan for the inevitable. Indeed, one book about crisis communication is subtitled, *Planning for the Inevitable.*[8]

It may seem impossible to plan for this kind of inevitability. How can you prepare for something that is likely to have unique characteristics? As we will see, crisis communicators can indeed plan to communicate for crises before they occur.

In sum, since crises are inevitable, communication during crises can affect the health of an organization, and planning for crises can affect the quality of communication during the crisis, it is imperative that organizations and crisis communicators prepare for them.

2. In case after case, transparent and honest communication has been proven to be a key to effective crisis communication

For pragmatic as well as moral reasons, an organization is compelled to be honest when communicating with its stakeholders. Dishonesty in the form of deliberate omissions, deception, and strategic ambiguity are not only inappropriate from an ethical point of view. In multiple cases, duplicity has been shown to undermine, not support, the crisis communication effort.

Readers who complete this book will discover many instances when a company's immediate reaction to crisis was to attempt to deny, cover up, or otherwise not be transparent with its audiences. Over and over, readers will see how these attempts—regardless of ethical considerations—simply did not work. Evasive responses, disingenuous communications, ambiguous responses, may have short-term positive effects, but may well have long-term negative effects. Whether the case is political like the Watergate break in, related to airplane or space travel like the horrific disasters of the Challenger and Columbia, medical like Dow Corning's crisis with its breast implants, industrial like Union Carbide's Bhopal crisis, or based on a natural disaster such as Hurricane Katrina—regardless of the nature of the crisis, the results repeatedly point to the pragmatic wisdom of transparency.

Consider a comment by P.M. Kearns in the practitioner journal *Communication World,* "Remember the ripple effect. A disappointed or disgruntled public has a long memory. Just as the concentric circles go outward, vast waves of potential customers and allies can, and will, go out of their way to boycott the companies who they perceive are not open and caring. They'll patronize and recommend the ones who are."[9]

3. When in doubt follow a golden-rule approach

This third principle is related to the prior one. Phillip Tompkins is a well-known scholar in the field of organizational communication and has written two books examining crisis communication incidents related to NASA and the Marshall Space Flight Center in Huntsville, Alabama. The aforementioned Steve Wilson is a practitioner whose book, *Real People, Real Crises,* discusses crisis communication from the perspective of a "real world" consultant. Both of these writers independently discuss the wisdom of what each calls a golden rule approach to crisis communication.

The golden rule approach as it relates to crisis communication is simple. When communicating with audiences ask yourself these questions:

If you were a member of the particular audience

    a. What would you want to know?
    b. What would you need to know?
    c. How would you want the messages communicated to you?
    d. What channels would need to be available to you if you had further questions or comments about the crisis?

The Schwan Food Company crisis will be discussed in more detail in Chapter 5, but it is appropriate here to explain the following. The Schwan Food Company faced a crisis when its food products became tainted and consumers of its products became ill. As you will see, the Schwan Food Company, as it turned out, was not really responsible for the problem. The problem cost them a good deal of money, but they could have—with some legitimacy—claimed not to be liable or responsible. Nevertheless, Alfred Schwan, the head of the company, demanded that all of his employees follow a single guiding rule in all of its communications related to the crisis. He told his employees to ask themselves this one question and make all decisions based on it. "If you were a Schwan customer, what would you expect the company to do?" Schwan took a golden rule approach and as the scholar Tompkins, the practitioner Wilson, and nearly every other author on this topic has suggested, a golden rule approach is a fundamentally wise one when communicating during a crisis.

4. AN ORGANIZATION'S CULTURE CAN DETERMINE CRISIS COMMUNICATION SUCCESS

An organization's culture, which has been called an organization's DNA, more than any communication strategy, will determine the success of a crisis communication plan. Consequently, creating a communication plan in the absence of a culture that will support its enactment is a valueless activity.

Some cases and studies demonstrate that organizations have prepared for crises effectively, but when faced with them the culture of the organization has undermined implementation. In the throes of a crisis, a plan to be transparent may collide with a tacit or explicit cultural value of "win at all costs" or "profit trumps safety" that had been etched into the consciousness of the organization. It can be easy to rationalize deception if the core of your enterprise rests on principles that allow for omissions and deliberate ambiguity. There is an irony here, because transparent communication tends to be in the best interests of the organization in the long run.

The notorious case of WorldCom, an enormously successful telecom company, is a sobering one. As Cynthia Cooper reports in her book, *Extraordinary Circumstances: The Journey of a Corporate Whistleblower,* while there may have been superficial acknowledgment that internal controls were important, the organizational culture at WorldCom overwhelmed any in-place process for internal assessment and straight shooting. The WorldCom case and others support the claim that a culture that condones duplicity will be duplicitous during crises despite a recorded protocol that is based on transparency. A more positive example is the often-cited Tylenol case. Tylenol did not even have a crisis communication plan in place when they were confronted with a situation that involved a psychotic who was placing cyanide in Tylenol capsules. However, a cultural value with Johnson & Johnson was to do the right thing and therefore the company defaulted to doing just that.

Therefore, nourishing and nurturing a culture that is conducive to effective crisis communication is a preliminary step when planning for the inevitable.

5. CRISIS COMMUNICATION REQUIRES TRAINING AND SKILL SETS THAT EVEN BRIGHT EXECUTIVES MAY NOT POSSESS

People can learn to be effective communicators if they acknowledge they have a need to learn, but not all people are naturally skilled. Knowing what to communicate does not guarantee being able to communicate well. Crisis communicators should practice, especially if they are not inherently skilled.

A CEO who is trotted out to speak for a company can do damage despite an intelligent plan. Students of communication know that orally communicated messages can be undermined by poor delivery, counterproductive body motions, even inappropriate facial expressions and eye contact. The following excerpt provides an illustration. In *Speaking Out,* Larry Speakes, the press spokesperson for former president Ronald Reagan, commented on a statement made by Reagan's secretary of state George Schultz after an unsuccessful summit meeting with the then Soviet Union.

> Schultz had given us a very upbeat analysis and he tried to sound upbeat before the press, using words like "magnificent" to describe the President's performance and stating that important agreements had been achieved. But Schultz's body language and words were two entirely different things—and his talk was transmitted live to a huge audience back home, as CBS and NBC interrupted their Sunday afternoon pro football games to put Schultz on. He was somber, downbeat, very deliberate, slow of speech, and tired. As [newscaster] Sam Donaldson said, Schultz "looked liked his dog had just been run over by a truck."[10]

Similarly, written communications can be affected by poor proofreading, misleading sentence structure, and even the font style used in the message. Well-considered messages can be embarrassments if written poorly.

Effective crisis communication requires skill, training, practice, and simulation. Intelligence, knowledge, and even humanitarian predispositions are limited assets if people assigned to articulate policy are inept. Thousands of years ago, Pericles commented, "those who think and cannot express what they think are at the same level of those who cannot think." Organizations that have planned for crises, are determined to be transparent, intend to follow the compass of the golden rule, and operate within a culture that is consistent with the communication plan can ruin the effort because they "cannot express what they think."

A study by David Guth suggests that only one-third of the companies that have crisis communication plans regularly practice or conduct training for those who are required to carry out the plan.[11] Training, practice, and simulation are essential for crisis communication to be effective.

Some readers may profit from the use of acronyms to help remind themselves of fundamental principles. Remembering the need for

- **S**kill in crisis communication,
- **T**ransparency,
- **I**nevitability of crises and therefore the imperative of precrisis preparation,
- **C**ulture an organizational that will not undermine the crisis plan, and
- **K**nowledge of the value of the golden rule principle for crisis communication may

allow these important planks to **STICK** with you as you read through this book and when you plan for crises as organizational women and men.

BOOK STRUCTURE AND FEATURES

An objective of this chapter is to stimulate reader interest in this subject by beginning to suggest the concerns of the crisis communicator. In the eight subsequent chapters readers will be exposed to facets of crisis communication study.

Chapters 2 and 3 provide definitions and theoretical underpinnings for crisis communication. In these chapters, myths about crisis communication are presented and dispelled, terms used in the language and research of crisis communication are defined and discussed, and theories germane to crisis communication are explained.

Chapters 4 and 5 present counsel pertaining respectively to proactive and reactive crisis communication activity. Chapter 4 examines how an organization can prepare for events yet to occur, and Chapter 5 discusses approaches to responding once a crisis has surfaced.

Chapter 6 deals with the important ethical considerations and choices crisis communicators are forced to make. As you will see, acting ethically in crisis communication is not solely a moral decision but is considered a pragmatic decision as well.

Much crisis communication activity is done in teams as opposed to being handled by a single representative of an organization. Chapter 7 examines issues relating to teams and crisis communication in terms of conflicts, interventions, and specific roles of crisis communication team members.

If an organization considers crisis communication activity important—and it should—it should consider how to train spokespersons to be effective when they are actually pressed into service to speak for the organization. As we have discussed, knowing what to say is not sufficient. Chapter 8 refers to training techniques when speaking to the press and other stakeholders.

In Chapter 9, we discuss some of the potential benefits of crises, examine the relationship of leadership and courage to crisis efforts, and recap the main points made in the text. Also in this final chapter, students are challenged to create a crisis communication plan for an organization with which they are affiliated.

CHAPTER FEATURES

In addition to the relevant counsel from scholars and practitioners, each chapter includes a case for analysis as well as references to other cases that are made to illustrate points. There is no shortage of crisis cases and in each chapter readers are challenged to evaluate the quality of communication as reflected by the behaviors of organizational representatives in times of crisis.

Readers will find three additional features in each chapter. The first is an exercise or exercises called "Apply the Principles." These are similar to the one presented previously in this introductory chapter. The second feature is an insert called "Practitioner Perspective." Some professional, either a communication, consultant, current corporate communication officer, company executive, lawyer, or some other person whose work is related to crisis communication presents her or his perspectives on an aspect of crisis communication. The third is a Point/Counterpoint challenge, which precedes the summaries for each chapter. In the Point/Counterpoint, two positions are presented to the reader. The first is consistent with a point made in the chapter. The second is a counterargument. Readers are asked to consider the counsel and the counterargument and write a one-page position paper identifying their position on the issue.

Communication during crises can and often does have a significant effect on an organization's health. Studies suggest that people tend to remember how a company communicates during a crisis as much as they remember the crisis itself. The remaining chapters describe theories, principles, and cases that will help readers to understand the nuances of effective crisis communication.

Point/Counterpoint

- Counsel—Transparency and honesty are cornerstones to effective crisis communication efforts. Deception and duplicity will erode the image of an organization in the long run.
- Counterargument—This is a nice claim in a fairy tale. The problem is that the real world is not a fairy tale. Companies can go out of business because of crisis. If transparency facilitates that demise, then the right thing for an organization to do, for its employees, its stockholders if applicable, and its community is to be disingenuous. Do you really want to be transparent if it means that workers in an entire town will lose their jobs?

Summary: A Toolbox

- All organizations face crises.
- In the wake of these crises, organizations must communicate with audiences inside and outside the organization.
- Effective communication can reduce problems related to the crisis. Poor communication can magnify the problem.
- General recommendations for crisis communicators include:
  - Planning for crisis. Organizations can anticipate crises and begin their communication activity prior to the onset of any crisis.
  - Being transparent. Crisis cases suggest that transparent communication is a wise approach in the long run if not in the immediate future of the organization.

(continued p. 16)

PRACTITIONER PERSPECTIVE: ED KLOTZBIER

Ed Klotzbier served on Massachusetts Governor Michael Dukakis's staff when the governor was the Democratic nominee for President of the United States in 1988. In 1986, Mr. Klotzbier worked for Governor Dukakis during the governor's successful campaign for reelection. Mr. Klotzbier holds a law degree and is currently the Vice President for Student Affairs at Northeastern University. Prior to this appointment, he was the Director for University Communications at Northeastern. One of his responsibilities involves participating on a committee that prepares for and responds to any organizational crises.

There are several factors that make crisis communicators effective. First, you have to prepare. There is an expression: You fix your roof on a sunny day. Similarly, the time to deal with a crisis is not when you are in one, but before you are immersed. We can and have created template strategies for crises. We might develop a template strategy for a natural disaster. When we are hit with something that is similar we use the template. Let us say we develop a template strategy for a blizzard. We use the template for a hurricane or flood or something else that is similar.

Another key to success is that you have to know your stakeholders and must be able to access them quickly. We have lists of our various constituencies ready so that in an emergency we can send a message out to them instantly. Also, you have to make sure you get the message right. By this I mean you want to make sure that you are clear about the four or five things you want to say, and stay on message. Your crisis team has to be on the same page. We in our crisis team work very closely together during crises, and therefore prior to crisis, we want to spend time together formally and informally in order to develop relationships and chemistry that is invaluable during crises.

There is no room for deception in crisis communication. Your credibility is so important that it would be foolish for that reason alone to be anything other than transparent. There may be times when we strategically omit something but that is because we want to be diplomatic with certain stakeholders; it is not for deception. To retain information to deceive by omission is not wise or right.

A problem some organizations have during crises is that they forget their internal audiences. You must remember your internal audiences. I get my messages to the internal audiences before the external. I want them to at least know I made an attempt to reach them before they read something in a newspaper.

What makes crisis communication approaches different in the 21st century than in prior ones is the rapid advance of technology and the 24/7 media coverage. We have to know how our constituencies get information and be aware of the realities related to how they get information.

- Using a moral compass. For pragmatic reasons as well as ethical ones, organizations should follow a "golden rule" guiding principle in crisis communication.
- Acknowledging the importance of organizational culture. An organization's culture can support or undermine the crisis communication effort.
- Training and simulations. Skill sets must complement any strategy for a crisis communication plan to work.

Exercises and Discussion Questions

1. Which of the five principles of the STICK list seem most important to you? What organizations have you been in to which this principle would apply?
2. Sixteen mini-cases were presented in this chapter. How many of these do you remember reading/hearing about in "real time," that is, when they actually occurred? How many have you read about in the course of studying or reading about them after they occurred?
3. Of those cases identified in question (2), what was your immediate reaction to the crises when you first heard/read about them. For example, did you think that JetBlue was irresponsible, or did you think that JetBlue was being unfairly criticized?
4. Do you think that organizational culture can change during crises such that the change can positively affect the crisis effort? For example, can a company that values the bottom line realize the importance of humanitarian concerns during a crisis and devalue the bottom line to ensure doing the "right thing."
5. Is there a crisis communication plan at your university? How is it communicated internally?

NOTES

1. http://vtap.com/wikitap/detail/Vt_massacre/WIKI10705678 found on July 22, 2009.

2. Original cspan video http://www.c-spanarchives.org/library/index.php?main_page=product_video_info&products_id=174100–1, July 23, 2009.

3. Micheline Maynard, "At JetBlue Growing Up Is Hard to Do," *New York Times*, October 6, 2008, Business Section, pp. 1, 12.

4. Story reported in the *Boston Globe* (as well as in many other places), February 2, 2009, p. c2.

5. Rene A. Henry, *You'd Better Have a Hose If You Want to Put Out the Fire* (Windsor, CA: Gollywobbler Productions, 2000), p. 2.

6. Steve Wilson, *Real People, Real Crises: An Inside Look at Corporate Crisis Communications* (Winchestor, VA: Oak Hill Press, 2002), p. 1.

7. Laurence Barton, *Crisis in Organizations II* (Cincinnati, OH: South-Western, 2001), p. 1.

8. Steven Fink, *Crisis Management: Planning for the Inevitable* (Cincinnati, OH: Authors Guild, 2002).

9. P.M. Kearns, "Protect Your Company's Image," *Communication World* 15, no. 7 (August–September 1998): 43.

10. Larry Speakes with Robert Pack, *Speaking Out: The Reagan Presidency from Inside the White House* (New York: Avon Books, 1988), p. 184.

11. David Guth, "Proactive Crisis Communication," *Communication World* (October 1995): 12–15.

Defining Crisis Communication

CASE 2.1: LAB SHOPPING

January 2009 did not mark the beginning of a happy new year for the Peanut Corporation of America (PCA). In late January the company was forced to recall many of its products because they had been found to contain salmonella poisoning. Reports indicated that over 500 people had been taken ill by the outbreak and 8 deaths were attributed to the toxins. The PCA felt compelled to "voluntarily" suspend operations in their plant in Georgia and, similarly, in early February "voluntarily" closed their plant in Plainview, Texas.

Anytime there are tainted foodstuffs and a product recall, damage is done to the company that produces the product. The problems for the Peanut Corporation of America, however, were compounded. Not only did its products contain salmonella poisoning, but according to a Food and Drug Administration (FDA) report, the company knew that its products were tainted before it distributed them.

In late January 2009, the FDA contended that the Peanut Corporation of America had tested its products as early as 2007 and discovered the salmonella poisoning. Instead of stopping production, however, the company conducted what is referred to as "lab shopping." This means that the PCA was accused of sending its products to labs until they could obtain a report that reflected a negative test result. Food industry analysts, as well as most consumers, argued that this was certainly not appropriate for a food manufacturer.

When interviewed, Tommy Irvin, Georgia's agriculture commissioner, said "They [the PCA] were trying to find a way to clear their product, so they can ship their product out." However, if two reports are contradictory—one positive and one negative—the protocol is that "You believe the one that is positive." The company's procedures were further besmirched when the FDA's director of the Center for Food Safety and Applied Nutrition contended that an inspection revealed that "no steps had been taken in terms of cleaning or cross–contamination' after the salmonella was found in the plant."[1]

Related companies and organizations quickly sought to distance themselves from the Peanut Corporation of America and issue communications. On the American Peanut Council's Web site, a posting relayed "shock and dismay" at findings that report the PCA knowingly released a product with potential salmonella contaminating the food supply. Peanut butter makers Skippy, Jif, and Peter Pan commented that their brands did not contain any products made by the PCA. On February 18, 2009, Skippy took out a multicolored half-page advertisement in major newspapers. A white banner headline appeared boldly against a red background.

SKIPPY PEANUT BUTTER IS **NOT** PART OF THE PEANUT RECALL[2]

The supermarket chain Kroger issued a recall for certain foods made with peanut products that they stock in the Kroger stores found in thirty-one states. The Federal Emergency Management Agency issued a statement saying that products that were sent to towns ravaged by weather in Kentucky and Arkansas may have contained tainted PCA products. The U.S. government suspended the PCA from doing business with the federal government for at least a year because of the transgression.

In a written statement, the Peanut Company of America denied that they were "lab shopping" to obtain a negative test result that would permit them to shop their product. On January 28, the company released a statement that read, "PCA categorically denies any allegations that the Company sought favorable results from any lab in order to ship its products."

On January 31, the company posted the following statement on their Web site:

> We at Peanut Corporation of America express our deepest and most sincere empathy for those sickened in the salmonella outbreak and their families. We share the public's concern about the potential connection to Peanut Corporation of America's products.
>
> Our top priority has been—and will continue to be—to ensure the public safety and to work promptly to remove all potentially contaminated products out of the marketplace. To that end, we have issued extensive recalls that broadly encompass potentially contaminated product.
>
> We understand that the media and public are eager to obtain facts related to that outbreak. Peanut Corporation of America's employees and attorneys are deeply engaged in the process of learning and understanding the facts and issues here. When they are prepared to discuss

those facts, additional information will be provided as appropriate. For Peanut Corporation to engage in any discussion of the facts at this point is premature.[3]

On February 4, the company issued another statement:

The Peanut Corporation of America continues to be deeply concerned about those who have been affected by salmonella contamination in the past weeks. The product recalls issued by our company continue to expeditiously remove all potentially harmful products from the marketplace, in the best interest of the public's health and safety.

There has been a great deal of confusing and misleading information in the media. We want the public to know that there were regular visits and inspections of the Blakely facility by federal and state regulators in 2008. Independent audit and food safety firms also conducted customary unannounced inspections of the Blakely facility in 2008. One gave the plant an overall "superior" rating, and the other rated the plant as "Meet or Exceeds audit expectations (Acceptable-Excellent)" ratings. Unfortunately, due to the nature of the ongoing investigations, we will not be able to comment further about the facts related to this matter at this time.

PCA is second to nobody in its desire to know all the facts, and our team is working day and night to recall affected products and to complete its investigation.[4]

The Food and Drug Administration announced that a criminal investigation had been initiated against the Peanut Corporation of America.

Questions for Analysis

- How do you think the PCA has addressed this crisis?
- Could the PCA have done anything proactively to be ready for this crisis?
- Will the culture of the PCA be a factor in the crisis communication effort?
- Should the PCA be transparent in its communications?
- Should the PCA follow a golden rule approach?
- How would skill sets help or sabotage the communication effort in this case?
- If you were an executive for the Peanut Corporation of America how would you proceed?
  - Apologize to the consumers?
  - Pledge to conduct your own investigation?
  - Who would be your primary audiences?
  - What would your messages be to them?
  - How would you get your messages out to these groups?
- What other organizations need to communicate regarding the crisis?
  - Should the FDA continue to communicate to stakeholders?
  - The local supermarkets?
  - Jif, Skippy, Peter Pan?
  - Which others?
    - What should these organizations express and to whom should they relay their messages?

NOTES

1. See www.cnn.com/2009/HEALTH/01/28/salmonella.outbreak/index.html.
2. *Boston Globe,* February 18, 2009, p. A12.
3. See www.peanutcorp.com/pdf/Statement by PCA 1–31–09.pdf.
4. See www.peanutcorp.com/pdf/PCA Statement 02 04 09.pdf.

DEFINING CRISIS COMMUNICATION

WHAT IS A CRISIS?

Is a flood in the basement of your business a crisis? If the CEO of your company suddenly leaves to join a competing firm, is that a crisis? If a longtime employee has been exposed as a Nazi sympathizer, does your organization face a crisis?

Understanding what the word crisis means in the context of crisis communication is an important initial step to take in the study of crisis communication. Crisis has been defined variously by researchers, practitioners, and consultants. Typically, however, there are common components in these many definitions. Let us consider four of these definitions.

A crisis is

- "A major, unpredictable event that has potentially negative results. The event and its aftermath may significantly damage an organization and its employees, products, services, financial condition, and reputation."[1]
- "An event that runs the risk of escalating in intensity, could fall under close media or government scrutiny, interferes with normal business operations, jeopardizes the current image of an organization, and damages the financial health of an organization."[2]
- "An unpredictable event which threatens important organizational values and which creates pressure for a timely response requiring effective communication."[3]
- "A major occurrence with a potentially negative outcome affecting an organization as well as its publics, services, products, and or good name."[4]

Little in these definitions or in the legion of others is antithetical to any other. They are clearly similar, and each one is distinct because of a nuanced variation or addition. Let us consider the recurring characteristics in these and other definitions of crisis.

1. Crises are atypical events that might be predictable, but are not expected when they occur.

   For example, while we know it is not impossible that key figures in our organization may abruptly leave the company, we might still be stunned when we read the resignation e-mails. An airline company is aware that horrific accidents are possible, but any specific incident is an unpredictable aberration. We know that hurricanes, and blizzards, and earthquakes are possibilities, but even with advanced meteorological technology the magnitude of storms can startle us.

2. Crises can be damaging to an organization or individuals within the organization.

   A flood may result in the loss of inventory and an inability to satisfy customers waiting for products. The departure of a CEO may cause a precipitous drop in stock prices. Community awareness that a local company has harbored a Nazi is likely to damage relationships the company enjoys with its internal and external communities.

3. Finally, a crisis compels organizations to communicate with various audiences in order to limit the damages that may be caused by crisis. The quality of these communications can ameliorate or exacerbate the situation.

   If a newspaper reports that a city official has embezzled funds, then the city must identify audiences and communicate with these audiences to reduce the effects of the theft. If a city does not respond or responds with an apparent lack of concern, the damage related to the crisis is magnified. Because of a sloppy communication effort, the reputations of all city officials may be sullied. Throughout the nation, the city may earn a reputation as a shady municipality and be seen as a place where corruption is tolerated. A crisis compels organizations to address audiences to limit and not magnify negative perceptions.

Let us capture these characteristics in a relatively concise definition. We define a crisis as *an anomalous event that may negatively affect an organization and requires efficient organizational communication to reduce the damage related to the event.*

If your university's basketball team loses a game you have no crisis in the context of crisis communication although members may consider the loss devastating. If the team's star player is injured you do not have a crisis in the context of crisis communication, although some people may worry how the injury will affect the revenues and fortunes of the team.

However, if it becomes known that members of the team were selling their complimentary tickets to scalpers, or the team members were conspiring with gamblers to alter the natural course of the games, then your university has a crisis. This situation would be an anomalous event. It would likely have a damaging effect on the basketball program, the university's students, and the university's image, if not its financial health. The illicit activities of the players would compel university officials to communicate with various audiences in order to reduce the effects of the crisis.

Apply the Principles

1. For each of the following types of organizations, identify an event that would qualify as a crisis:

   - Department store such as Target or Wal-Mart
   - Software company
   - Convenience store
   - Delicatessen
   - Public school
   - Museum
   - Public transportation system
   - County government

2. What would be your primary communication challenge in each of the events identified in part 1 of this exercise?

TYPES OF CRISES

Several writers have attempted to identify categories of crises. Below is a list of these categories with examples for each type.

Natural Disaster

- Hurricane Ike destroys communities as it wreaks havoc upon towns in Texas during the weekend of September 13–14, 2008.

Management/Employee Misconduct

- WorldCom executives are accused of deliberately presenting inaccurate data about the company, which has devastating effects on investors and employees at WorldCom itself.

Product Tampering

- On September 15, 2008, Chinese police arrest two brothers suspected of adding a dangerous chemical to milk they sold to a company that produced infant formula. Two babies die and more than 1,200 others become ill.

Mega Damage

- The *Exxon Valdez* crashes. The oil it was carrying spills into pristine waters, destroying wildlife in Alaska.

Rumor

- A widow is a guest on Larry King and claims that cell phone effects were the cause of her husband's fatal cancer. Motorola's stock drops precipitously as a result of this unsubstantiated claim.[5]

Technical Breakdown/Accident

- The crash of computers storing information about applicants to a university renders prior admissions decisions worthless. The university is unaware of who has been accepted and who has been rejected.

Technical Breakdown/Not Entirely Accidental

- Intel is compelled to recall its computers because of a problem with a program that miscalculates numbers. This problem is aggavated when it is revealed that Intel had been aware of the problem and did not immediately recall the flawed products.

Challenge

- Wal-Mart is confronted by a consumer group that argues that there is a "high price for low cost." A movie is produced with that title and the producers arrange to have the film shown in various locations.

Human Error
- Automobile tires are defective. Driving fatalities are attributed to problems with the manufacturing of the product.

Workplace Violence
- A postal worker in Enid, Oklahoma, enters the workplace and murders coworkers at the facility.[6]

WHAT DO CRISIS COMMUNICATORS DO?

Crisis communication involves identifying internal and external receivers who must receive information during times of crisis. Crisis communicators conceive, create, and disseminate messages to these internal and external receivers, and prepare to receive and respond to feedback from these audiences.

More specifically, crisis communicators:

- **Prepare for crises**. While crises are not normal events, one can prepare for them by developing relationships with internal and external organizational audiences, anticipating potential crises, and considering, ahead of time, how to address types of crises that can be anticipated.
- **Identify audiences**. An effective crisis communicator considers who needs to receive information from the organization during times of crisis. These audiences will be external to the organization as well as internal. For example, in early September 2008, when Hurricane Gustav forced the closure of companies in New Orleans and all along the Gulf Coast, crisis communicators needed to consider who within their organizations required information about emergency procedures, and which suppliers, customers, government agencies, and other external audiences needed information about the storm.
- **Conceive and construct messages** to be communicated to audiences. Crisis communicators identify units of information that they wish to relay to the identified audiences. Communicators then create messages that are composites of these units of information. The University of Louisiana at Monroe, for example, readying itself for Hurricane Gustav, had to inform students about class cancellations and temporary housing. These units of information—when class would be canceled, where students would be housed—had to be incorporated into composite messages that explained the crisis procedures.
- **Select the media or medium to be used to relay information**. A crisis communicator evaluates methods for communicating, and selects the best method for relaying information. What is the best way to convey a message? Should a representative deliver a speech; hold a press conference; use a social network such as Facebook or LinkedIn; post a notice on the Internet; place an advertisement in a trade magazine? Should an e-mail be blasted to all relevant audiences? Should the organization request time on an interview program to present its perspectives? The best method will depend on a number of factors, among which are the nature of the audience; the crisis itself; the organization's history of responsibility dur-

ing crisis; relationships the organization has formed with the audience prior to the crisis; and the nature of the message content.

- **Respond to feedback** from internal and external audiences during crises. Crisis communicators acknowledge, or should acknowledge, that audiences will have questions and reactions that pertain to the information generated by the organization. Crisis communicators must be prepared to respond to the feedback from these internal and external audiences.
- **Evaluate the success** of crisis communication efforts. After the immediate problems related to the crisis have passed, crisis communicators must assess the effort, discuss how they could have been more effective, and record plans for activity if faced with similar crises in the future.

MYTHS ABOUT CRISIS COMMUNICATION

Eric Dezenhall and John Weber's 2007 book *Damage Control* is subtitled *Why Everything You Know About Crisis Management Is Wrong*. Theirs is a peculiar subtitle. It is remarkably presumptuous since the pronoun, one assumes, refers to the reader. It is arrogant for the authors to assume that all readers are ignorant or have been misguided and that the lone bearers of wisdom are the authors themselves. In fact, research and case studies do not support all of the authors' claims. Nevertheless, Dezenhall and Weber are correct when they suggest that there are misconceptions about how organizations should communicate during crises. A review of how some organizations behave during crises makes this point well.

Organizations have addressed crises by pretending that they will go away; by stonewalling the media; by denying what could not possibly be plausibly denied; and even by attempting to intimidate those casting legitimate doubts about the company's culpability. Companies have said, "no comment" when confronted with challenges. They have assumed that these two words would avoid complications when in fact the defensive phrase has dug them in deeper. Organizations have attempted to displace responsibility on some third party assuming that this will peremptorily remove guilt, when in fact such communications have reduced the respect and credibility the public attributes to these shortsighted organizations.

Misconceptions about crisis communication are problematic not only because they are logically flawed but also because the inaccurate notions become floorboards for communication plans that could not possibly be supported by the warped foundation for construction. Inept communications become part of the crisis itself. Like cement caked on a flat tire, poor communication behavior compounds the original problem. Instead of a tire that needs to be fixed, the company now has to remove the cement from the tire to clear the way for repair. To extend the metaphor, the drivers of the communication plan are at risk because the problems with the tires can create additional accidents.

Both researchers and practitioners identify specific instances when this compounding has occurred. They have argued that audiences, in fact, may remember less about the actual crisis incidents and more about how an organization responded to the incident. In the case most frequently cited as a positive example, Johnson & Johnson is recalled more for how it communicated in the Tylenol tragedy than for what actually occurred during the crisis. Johnson & Johnson did have some advantages that other companies in crisis do not have. They were, in fact, not at all responsible for the tragedy so that their image restoration efforts did not have to address perceptions of irresponsibility. Nevertheless, the communication behavior during that crisis is what people remember, not the details of what occurred. In what is often identified as a poor approach to crisis communication, President Richard Nixon's Watergate scandal is recalled more for how the president and his associates communicated during it than for the actual burglary. Watergate is so named because the break-in took place at the Watergate apartment/office complex in Washington D.C. But what Watergate has come to mean is the entirety of executive behaviors carried out in an attempt to reduce the damage pertaining to the crisis. In this case, nearly all of these behaviors were counterproductive to the realization of the ostensible goal: the exoneration of the president. Toward the end of the Watergate crisis, the United States House of Representatives Judiciary Committee voted to recommend to the larger body that the president be impeached. Two of the three articles of impeachment relate not primarily to the burglary, but *to the inappropriate communication behavior* after the burglary.[7]

Since ineffective crisis communication can exacerbate crises, and since these ineffective communication efforts may be based on misconceptions, it is important to understand fully not only what crisis communication is but also what it is not. Consider the following five common myths about crisis communication.

MYTH 1—CRISIS COMMUNICATION IS SOLELY A REACTIVE ACTIVITY

Crisis communication does, of course, involve responding to crises. However, as we mentioned briefly in Chapter 1, the successful crisis communicator can prepare for, and in some instances preempt, crises because of proactive planning.

It makes sense that one's initial reaction to thinking about crisis communication would be to consider it as a reactive enterprise. A company has a crisis. What does it do to respond? While this conception can seem correct or merely benignly short-sighted, it is neither. It is actually an insidious misconception.

It is insidious because a reactive conceptualization precludes taking preparatory steps that enable an organization to communicate effectively during crisis. For example, relationships with stakeholders are key factors in determining the success of crisis communication efforts. Assuming that crisis communication is a reactive enterprise may mean that positive relationships that could have been developed before any crisis have not been established until there is a crisis. It may even mean the company has disregarded some audiences and this disregard has created negative relationships. Consequently audiences that may have been inclined to be supportive or just receptive during a time of crisis may be neither. These audiences might be less inclined to believe organizational messages than they would have been had crisis communicators conceived of crisis communication as more than a reactive activity.

On page 15 you will see an interview conducted with Ed Klotzbier, who served for years as Director of University Communications for Northeastern University. Now

Klotzbier is the vice president for student affairs at the school. Before assuming his university posts, Klotzbier completed a law degree and also worked for Governor Michael Dukakis's 1988 presidential campaign. You will note that in the interview Klotzbier repeatedly makes the following claim about crisis communication activity.

> You fix your roof on a sunny day.

Similarly, Norman Augustine, former Lockheed Martin chairman and CEO, made the following comment: "When planning for a crisis, it is instructive to recall that Noah started building the ark before it started to rain."[8] Conceiving of crisis communication as solely a reactive activity precludes proactive planning.

MYTH 2—CRISIS COMMUNICATION IS SYNONYMOUS WITH MEDIA RELATIONS. THE PRIMARY ACTIVITY OF CRISIS COMMUNICATORS INVOLVES DEALING WITH THE MEDIA

What is collectively referred to as "the media"—television and radio, newspapers, magazines, and in the twenty-first century the Internet—are very important players in crisis communication. The media are important to crisis communicators because the media can quickly disseminate influential messages to mass audiences and also because experienced crisis communicators can engage the media to actually assist with the crisis communication effort. This was evidenced in a case that involved the small town of Jasper, Texas. In brief, the town was confronted with a severe image problem because of the egregious behavior of some of its citizens. The town employed the local newspaper, the *Jasper Newsboy,* as an aid in their crisis communication effort.[9]

However, the media are not the only important audience or player in crisis communication. The media may not even be the primary audience in a crisis situation. This is often misunderstood by organizations and is reflected in common crisis communication behavior. Pauchant and Mitroff write critically, "[the] priority [often] is to get good press from a bad situation rather than reduce the impact of the crisis on stakeholders and on the environment."[10] The awareness of stakeholders other than the media was something Aaron Feuerstein recognized during the challenges surrounding the Malden Mills case that is described on pages 87–88. He realized and demonstrated—whether by strategy or simply because of his character—that the local community and the workers were the primary stakeholders and the media representatives were secondary stakeholders.[11]

There are at least two reasons not to consider crisis communication to be synonymous with media relations. The first is that considering the two as synonymous means, inevitably, that an organization will be ignoring other key audiences when considering their communication efforts. When Virginia Tech faced its crisis because of the tragic shootings on its campus, it did indeed have to communicate with the media. However, it had other very important audiences. Parents of students, friends of the victims, faculty on campus, dormitory directors, the counseling center at the school—all of these audiences were crucial and care had to be taken to ensure that sensitive messages were relayed to them. Considering the audience to be the media would inevitably relegate these other important stakeholders to minor status.

A second reason to see media relations and crisis communication as distinct is that if an organization defines crisis communication and media relations synonymously, it might assume that *it does not have a crisis unless the media become involved.* The results of such a parochial conception can be catastrophic and are ironic. Incidents that became media events might never have become such if the organization assumed it had a crisis on its hands regardless of whether the media were yet involved. The Catholic Church had crises when they became aware that clergy were acting inappropriately. By assuming they did not have a crisis until the crisis became grist for media exposure, the Church was complicit in magnifying its crisis situations.

A positive example of acknowledging the importance of audiences other than the media occurred just moments before I began writing this section of the book. I received an e-letter from a university official informing me that students who had been studying at another institution as part of an exchange program had been hazed by members of that cooperating institution. I am not, at least as it relates to this matter, a member of the media, but as a professor I am an important audience. My university was wise to know that before I heard anything through a fast moving informal network, or before any media outlet should publish information about the event, I should be aware of what transpired, what actions the university had taken, and what steps the university planned to take to ensure that such an event does not recur. In the days following the e-mail, the event, in fact, gained limited media exposure. Nevertheless, my organization rightfully acknowledged the importance of communicating to its faculty and staff as an example of efficient crisis communication.

MYTH 3—CRISIS COMMUNICATION IS ABOUT SPIN CONTROL. THE JOB OF THE CRISIS COMMUNICATORS IS TO SPIN A NEGATIVE SITUATION SO IT APPEARS TO BE A POSITIVE ONE

My intention was to title this book, *Spinning Just Makes You Dizzy: Crisis Communication Theory and Practices.* In the final analysis we decided to abridge the title and leave out the first several words. However, the original idea for the title reflects the correct perception of what crisis communication is and is not. The job of the crisis communicator is not to spin and it is counterproductive to think of crisis communication in this way.

Spinning is a term that has become a metaphor for taking a reality and changing it—spinning it so that it will be seen from a different vantage point. Spinning the event may make it seem to be something other than what it is. Take a negative event and spin it a different way and it may become a positive one—or so claim the advocates of spinning. The event is no longer what it was, but a more palatable and attractive variation.

If a senator is accused of taking expensive junkets to other countries on taxpayer money, a spin doctor may attempt to portray the trip as *a fact-finding mission intended to discover whether energy planning in these other countries can be used to model alternative behaviors in this country, consequently saving hard-working taxpayers' money at the fuel pump.*

The collapse of a mutual fund's value because of foolish decisions by a fund manager is not a reflection of incompetence at best and corruption at worst when it is spun, *but suggestive of an aggressive approach to investing that has, over the long run, resulted in great profits for all customers of the financial institution.*

It is a myth to think of crisis communication and communicators as those responsible for spinning. As do the other myths in this section, this misconception can have harmful effects even if these effects are not initially identified. A careful reading of the scholarly research conducted on crisis communication advises practitioners to avoid spinning. In addition, a careful reading of books and articles written by practitioners suggests that spinning is harmful to an organization and to the crisis communication effort. The almost universal conclusion by all—practitioners and academics alike—who have studied cases in crisis communication is that spinning, in fact, does make an organization dizzy because in the final analysis it disorients the organization, making it difficult to see clearly the crisis and the role of communication during it. We address this in greater detail in Chapter 6, where we discuss a phenomenon that sociologist Diane Vaughan has called the "normalization of deviance."

It is the knee-jerk, uneducated, or frightened managers who sit in a war room and try to put a positive spin on a negative situation. And there are many such managers. Wilcox, Ault, and Agee comment that organizations have a tendency to "deny that a crisis exists, refuse to answer media questions, and resist involvement by appropriate government agencies. . . . [Companies release] partial, often inaccurate and delayed information while concealing unfavorable facts."[12] Williams and Treadway write "Honesty and openness about the crisis along with evidence of sincere attempts by the organization to resolve it are the keys to establishing or enhancing credibility with the press and public."[13]

There are at least two reasons why spinning is inappropriate. The first is that spinning is inherently unethical. It is an attempt to confuse an audience by distorting reality. I have to date, never met anyone who enjoys being deceived. I have never heard someone suggest that once duped they admired the subterfuge and the dissembler's prowess. It is wrong to spin, simply because we ourselves do not like being spun.

The second reason is that, from a pragmatic perspective, spinning actually makes crisis communication efforts more difficult. Truth typically does surface and when truth is juxtaposed with spun reality, the communicators who attempted to present the distorted view lose credibility. As we will see, an important criterion for crisis communication success is organizational reputation. Reputation is typically enhanced by candor and damaged by duplicity. Reputation is sullied by the realization that deliberate deception was practiced. In contemporary society with its broad access to the Internet, citizens are no longer passive receivers (to whatever extent they had been only passive receivers) of information. Citizens contribute to the dissemination of information by blogs, postings on Web sites, and other methods. Within minutes of a politician's speech, consumers are offering their criticisms and questioning the honesty of the message.

Spinning makes you dizzy. It is unethical, and, just as significantly, makes the work of the crisis communicator much more difficult in the long run. A good example of an organization that has been troubled by reputation and spinning is NASA. NASA has suffered four major crises with the Apollo, Hubble Space Telescope, Challenger, and Columbia disasters. In all of these instances, NASA made spinning-related mistakes that made efforts in subsequent crises more difficult. In particular in the Hubble case, the spinning of messages created the crisis itself.

There is no doubt that some crisis communicators spin. It is a myth to think that spinning is what these crisis communicators should be doing.

MYTH 4—CRISIS COMMUNICATION INVOLVES COMMUNICATING ONLY TO EXTERNAL AUDIENCES

Even those who acknowledge that media members are not the primary audience for communication sometimes assume that crisis communication is about public relations, that is, about dealing with external publics. While an airline tragedy requires communicating with victims' families, other carriers, air traffic control officers, and travel agencies, it requires communicating to internal audiences as well. Pilots and technicians must be made aware of any new safety policies. Staff must become aware of compensation for families who have lost loved ones in the tragedy. Internal publics need to be made aware of external communication efforts. In the America West case described briefly in Chapter 1, messages had to be sent immediately to other pilots that (a) described the event, (b) identified a zero-tolerance policy for such behaviors, (c) explained the punitive actions taken against the pilots, and (d) articulated new policies intended to ensure that no other offenders work for the airline. Similarly, salespeople, flight attendants, and security personnel who worked for the airline, and other internal stakeholders needed to be contacted.

While some people who deal with public relations are aware that internal publics are important, and while some external publics are crucial to effective crisis communication, it is essential to remember that crisis communication addresses internal as well as external audiences and that crisis communicators must deal with internal as well as external publics. Readers will note that several practitioners in the practitioner-perspective feature of the text refer to the importance of acknowledging internal audiences.

MYTH 5—CRISIS COMMUNICATION IS A LINEAR ACTIVITY

A common misconception in all matters related to communication is that communication is a linear activity. That is, there is an assumption that communication goes one way—from sender to receiver. Communication is a nonlinear activity. Receivers of information more often than not respond to messages that are sent to them. The process of communicating does not end once a message has been generated.

The editor of the *Journal of Employee Communication* once commented that the definition of communication is "to get in your head, what is in my head." While this may be a goal of communication, and often the goal of crisis communicators, it is important to understand that realizing the goal is not solely a function of generating a message. What settles as a message received is a function of a nonlinear process of reaction to the original message and ongoing interaction. All communicators—not just crisis communicators—are mistaken if they believe that by virtue of sending a message, the process of communicating has ended.

For example, practitioners and researchers counsel spokespersons not to say "no comment" when confronted with questions about a crisis. It is beyond shortsighted, and borders on the stupidly foolish, to assume that because you say, "No comment" a receiver will simply absorb this message. People do not take in messages like a bullet to the chest. Receivers will not hear, "We have no comment on this matter" as "They have no comment on this matter." Receivers will respond with a host of speculations, such as "Perhaps they have something to hide" or "They do not have their act together." There will likely be follow-up questions if not to a particular spokesperson then to others who may be perceived by receivers as those in the know.

America West could not assume that by sending out a message to its regular customers assuring them that the pilots had been fired, it had comforted its passengers about their safety. Kobe Bryant could not declare that the relationship he had in Colorado was consensual and consider that the message would be consumed as desired. Howard Dean could not assert that his wild reaction to defeat in Iowa was an aberration and that he was really a calm individual capable of leading the nation. Communication is not linear. There is a back and forth that affects what is internalized by stakeholders.

Apply the Principles

- Review the Peanut Corporation of America case that begins this chapter.
- Which of the five myths just discussed could do the most damage to PCA if it assumed this myth to be a truth? Explain.
- Would any of the other myths in this section do significant damage if they were held by the company to be truths?

KEY CRISIS COMMUNICATION TERMS

In addition to defining crisis and crisis communication, it is necessary at this point to define certain terms that regularly surface when discussing crisis communication. As is the case in many fields, jargon is used in this area of study. Some of the terms identified and described in the pages that follow will be more familiar to scholars than practitioners, and some may be more familiar to practitioners than scholars. But all of the terms are relevant to other sections of this book. These terms are also important to know if you plan to read research studies in crisis communication or intend to pursue a career in this area.

STAKEHOLDERS

In the language of crisis communication, the word "stakeholder" refers to the audiences who receive messages pertaining to crises. The word "stakeholder" is used instead of "audience" to be more precise about the characteristics and nature of the receivers. Either stakeholders have a stake in the issues germane to the crisis or the organization wants these receivers to have a stake in the organization and the crisis. Internal stakeholders are people within the focal system. In other words, they are inside the organization the consultant or researcher is examining. External stakeholders are people outside of the focal system.

In the Kobe Bryant case, internal stakeholders would include members of the Los Angeles Lakers basketball team. External stakeholders would include Lakers' season ticketholders. If a fire damaged property and affected the health of students in a dormitory, then internal stakeholders would include students in the dormitory, the head of residential life, campus security, and the infirmary staff. External stakeholders would include local fire officials, representatives from the board of health, parents of students in the dormitories, prospective students at the university, and contractors who install fire prevention equipment.

STAKEHOLDER THEORY

Stakeholder theory refers to the assumption that during crises there are multiple stakeholders and each discrete group likely needs to receive different messages. In his article, "Corporate Publics and Rhetorical Strategy," addressing the Union Carbide Bhopal tragedy, Ice makes this point explicitly.[14] A message intended for the Bhopal receivers was inappropriate for Union Carbide employees located in the United States. The company did not acknowledge the multiple stakeholders that would be consuming its messages. Ice's contention is hardly an isolated one. A 2007 article in the *Journal of Applied Communication Research,* for example, discusses marginalized publics who were excluded from consideration in the events surrounding Hurricane Katrina.[15] When identifying stakeholders all internal and external audiences need to be considered and the appropriate messages for these audiences need to be created and disseminated.

Teammates of Kobe Bryant should receive a message different from that communicated to season ticketholders of the Lakers. The idea of blasting an e-mail to all affected individuals may be clearly inappropriate to readers studying this subject, but it is not an uncommon practice in crisis situations. Stakeholder theory suggests to crisis communicators that a preliminary step in responding to crises is the identification of all stakeholders and then separating these populations into distinct groups that need to receive discrete messages.

Thus, in the case of a dormitory fire, a crisis communication team would be unwise to identify "students" as a group of stakeholders. The team must identify distinct groups of students who are to receive discrete messages. Those who live in the affected dormitory would get one set of messages; those who live in other dormitories another; students who live off campus might receive a third. While the messages would likely contain some similar content, the messages to each group would be distinct, reflecting the basis of stakeholder theory: there are various internal and external publics.

LEGITIMACY

"Legitimacy" is a term used often in the crisis communication literature. It refers to stakeholder perception of an organization's behavior. "Threats to organizational legitimacy occur when perceived responsibility and response are not congruent."[16] In other words, when an organization is perceived as acting appropriately it is seen as legitimate; when it is perceived as behaving inappropriately it loses legitimacy.

If, for example, an organization is honest in dealing with stakeholders; complies with the law; takes safety precautions; prices fairly; and treats its employees well, it is likely to maintain a perception of legitimacy among stakeholders. If an organization operates bait-and-switch operations, produces products that are health hazards, and/ or advertises deceptively, it is likely to lose legitimacy. An organization does not have legitimacy as much as legitimacy is attributed to them. Seeger, Sellnow, and Ulmer comment, "having a noble purpose . . . is no guarantee that an organization will be perceived as legitimate."[17] Legitimacy is an attribution, a function of perception.[18]

During crises for reasons related to the crisis itself or to communications about the crisis, an organization either gains or loses legitimacy. If a company is not prepared for a power outage, runs out of product, serves uncooked meat, hires and harbors a sexual predator, then perceptions of legitimacy will erode. The objectives of crisis communication are to restore legitimacy when necessary and to ensure that a company does not lose legitimacy in those instances when stakeholders are temporarily withholding judgment.

In the America West case, stakeholders might have wondered whether America West had been victimized by its pilots. However, America West lost legitimacy the instant it was revealed that one of the pilots had a documented history of alcohol abuse. Passengers could reasonably assume that an airline would be extraordinarily careful not to hire pilots who had substance abuse problems. Since apparently America West was not so careful, they lost legitimacy in the parlance of crisis communication. In a 2004 article published in the *Journal of Business Communication,* Dean clearly and concisely explains the responsibility of crisis communicators in terms of organizational legitimacy. "To counter any loss of legitimacy, the organization must reestablish congruency between the values implied by its actions and accepted social norms."[19]

IMAGE RESTORATION THEORY

Image restoration theory posits that when an organization loses legitimacy it can restore its image by the use of symbols. In other words, when one loses legitimacy, stakeholder perceptions can be improved or restored by using language to communicate messages to audiences. Image restoration theory identifies several different types of messages that can be employed toward this end. These approaches include denial, apology, attack, transcendence, bolstering, intimidation, corrective action, compensation, ingratiation, minimization, displacement, mortification, compassion, suffering, and differentiation. Each of these image restoration strategies is discussed and explained in Chapter 5.

FOUR RS

Relationships, reputation, responsibility, and response are four variables examined in crisis communication research. The fact that relationships and reputation are considered significant supports the perspective that crisis communication is not solely a reactive activity.

Relationships in this context refer to the connection between the organization and its various stakeholders. While these relationships are established or exist prior to any crisis, they are still variables that affect crisis communication efforts.

Reputation refers to the extent to which the organization is seen as legitimate. Similarly, reputation is established or exists prior to any crisis and is strengthened or tarnished on the basis of the crisis and crisis communication activity.

Responsibility refers to the extent to which the stakeholders consider the organization responsible for the crisis. If a madman indiscriminately shoots coworkers, assuming that the perpetrator had no previous mental history, the organization is not likely to be seen as responsible. However, if another company indiscriminately hires criminals with records of violent activities they may be considered irresponsible. If a company's product is delayed because of an unforeseen blizzard that company is not likely to be seen as irresponsible. However, if an organization does not take precautions to stop pipes from freezing in a frigid climate, then it may be perceived as responsible for transportation delays when pipes burst and shut down a factory.

Response, predictably, refers to how a company has responded to the crisis in terms of its behavior and communication efforts.

As is likely apparent, each of these variables can affect the others. The reputation an organization enjoys may affect the relationships that a company has with its stakeholders. Relationships may affect the extent to which stakeholders will accept a response. The extent of responsibility for a crisis will affect the nature of the response. The response during a crisis will affect the reputation after the fact.

ATTRIBUTION THEORY

Attribution theory is based on the assumption that when an event occurs, people need to or tend to attribute causes and responsibility for the events to other individuals or organizations or to themselves. "Attribution theory posits that people look for the causes of events, especially unexpected and negative events."[20] Since crisis communication by definition involves unexpected events and since these events often have negative effects, attribution theory is relevant to crisis communication study.

Tires explode on automobiles and people are injured. People want to know who is at fault. Is it Ford or is it Firestone who makes the tires?

If a mentally ill worker randomly shoots colleagues, stakeholders want to know whether the organization is accountable somehow for not making the environment safe. Is some psychiatrist who cleared the employee for work responsible for conducting a superficial examination?

A blizzard paralyzes a city, leaving roads littered with cars that ran out of fuel, creating gridlock. Citizens attempting to walk miles to their homes succumb to exposure and perish. Was the city derelict in not anticipating the storm and mobilizing snow removal teams? Were the downtown business owners responsible for not having the foresight to let workers out early to beat the inevitable traffic snarl caused by the snow? Were the meteorologists to blame for predicting a dusting when a blizzard was looming?

In crisis communication the application of attribution theory affects how the organization should attempt to restore legitimacy. In other words, an organization's communication approach will depend on stakeholders' attributions of responsibility. Three factors that affect attribution of responsibility in crisis communication are stability, external versus internal control, and personal control.

STABILITY

"Stability" is a term that has a counterintuitive meaning in the language of crisis communication. Stability refers to how frequently an organization has crises. Therefore, a company that has regularly experienced crisis problems is considered a company with high stability. There is an obvious correlation between reputation and stability: the greater the stability the higher the likelihood of a weak reputation. There is also a correlation between stability and perception of responsibility. Higher stability increases the chances that an organization will be considered responsible for a subsequent crisis. Finally, there is a correlation between stability and the requirements for responses during crises: the higher the stability, the more challenging the requirements for crisis communicators.

Stability is an important factor to consider in crisis communication. The effects of stability are discussed in a 2004 *Journal of Business Communication* article titled "Impact of Past Crises on Current Crisis Communication." The first two sentences of the article speak to the importance of stability as a crisis communication factor.

> On Monday March 27, 2000, a deadly blast ripped through the Phillips Petroleum Company facility in Pasadena, Texas. That day, Phillips's managers faced not just one crisis, but three. Newspaper reports mentioned a 1989 explosion that killed 23 workers and a 1999 incident that killed two workers and injured four others.[21]

EXTERNAL VERSUS INTERNAL CONTROL

These two phrases pertain to whether a crisis is controlled or fueled by someone inside or outside the organization. An earthquake is an example of an externally controlled crisis. Embezzling of funds in an organization is internally controlled.

PERSONAL CONTROL

This refers to whether an actor involved with the crisis could have controlled the event. An organization that defrauds its clients by using moneys to fund personal investments or to invest in some Ponzi scheme, would have high personal control of the crisis. If pipes burst in a facility because of atypically cold temperatures, there would be relatively low personal control. Coombs and Holladay conducted a study that proved, to the extent it needed to be proven, that an internal crisis with high personal control in an organization with high stability would have to be addressed using different image restoration techniques than a crisis with low stability that was external and had low levels of personal control.[22]

EMOTIONAL STABILITY

Coca-Cola faced a crisis in June 1999 when consumers in Belgium became ill after drinking the product. A study by Verbeke, Wim, and Van Kenhove published in the *Journal of Health Communication* discussed the concept of "emotional stability" in their analysis of the case.[23]

The researchers conjectured that the psychological variable of a stakeholder's emotional stability would affect how much information that stakeholder needed. Receivers with low emotional stability might reject reassuring messages from a company; require more authority-based assurances; or need information faster than other groups. The researchers conclude, as might be expected, that fast and transparent communications to lower emotional stability groups is recommended in similar food and health situations.

This does not suggest that high emotional stability groups do not require fast and transparent communication. Rather it simply suggests that the notion of emotional stability is a variable that should be considered. Crisis communicators with high emotional stability may not be sufficiently sensitive to the fact that others may be less emotionally stable. What appears to be unnecessary may well be necessary for those hungry to be comforted about discomforting news.

COUNTERFACTUALS

An objective for crisis communicators is to reduce counterfactuals. In laypeople's terms a counterfactual is a reaction by stakeholders that reflects their feeling that a company could or should have done something differently as it relates to the crisis. Had they done something differently the outcome would have been different.

These "coulda," "shoulda," and "woulda" reactions are all counter to the facts. The facts are that the company did not do what the stakeholder might think the company could have done. An effective crisis communication effort reduces stakeholders' consideration of these counterfactuals. A 2004 study in the *Journal of Business Communication* attempts to assess the extent of counterfactuals on the basis of perception of response, responsibility, and reputation for an event.[24]

SLEEPER EFFECT

The sleeper effect is described in a 2004 article by Lyon and Cameron that examines the effects of prior reputation on success of an organization's immediate response to a crisis. As discussed in the "four R" section earlier, reputation can affect the success of an organization's response. The sleeper effect suggests that in certain situations the effect of reputation may be short term. If person A has a weak reputation and makes a claim that the cause of X was Y, a stakeholder may dismiss the validity of the claim because of what she or he knows about A. However, the sleeper effect suggests that in time stakeholders forget who made the claim. They recall the claim that X was caused by Y, but forget the source. While the sleeper effect is often identified, Lyon and Cameron raise doubts about its application in crisis communication scenarios. In classic phrasing for scholarly research, the authors conclude their study by arguing, "Failure to consistently find an absolute sleeper effect represented by a rise in persuasive impact over time called into question the robustness of the sleeper effect."[25]

SCCT/CLUSTERING

SCCT stands for Situational Crisis Communication Theory. It has been advanced by W. Timothy Coombs, a crisis communication researcher. Coombs suggests that crises can be clustered into victim, accidental, and intentional groupings (See Table 2.1, page 45).

Crises in the victim cluster would include natural disasters, product tampering, rumors, and workplace violence. Crises in the accidental cluster include, for example, the NASA Columbia accident, which occurred when a piece of the space vessel broke away and damaged another portion of the vessel. Intentional crises occur when a manager embezzles funds, sexually harasses coworkers, or deliberately allows cost to trump safety standards when manufacturing vehicles.

SCCT argues that on the basis of clusters, crisis communicators can use image restoration approaches that have been shown to be effective for these crises. A problem with SCCT is that several factors in a crisis situation render any individual crisis unique. While it may be possible to categorize a crisis in a cluster, too many variables can influence the wisdom of applying one or another approach. Therefore, the assumption that clustering can allow for correlated rhetorical strategies has value assuming that those who apply the theory are aware of its limitations.

INSTRUCTING INFORMATION

When a crisis involves a health risk, organizations need to communicate about how to address that risk. Information that instructs a stakeholder about where to go in case of a hurricane, how to ascertain whether a toxin has affected him, what to do if his automobile exhibits certain tendencies, are all examples of instructing information. The quality of instructing information can affect perceptions of legitimacy and the overall crisis communication effort.

NUGGETS

The word "nuggets" is used by practitioners to refer to specific messages that crisis communicators want to convey to audiences. In simple terms, a nugget is a vital piece of a message.

Crisis communicators are encouraged to identify nuggets that will be relayed to each group of stakeholders and to stay on message when communicating to audiences. For example, when Howard Dean was faced with the fallout from the Dean Scream, he and his campaign associates had to determine what units of information had to be relayed to internal and external stakeholders. When you completed the exercises at the beginning of the previous chapter you were essentially identifying the nuggets for the Dean case and others. After the nuggets are determined, crisis communicators create messages that are made up of these nuggets. Spokespersons and writers are urged to stay on message, which means to state and restate the key units of information—the nuggets—when communicating with stakeholders.

HALO AND VELCRO EFFECT

The halo effect is the tendency for some positive attribution of a company to remain with the company subsequently. Because of its behavior during its crisis, the Schwan Food Company has enjoyed a halo effect. Because of the Tylenol case nearly twenty-five years ago, Johnson & Johnson has been blessed with an enduring halo effect.

The Velcro effect is the tendency for negative attributions to stick to a company because of negative performance history. As Coombs and Holladay write, "A performance history is like Velcro; it attracts and snags additional reputational damage."[26]

Performance history is defined, predictably, as the residual of past relationships and the quality of a company's work. Companies that have a negative performance history because of high stability or other factors are attributed low levels of legitimacy. This poor relationship history will, like Velcro, snag greater perceptions of crisis responsibility in future crisis cases. Consequently, a company with poor performance history is likely to have greater reputational damage when faced with a crisis because of the Velcro effect than another company faced with the exact same crisis, if that other company is enjoying the halo effect.

SUPPORTING BEHAVIOR AND HONORING THE ACCOUNT

Because of a positive relationship with a company, stakeholders are more likely to honor the account than had there been a negative relationship. Honoring the account means to believe and accept the account. Sometimes the relationship between stakeholder and organization is so good that the stakeholder will act as an agent of the company and spread the nuggets in informal and formal conversations with other stakeholders. Devoted partisans may be willing to honor the account of a senator accused of chicanery and attempt to spread the image restoration approaches employed by the senator's office. The very same behavior evidenced by a representative of a rival's party is not likely to enjoy the benefits of supporting behavior nor should she or he expect a natural honoring of their accounts.

MEDIA RICHNESS

The phrase "media richness" refers to the value of a particular medium as a method of communicating. Some methods are richer than others, that is, some methods have a greater chance of effectively communicating information.

Three factors determine the richness of a medium. The first is whether the medium allows for immediate feedback. A face-to-face interaction is considered richer than a memorandum, assuming that the author of the memorandum is not present at the time the receiver is reading the memorandum.

The second criterion is the availability of multiple communication cues. Audiences decode communications. It is easier to decode a message if in addition to whatever words are relayed, there are nonverbal complements that help the receiver understand the message. Words can be italicized in a written message or boldfaced for emphasis but these written complements are not as valuable as the multiple communication cues present in face-to-face interactions. Body motions, hand gestures, facial expression, physical distance, touching behaviors, eye contact—all contribute to whatever is perceived as meaningful by a receiver.

The third criterion that determines media richness is the ability to use the medium to personalize the message. A broadcast e-mail cannot be as rich as a teleconference or a phone call, or a meeting with a few persons.

RHETORICAL/PARALINGUAL SENSITIVITY AND SPEECH ACCOMMODATION THEORY

Rhetoric has been defined in so many diverse ways that the very number of definitions has rendered the term difficult to understand. For our purposes here we can define rhetoric as the study of language or other symbols and the analysis of how language/symbols are used to convey meaning.

Paralanguage refers to how one says what one says. A person who sounds lethargic and is barely audible is likely to convey a different message when she says "I am having a good time" than someone whose voice reflects enthusiasm.

The phrase "rhetorical sensitivity" means that language needs to be sensitively selected to meet the expectations of the situation and the audience. Representatives may speak or write about "damage control" and because of word choice sound less concerned with the victims of the spillage and more concerned with how the spillage may affect the stock price of the organization. Similarly, spokespersons may use highly technical words in explaining problems. The choice of language then might not be comforting to citizens who are unfamiliar with the terms, may have low emotional stability, and need to hear words they can decode.

Paralingual sensitivity refers to care in how you say what you say. Spokespersons can desire to express how their organization is on the case in cleaning up an industrial waste spill, but may sound dismissive or condescending because of tone, rate, and volume of speech.

Speech accommodation theory posits that people have a tendency to accommodate their language because of the audience with whom they are speaking. This needs to be not only in terms of word choice but also in terms of syntax. For example, an extreme case of speech accommodation occurs when a person who is fluent in a language employs broken language when conversing with, for example, a family member who speaks broken English. An executive who can discuss policy quite eloquently with her subordinates finds herself conjugating verbs incorrectly or placing adjectives after nouns when she speaks with her immigrant grandparents. Speech accommodation theory is less a strategy than a phenomenon, but spokespersons in crisis situations need to be vigilant about not being so accommodating in either word choice or paralingual behavior as to miss relaying the nuggets that have been determined to be essential in order to restore organizational legitimacy.

Apply the Principles: Test Yourself

Again, review the case that begins this chapter regarding the Peanut Corporation of America. Each of the nineteen terms described in detail above appear in a bulleted list below. Each of the terms can be applied to the Peanut Corporation of America case. Explain the relevance of the terms to this case.

- Stakeholders
- Stakeholder theory
- Legitimacy
- Image restoration theory
- Four Rs
- Attribution theory
- Stability
- External versus internal control
- Personal control
- Emotional stability
- Counterfactuals
- Sleeper effect
- SCCT/Clustering
- Instructing information
- Nuggets
- Halo and Velcro effect
- Supporting behavior and honoring the account
- Media richness
- Rhetorical/paralingual sensitivity/speech accommodation theory

---

CRISIS COMMUNICATION AND ORGANIZATIONAL COMMUNICATION

Crisis communication is a subcategory of a broader area of study called "organizational communication." Courses and programs in organizational communication are typically offered in departments called "Communication Studies" at colleges and university. At some schools, curricula in organizational communication are found in colleges of business.

Organizational communication is a relatively new field of academic inquiry. The first textbook in this area was written only some forty years ago. Only recently—during the past twenty years—have organizational communication courses become staples of Communication Studies programs. Until the 1980s, it was not at all uncommon for students in communication programs to complete their degrees without having been exposed to a single course in organizational communication.

WHAT IS ORGANIZATIONAL COMMUNICATION?

Since organizational communication study is relatively new, many people are unaware of what the phrase, *organizational communication,* means. Incoming students to universities sometimes think that organizational communication refers to how to organize communications. Sometimes people confuse organizational communication with public relations. Others assume that organizational communication is about mastering the skill sets of writing and speaking. Organizational communication study can and does include public relations and an effective communicator in organizations is aware of the importance of organization for communication success. Organizational communication also involves an examination of skill sets necessary for quality communication.

However, organizational communication study is broader and more nuanced than these narrow perceptions. Organizational communication is the study of why and how organizations send and receive information in a complex environment. Crisis communication is a subtopic of organizational communication that examines issues pertaining to a specific organizational situation: crisis. Those who study organizational communication typically examine four areas: communication skill sets, communication culture and climate, communication networks, and information management. Each of these is relevant to crisis communication practitioners and students.

COMMUNICATION SKILL SETS

Organizational men and women have to be able to speak, write, read, listen, and use communication technology. Crisis communicators must be adept in each of these areas with the added dimension of being proficient under time pressures. Crisis communicators must demonstrate that they

- can speak under pressure,
- respond efficiently to questions,
- write efficiently,
- conduct meetings with crisis communication teams and members of various stakeholder groups,
- utilize new technologies to complement conventionally disseminated messages, and listen meaningfully to feedback from stakeholders.

COMMUNICATION CULTURE AND CLIMATE

Researchers in organizational communication examine the interdependent relationships between communication and organizational culture and climate. As discussed in the previous chapter, this is an extraordinarily important area of study for crisis communicators. A company's culture can reduce the chances that crises will surface or increase the chances that problems will fester and become crises. The culture of an organization can facilitate quality communication during crisis, but it also can undermine the best of plans. Cultural theory is discussed in detail in Chapter 3.

COMMUNICATION NETWORKS

In order to drive from one place to another, motorists need highways. Without Interstate 90 or other alternate routes, it would be difficult to drive from Buffalo to Cleveland. It would not matter whether motorists drove old Chevrolets or state-of-the-art

Cadillacs, they would still have trouble getting to Cleveland by car if there were no viable routes. Similarly, organizations require routes to facilitate the transportation of information. Organizations must create, cultivate, and nourish these networks in order to permit the flow of information. Networks do not refer to specific messages such as an interoffice memo or a broadcasted e-mail. These examples are analogous to the Chevrolets and Cadillacs that use the highways. The networks refer to the highways themselves. The networks refer to the existence of navigable channels that permit the use of communication methods such as interoffice memos and e-mailings. An organization is made up of interdependent units. Linking one unit to another is essential for organizational success. Organizational communication study involves the analysis of inter- and intradepartmental networks, and networks that link subordinates to superiors.

It is essential during times of crisis that these networks exist and are available to crisis communicators. If there is an urgent need to get information to a certain internal or external population, an organization needs to have a network to transport the messages. During a crisis you do not want to construct the highway, you need to drive on it.

INFORMATION MANAGEMENT

Information management refers to identifying what needs to be communicated within organizations and how to communicate what needs to be communicated most efficiently. Essentially, what messages do people need to get and how should we get the information to them?

Information management identifies five characteristics of efficiently communicated messages. Messages need to be accurate, credible, pertinent, timely, and clear. Instructing information, for example, is a label for messages disseminated during a crisis that involves risk. If people have become sick due to consumption of a contaminated food product, then an organization has to explain to the consumers what to do. This information has to be accurate, believable, relevant to the audience, timely so that the effects of ingestion do not get worse, and clear.

Apply the Principles

It is the job of crisis communicators to prepare for crises and respond to them. Consider the thirteen scenarios listed next. For each one

1. Describe what might have been done to prevent the crisis.

2. Assuming that the event has occurred,

   - Identify the two groups of internal and two groups of external stakeholders who are most important.
   - Identify the two most important units of information that you would need to relay to these audiences.
   - What would be the appropriate method for communicating this information?
   - Identify the responses you could anticipate from the stakeholders.
   - Suggest how you might react to the predicted responses.

13 Scenarios

1. Two employees assert that they have been sexually harassed at work and intend to take their case to the media if the situation is not rectified.
2. A citizen's group boycotts/pickets your store because your organization has donated money to an abortion rights group.
3. It has been determined that an internal accountant has manipulated the income statement and your declared profits are now identified as bogus.
4. Employees have declared their intention to strike because of demeaning treatment by their employers.
5. An accident related to equipment at your plant has killed seven workers.
6. A blizzard has rendered your company powerless and you cannot meet orders that customers are expecting.
7. You will have to close one of your three plant facilities, requiring the layoff of hundreds of workers.
8. Several employees complain of ill health due to noxious odors that are somehow escaping into their offices.
9. Your company is merging with another and employees are fretting about the implications for their work.
10. It turns out that an employee is a psychopath; he enters your office and randomly murders five employees.
11. You are a superintendent of schools. You discover that a forty-year-old high school English teacher is having a consensual affair with a sophomore at the high school.
12. The Federal Trade Commission has contacted your organization claiming that your advertisements contain faulty and misleading advertising.
13. It is late October. It is revealed that your candidate for mayor has listed on a resume that he has a master's degree from Cornell University. He has no such degree.

PRACTITIONERS AND ACADEMICS

It is common for persons to draw a distinction between those who study phenomena and those who have to deal with phenomena. Academics are sometimes referred to disparagingly as people who live in an unreal world and operate in what is referred to as an ivory tower. By contrast, practitioners are said to be in the real world, have hands-on experience, and are less encumbered by ethereal notions. The prevailing opinion is that, unlike academics, practitioners have actually experienced phenomena and are thus aware of what actually occurs as opposed to what sequestered academics might conjecture.

As it relates to crisis communication, however, most practitioners who have written about crisis communication and most crisis communication scholars preach from the same altar. Their counsel is remarkably similar. Study after study supports the wisdom of successful crisis communication practitioners. This book will describe both the theory and practice of crisis communication and show how theory provides the foundation for practice. A good deal of literature in academic journals discusses cases of crisis communication. This research will be presented on the following pages and readers will see the remarkable similarity between academic research and the writings of practitioners on the subject.

The next chapter discusses the theoretical underpinnings of crisis communication.

Point/Counterpoint

In this exercise, two positions are presented. The first is consistent with a point made in the chapter. The second is a counterargument. Consider the counsel and counterargument. Then write a one-page position paper identifying your position on the issue.

- Counsel—Stakeholders remember how you communicate as much as they remember the crisis itself.
- Counterargument—This is a notion promulgated by crisis communication professionals to advance their consulting careers. The American Peanut Corporation will be remembered because of the contamination not because they denied that they knew about it. WorldCom executives will be remembered for their fraud not for how they communicated regarding their behavior. Kobe will be remembered for his indiscretion not for how he did or did not communicate about it.

Summary: A Toolbox

- Inaccurate conceptions can skew crisis communication efforts and result in inadequate planning and implementation. Accurate conceptions include
  - Crisis communication has proactive as well as reactive dimensions.
  - Crisis communication is not about spinning reality. Spinning can actually be counterproductive.
  - Crisis communication involves interacting with internal as well as external audiences.
  - Crisis communication is not synonymous with media relations. Many nonmedia stakeholders are crucial to the crisis communication effort.
  - Crisis communication efforts do not end once a message is sent. Communicators must be aware of the nonlinear nature of communication and be ready to respond to reactions to messages.
- Crisis communicators should be familiar with the following terms and concepts.
  - Attribution theory
  - Counterfactuals
  - Emotional stability
  - External/internal/personal control
  - Four Rs: relationships, reputations, responsibility, response
  - Honoring the account
  - Image restoration theory
  - Instructing information
  - Legitimacy
  - Media richness
  - Nuggets
  - Paralingual and rhetorical sensitivity
  - SCCT/Clustering
  - Sleeper effect
  - Speech accommodation theory
  - Stability
  - Stakeholder theory
  - Stakeholders
  - Supporting behavior
  - Halo and Velcro effect
- Crisis communication is a division of organizational communication study. Organizational communication addresses
  - Communication networks and networking including new social network technology
  - Information management
  - Organizational climate and culture
  - Communication skill sets

PRACTITIONER PERSPECTIVE: CAROLINE SAPRIEL

Caroline Sapriel is the founder and Managing Director of CS&A, a specialist risk and crisis and business continuity management consulting firm with offices in Hong Kong, the United Kingdom, Belgium, The Netherlands, Italy, Singapore, and the United States. Caroline Sapriel has over twenty years of experience in risk and crisis management working with multinational organizations across industry sectors globally. Prior to establishing her own consulting firm, Caroline Sapriel held senior management positions with a number of international public relations firms, including The Rowland Company and Hill & Knowlton.

Crisis communicators must remember that they will not be able to control the crisis events, but can certainly control their credibility by remaining truthful throughout. It is also important to remember the three F's: Fast, Frequent, and Factual. These keys are especially relevant during the early hours of the crisis when everyone is screaming for information.

Substance is crucial. Empty messages will not work and can even be counterproductive. Denial and downplaying exacerbate the impact of the crisis. "Knee-jerk" reactions are also counterproductive. Crisis communicators should hold the course and follow their plan. Many aspects of a crisis are outside of the organization's control. Focusing the efforts on those areas of the crisis and those stakeholders that can be influenced, and monitoring those that cannot, will help optimize resources and keep the team motivated.

An apology is required and appropriate when there is a clear case of guilt. How and when this is expressed is very much dependent on the culture/environment where the crisis is taking place (Japan versus the United States, for instance). In all cases, a heartfelt expression of regret for what is happening or has happened is required. This is particularly critical when there are victims or when the environment is greatly affected. The expression and demonstration of responsible behavior, care and ownership of the problem throughout the crisis is essential, and will help protect reputation.

An organization can absolutely plan for crises. Besides having a plan in place that describes escalation and mobilization procedures, assigns crisis communications roles and responsibilities, and provides as many templates as practical (holding statements, Q&A's, log sheets, and so on), I believe the best way to prepare is for the team to practice stakeholder mapping and scenario planning skills through training and exercises. Today's crises are incredibly complex, highlighting the interdependence of stakeholders. To lead their organizations through a crisis effectively, crisis teams must understand and be able to map stakeholder behavior and build strategies quickly through the development of "what-if and what-next" scenarios. Frequent and regular practice is necessary. Thankfully, crises do not occur often, so if the team waits for one before practicing, it will be rusty at best and ineffective at worst when the time comes.

Leadership and organizational culture are 100 percent crucial for the successful crisis communication effort. Crisis management and communication should be integrated into corporate management systems, tested and maintained very much like a life jacket—ready to be deployed effectively at any time when needed. Regrettably, despite having the "right" culture, an organization's change of leadership can shift the focus of crisis preparedness and response from pro-active to reactive, and this is when the organization becomes more vulnerable.

Table 2.1

SCCT Recommendations for Crisis Response Selection

1. Provide instructing information to all victims or potential victims in the form of warning and directions for protecting themselves from harm.
2. Provide adjusting information to victims by expressing concern for them and providing corrective action when possible. Note: Providing instructing and adjusting information is enough of a response for victim crises with no crisis history or unfavorable prior reputation.
3. Use diminishment strategies for accident crises when there is no crisis history or unfavorable prior reputation.
4. Use diminishment strategies for victim crises when there is a crisis history or unfavorable prior reputation.
5. Use rebuilding strategies for accident crises when there is a crisis history or unfavorable prior reputation.
6. Use rebuilding strategies for any preventable crisis.
7. Use denial strategies in rumor crises.
8. Use denial strategies in challenges when the challenge is unwarranted.
9. Use corrective action (adjusting information) in challenges when other stakeholders are likely to support the challenge.
10. Use reinforcing strategies as supplements to the other response strategies.
11. Victimage response strategy should only be used with the victim cluster.
12. To be consistent, do not mix denial strategies with either the diminishment or rebuilding strategies.
13. Diminishment and rebuilding strategies can be used in combination with one another.

Source: W. Timothy Coombs. 2007. *Ongoing Crisis Communications: Planning, Managing and Responding*. Thousand Oaks, CA: Sage Publications, p. 143.

Exercises and Discussion Questions

1. Are counterfactuals inevitable regardless of crisis communication planning? Do stakeholders default to considering and proposing counterfactuals?
2. Of relationships, reputations, responsibility, and response, which R is the most significant for the crisis communication effort? Which R was the most significant for the PCA?
3. How significant is emotional stability in determining the ability of stakeholders to perceive messages?
4. Have you ever experienced the sleeper effect? Halo effect? Velcro effect?
5. In your experience—of paralingual and rhetorical sensitivity, which can have the more significant positive effect on restoring legitimacy among stakeholders?
6. In your experience—of paralingual and rhetorical sensitivity, which can have the more negative effect when a group meets to solve a problem?

NOTES

1. Laurence Barton, *Crisis in Organizations: Managing and Communicating in the Heat of Chaos* (Cincinnati, OH: South-Western, 1993), p. 2.

2. Steven Fink, *Crisis Management: Planning for the Inevitable* (Cincinnati, OH: Authors Guild, 2002), pp. 15–16.

3. D. Fishman, "Crisis Communication Theory Blended and Extended," *Communication Quarterly* 47: 345–75.

4. Kathleen Fearns-Bank, "Crisis Communications: A Review of Some Best Practices," in *Handbook of Public Relations*, ed. R.L. Heath (Thousand Oaks, CA: Sage, 2001), pp. 479–485.

5. Eric Dezenhall and John Weber, *Damage Control: Why Everything You Know about Crisis Management Is Wrong* (New York: Penguin, 2007), p. 7.

6. The list of categories is derived from a combination of two articles. The examples for each category are mine. The two articles are W. Timothy Coombs, "Impact of Past Crises on Current Crisis Communication: Insights from Situational Crisis Communication Theory," *Journal of Business Communication* 41, no. 3: 270; and Timothy W. Coombs and Sherry J. Holladay, "Helping Crisis Managers Protect Reputational Assets," *Management Communication Quarterly* 16, no. 2 (November 2002): 170–71.

7. See http://watergate.info/impeachment/impeachment-articles.shtml. One could make a reasonable case that all three of the articles, at least peripherally, dealt with communication issues after the crisis.

8. Quoted in Fink, *Crisis Management*, p. x.

9. Jack Glascock, "The Jasper Dragging Death: Crisis Communication and the Community Newspaper," *Communication Studies* 55, no. 1 (Spring 2004): 29–47.

10. T.C. Pauchant and Ian Mitroff, *Transforming the Crisis Prone Organization* (San Francisco: Jossey Bass, 1992), p. 101.

11. Robert Ulmer, "Effective Crisis Management Through Established Stakeholder Relationships: Malden Mills as a Case Study," *Management Communication Quarterly* 14, no. 4 (May 2001): 597.

12. D.L. Wilcox, P.H. Ault, and W.K. Agee, *Public Relations Strategies and Tactics* (New York: Harper and Row, 1986), p. 310.

13. David Williams and Glenda Treadway "Exxon and the Valdez accident: A failure in crisis communication." *Communication Studies* 43; no. 1 (Spring 1992): 56–64.

14. Richard Ice, "Corporate Publics and Rhetorical Strategies: The Case of Union Carbide's Bhopal Crisis," *Management Communication Quarterly* 4, no. 3 (1991): 341–62.

15. Damion Waymer and Robert Heath, "Emergent Agendas: The Forgotten Publics in Crisis Communication and Issues Management Research," *Journal of Applied Communication Research* 35, no. 1 (February 2007): 88–108.

16. Ibid., p. 92.

17. Matthew W. Seeger, Timothy L. Sellnow, and Robert R. Ulmer, "Communication, Organization, and Crisis," *Communication Yearbook* 21: 231–75; the section dealing with this appears on page 254 of the article. The authors attribute this sentiment to K.M. Hearit, "'We Didn't Do It' to 'It's Not Our Fault': The Use of Apologia in Public Relations Crises," in *Public Relations Inquiry as Rhetorical Criticism: Case Studies of Corporate Discourse and Social Influence* (Westport, CT: Praeger, 1995), pp. 117–34.

18. Many, if not all authors who write about legitimacy make this claim. See, for example, Myria Watkins Allen and Rachel H. Callouet, "Legitimation Endeavors: Impression Management Strategies Used by an Organization in Crisis," *Communication Monographs* 61, no. 1 (November 1994): 44–62.

19. Dwayne Hal Dean, "Consumer Reaction to Negative Publicity: Effects of Corporate Reputation, Response, and Responsibility for a Crisis Event," *Journal of Business Communication* 41, no. 2 (April 2004): 193.

20. W. Timothy Coombs "Attribution Theory as a Guide for Post-crisis Communication Research," *Public Relations Review* 33 (2007): 135–39.

21. Coombs, "Impact of Past Crises on Current Crisis Communication," p. 265.

22. Coombs and Holladay, "Communication and Attributions in Crisis," pp. 279–95.

23. Wim Verbeke and Patrick Van Kenhove, "Impact of emotional stability and attitude on consumption decisions under risk: The Coca-Cola crisis in Belgium," *Journal of Health Communication.* 7, no. 5 (October/December 2002): 455–472.

24. Dwane Dean, "Consumer reaction to negative publicity: Effects of corporate reputation, response, and responsibility for a crisis event," *Journal of Business Communication.* 41, no. 2 (April 2004): 192–211.

25. Lisa Lyon and Glen Cameron, "A Relational Approach Examining the Interplay of Prior Reputation and Immediate Response to a Crisis," *Journal of Public Relations Research* 16, no. 3: 220.

26. Timothy W. Coombs and Sherry Holladay. 2001. "An Extended Examination of the Crisis Situations: A Fusion of the Relational Management and Symbolic Approaches," *Journal of Public Relations Research* 13, no. 4: 335.

3 | Organizational Theory and Crisis Communication

Chapter in a Nutshell

Good theories can help people understand various phenomena. Several theories about communication and organizations are relevant to crisis communication study. Understanding these theories can help practitioners (1) preempt crises and (2) respond to crises when confronted with them. In this chapter, we review several theories and discuss why and how they are relevant to crisis communicators.

Specifically, at the end of this chapter, readers will be able to

- Define the term "theory."
- Describe the following theories and explain their relevance to crisis communication study
  - Systems theory
  - Cultural theory
  - Classical and human resources theory
  - Chaos theory
  - Critical theory
- Explain applicable communication theory principles.
  - Transmission and constitutive definitions
  - Receiver–audience-centered perspective
  - Nonlinearity
  - Irreversibility
  - Verbal and nonverbal symbols
- Identify crisis communication cases that illustrate the relevance of theory.

CASE 3.1: A NEW SUPERSTAR

On February 9, 2009, Alex Rodriguez—a baseball superstar who plays third base for the highly visible New York Yankees—admitted that several years earlier he had taken an illegal substance to enhance his performance as an athlete.

Rodriguez's acknowledgment was not made because he suddenly had a pang of moral remorse. He did not wake up on February 9 and say, "I have been fooling the public too long. It is time to come clean." Rodriguez was essentially compelled to admit his guilt in order to salvage some semblance of his prior reputation. Two days before the admission a report appeared in *Sports Illustrated* magazine claiming that there was evidence indicating that Rodriguez had tested positive for steroids—a banned substance for baseball players. Once this information leaked, reporters scrambled to find old video clips of Rodriguez denying his involvement with illegal drugs. On Sunday, February 8, television stations ran segments of a 2007 interview with Rodriguez by CBS *60 Minutes* reporter Katie Couric. In the interview, Rodriguez answered Couric's point-blank question unequivocally. No, he did not take banned substances. On February 9, 2009, Rodriguez was forced to admit that he had lied then and had been, in fact, a cheat.

This revelation was not just a blow to Rodriguez. It was another blast to the image of major league baseball. A bold headline appeared on the front page of the February 10 *Boston Globe* sports section: **A-Rod Admits Steroid Use**. The first line of the article began with the following words:

> "Baseball's hall of shame gained a new superstar yesterday as Alex Rodriguez outed himself as a drug cheat . . ."

In 2008 the so-called Mitchell report—named for the chair of a congressional investigation committee—indicated that no fewer than 104 baseball players had used illegal drugs to boost performance. Barry Bonds, the all-time leading home run hitter, and Mark McGuire, the first player to break Babe Ruth's longtime record for home runs in a single season, had both been identified as drug cheats. McGuire had tearfully acknowledged his complicity during a senate hearing. The records of both Bonds and McGuire were now tainted. The results of all of the games they had played in were tainted. In fact, the results of all games that any of the 104 players played in were tainted. Baseball, the national pastime of the United States, a game revered by children and adults alike, seemed to be reeling from accusations surfacing monthly about one player or another who had been cheating while playing a game that ostensibly represented all that was good and pure. After the Rodriguez acknowledgment, President Barack Obama, less than one month into his presidency, commented that this latest admission "tarnishes an entire era" and affects children's perception of what it means to be honest. The baseball commissioner, Bud Selig, had no immediate comment on the Rodriguez admission.

In an attempt to reduce damage related to his involvement, Rodriguez apologized to sports fans. The *Globe* commented that Rodriguez "borrowed a page from Jason Giambi and Andy Pettitte who regained much of their popularity after admitting they used banned substances." Rodriguez acknowledged that the fans "will never look at me the same." In his remarks Rodriguez claimed that he was "young and stupid and naive" when he took the drugs and is now "very sorry." He also claimed that he knows now that "the truth will set me free." Rodriguez even commented that something good would come out of this crisis. "I'm beginning to grow up. I'm pretty tired of being selfish and stupid."[1]

Questions for Analysis

Is it possible that

- Insufficient information had been sent to players describing the rules about using certain drugs?
- The channels of communication from players to management were clogged and therefore management was unaware of drug usage?

- The trainers for the players were not sufficiently linked to the team coaches and therefore there was limited communication between the two groups?
- The organizational culture of major league baseball affected the evolution of this crisis?
- In the previous chapter we discussed several terms related to crisis communication. How would you analyze this case in terms of
  - Stakeholder theory?
  - Legitimacy?
  - Stability?
  - Halo and Velcro effect?
  - Four Rs?
- Does Alex Rodriguez need to continue to communicate to audiences?
- Rodriguez is a member of the major league baseball player's union. Does the union need to communicate a message to any audience?
- Rodriguez plays for the New York Yankees. Do the Yankees need to communicate about this issue?

If you answered yes to any of the preceding three questions:

- Why do these people/organizations need to communicate information?
- Who must be contacted?
- What is the message to these audiences?
- How should the messages be relayed?
- Will these communications affect the perception of Alex Rodriguez?
  - Major League Baseball?
  - The New York Yankees?
  - The Major League Baseball Players Association?

Will Rodriguez's apology on February 9, 2009, help restore his image?

NOTE

1. Bob Hohler, "A-Rod admits steroid use—Slugger was doping during Texas years" *Boston Globe*, section C, p. 1., February 10, 2009.

PRACTICAL THEORY

The word "theory" is unfortunately laden with a negative connotation. People often refer to the distinction between theory and practice and argue that conceptualizations may make sense "in theory" but have limited practical value. Practitioners will sometimes dismiss theory as the musings of academics who are not grounded in the nuances of reality.

Some theories are, in fact, less than practical, and often theories are poorly described so that whatever value they may have is inaccessible to those who might otherwise like to apply them. It can be thankless work to plow through a complex article about theory just to reach a conclusion that seems irrelevant or self-evident. Dismissing theory for these reasons, however, is a good example of throwing out the baby with the bathwater. If expressed effectively, theories can be valuable and can help practitioners in organizations understand phenomena.

WHAT IS A THEORY?

A theory is essentially a speculation, an educated guess based on study or experience.

People conduct research studies that test hypotheses. "Hypo" is a prefix that means "under." Hypotheses are literally under the theory—foundational assumptions that are tested. The results of the test/study form the bases for a theory. A hypothesis in a series of studies might be that an organization's internal stakeholders need more information than external stakeholders during a crisis. Researchers would conduct studies to determine whether this hypothesis can be supported. If the hypothesis is supported, then a theory might be developed about how to proceed during crises. The theory might assert that internal stakeholders need information more quickly and more completely than external stakeholders.

Theories are different from laws. A law, for example the law of gravity, is an immutable truth. Theories are conjectures about truth that are based on experimentation and observation. The law of gravity is not a conjecture. It is not a theory. It is a law. Drop a book and it will hit the floor. Someone even at the University of California at Berkeley will not have a contrary opinion (and this is the acid test). Theories—even though they are not immutable truths—can be valuable for people who study phenomena. They can help people think about events and can help people contemplate what should be done in problem situations.

Several organizational theories are relevant to the study of crisis communication. In the following pages these theories are discussed. Each section includes (a) a brief description of the theory, (b) a discussion concerning how the theory relates to crisis communication, (c) an explanation of the theory's key principles, and (d) some applicable crisis case examples for your analysis.

SYSTEMS THEORY

WHAT IS SYSTEMS THEORY?

The basic tenet of systems theory is that organizations are comprised of interdependent units that should work interdependently not independently. In a medical facility, pediatricians work in one unit, pharmacologists in a second, accountants in a third, maintenance staff in a fourth, human resources in a fifth, and executives in a sixth. Systems theorists argue that each of these units is dependent either directly or indirectly on another and no unit should act autonomously. In order to satisfy the needs of patients that visit the facility as well as the needs of individuals who work within the facility, the organization must see itself as an interdependent whole, otherwise the organization will not reach its potential.

HOW IS SYSTEMS THEORY RELEVANT TO CRISIS COMMUNICATION?

In essence, the effect of units acting independently and not interdependently can create crisis situations and limit the effectiveness of organizations when confronted with crisis. It is not difficult to imagine how a crisis could surface if pediatricians in a medical facility do not share information with pharmacists.

People in organizations gather information, relay and receive information from others, and store information for later use. Researchers such as Egelhoff and Sen have made the case that crisis management should be seen from the perspective of an information processing model.[1] Information that is inadequately transferred, or not transferred at all, deprives departments of information that may be essential in order to operate efficiently. Operating inefficiently can create crises. Operating efficiently will prevent them.

Systems theory applies not only to the prevention of crises but also to the ability to communicate when crises arise. When information is not transferred from one unit to another, executives are deprived of knowledge they need to respond intelligently to inquiries made during crises. Weick has argued that "crisis situations impede an organization's sense making process by straining its information systems."[2] This impediment is far more problematic in an organization that does not link its departments as a matter of daily operations. Understanding systems theory and applying its tenets results in the creation of an information system that has a chance of carrying the urgency and deluge of information during crises.

WHAT ARE THE KEY PRINCIPLES OF SYSTEMS THEORY?

Hierarchical ordering

A premise of systems theory is that an organization is composed of systems and subsystems arranged in a hierarchy. Any system within an organization has subsystems, and each subsystem, its own subsystems. These hierarchically ordered subsystems need to interact with all other subsystems in the environment.

Your college probably has several departments. Each department could be considered a subsystem of the larger system, your college. The Communication Studies Department within your college, a subsystem of the college, will likely have its own subsystems. There may be streams of study in Rhetoric, Media Studies, Organizational Communication, and Performance Studies. Within any of these subsystems can be further subsystems. For example, within Media Studies, one subsystem might explore media effects while another examines media production. A business may have advertising, marketing, production, human resources, and legal departments. Within human resources there could be subsystems dealing with grievances, training, and employee benefits.

In systems theory, the phrase *focal system* refers to the subsystem that one is studying within an organization—in other words, the subsystem that one is looking at, that is, focusing on. If you are examining your college, the focal system is the college. If you are examining a university with many colleges, then the focal system is the university and the college is a subsystem.

Each subsystem in an organization is said to be linked horizontally and vertically with other subsystems. That is, each subsystem in an organization is horizontally linked to other subsystems on the same level of the organization and vertically linked to systems below it and above it on the organizational hierarchy (see Figure 3.1). The absence of linkages could prove catastrophic for the organization's customers and employees as well as for the organization itself.

If major league baseball does not acknowledge the various ball clubs as subsystems and the need for these subsystems to interact not only with a central administration but also with each other, then the focal system—major league baseball—is more susceptible to crises. If each team does not acknowledge its subsystems and the need for those subsystems to be linked not only to management but also to each other, then the focal system—the team—is more susceptible to crises. If, for example, Alex Rodriguez is using steroids and the medical staff of a baseball club is not linked to the coaches, then managers may be out of the know and not able to make intelligent decisions. Of course, there are reasons why the medical staff might be linked to the coaches, but information may still not get through to them. The reasons for this, in the vernacular of systems theory, are related to permeability and requisite variety. Both of these systems theory tenets are important for crisis communicators to consider.

Permeability

All subsystems within an organization need to have permeable boundaries. Information from one subsystem must be able to penetrate the walls of other subsystems. If a subsystem has impenetrable boundaries then information that needs to be shared cannot reach essential receivers who might, despite their reluctance to make the boundaries permeable, absolutely need the information.

Every subsystem in an organization has to be able to get information from the outside and send information to the outside. Systems theorists refer to open and closed systems. A closed system does not have permeable boundaries. It will not function as well as it might and could atrophy or expire in the same way that a body organ might atrophy or expire without nourishment from its external environment. For example, if there are natural linkages between trainers and coaches on a baseball team, but coaches do not desire to hear what the trainers wish to tell them, systems theorists would say that the subsystem is not permeable. The focal system, the team, may suffer if not immediately, then over time.

Organizational penetration is a term used by Phillip Tompkins in his book *Organizational Communication Imperatives* and then again in a sequel.[3] In these books Tompkins describes the need for organizations to see external contractors as units within an organization and penetrate these units in order to be aware of the activities of the contractors. By extension organizational penetration is used to describe the practice of learning as much as one can about other subsystems internally so that each unit can act with the knowledge of these inherently related entities.

The importance of this point is that crises often arise when an outside contractor or vendor is not connected to the hiring organization. The linkages may not exist or, even if they do, the boundaries may not be permeable. Sometimes it seems convenient for an organization to blame a contractor for a crisis. In the language of crisis communication this is a form of *displacement*. "It is not our fault. We hired THEM to handle this and THEY messed up." Certainly, all organizations prefer not to have a crisis rather than

Figure 3.1 **Organizational Focus System and Subsystems**

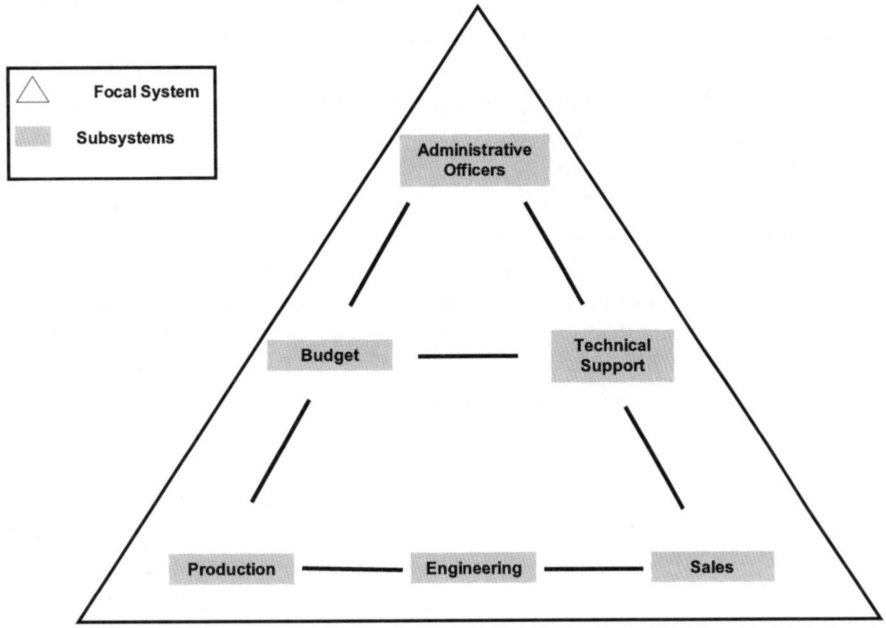

The subsystems within any focal system should have permeable boundaries to allow for communication between these interdependent units.

to be put in a position where they feel they must—foolishly and myopically—blame someone else for the tragedy. (For more about displacement, see Chapter 5.)

Permeable walls must be characteristic of all subsystems, even those that may not be officially on the organization chart. Otherwise, as was the case with the Challenger disaster, a lack of permeability can create crises. The Challenger should not have launched. It was too cold to launch. The contractors at Morton Thiokol advised against the launch. However, the focal system, the Marshall Space Flight Center (MSFC) had abandoned their policy of penetrating the contractor. In effect, they had abandoned a policy that recognized the importance of permeability and the inherent relationships between subsystems. When Thiokol recommended against launch, the suggestion made at MSFC was that Thiokol rethink its position. Thiokol was told to put on its "management hat and not its engineering hat." Had the MSFC created permeable walls, and had they penetrated Thiokol, they would have known themselves that it was too risky to fly at cold temperatures. The absence of interaction and the presence of discrete subsystems operating independently precluded an understanding of the risk. More about the Challenger crisis appears in Chapter 4.

If subsystems within organizations are not permeable the result is a silo effect, in which each subsystem operates autonomously not knowing or caring what another related department is doing. Silos on farms are long tall structures that are used as repositories for grain. Often several of these silos stand adjacent to one another and are not connected in any way. The silo effect is a phrase used to describe departments that, like silos in a field, stand adjacent to one another and are not connected. Sometimes silos are created because of competition between units. Other times these silos are created because the organizational culture perpetuates the notion that if every unit does its job, the organization as a whole will operate seamlessly. This is counterintuitive to anyone who considers it. Seamless functioning requires connectivity that can occur only with efficient communication and a culture that supports interactions between departments. It should be apparent that information stored in silos undermines the applications of systems theory.

Return for a moment to a case introduced in Chapter 1. Review it now.

> Reebok, a company that prides itself on innovation and cutting-edge chic, named a new brand of sneaker the *Incubus*. This was a bewildering name choice. The word "incubus" has sexual connotations with which Reebok, one assumes, would prefer not to be associated. An incubus, by definition, is a ghost that has unsolicited intimate relations with a woman while she is asleep. Reebok claimed to be unaware of the meaning of the word when it was chosen as the name for the shoe. This claim made audiences wonder about the intelligence, internal communication structure, and/or credibility of the company.

How can the Reebok crisis be seen from the perspective of an absence of permeability? As you read through the next section, think about how the Reebok crisis can be seen as a function of the absence of requisite variety.

Requisite variety

Even if walls are permeable, subsystems may fail to communicate adequately if the subsystem is not equipped to deal with the information coming into and flowing out of the subsystem. Requisite variety means that, in terms of processing information, each subsystem has to be as complex and sophisticated as the relevant external environment.

The sales department within a car dealership may receive information from vendors, customers, clients, media personnel, job applicants, government agencies, delivery systems, other dealers, lawyers, and the dealership's own service and parts units. The walls of the sales department may be permeable, but if the system for addressing the influx of information from these various other sources is not sophisticated enough, then communication can and will break down. The hasty remedy for this is to render the walls nonpermeable, that is, to make it difficult for information to get into the subsystem to avoid being subjected to the deluge. This is, of course, a shortsighted solution. The long-term solution is to ensure that all meaningful information can be addressed by maintaining a system for communicating as complex as the environment external to the subsystem. If a Wal-Mart store hired a single temp to handle all external communications "to ensure" permeability, it would likely plant the seeds for crisis and the act itself would help create a culture that devalues organizational communication.

The relevant environment is the part external to the subsystem that is relevant to the system. One could argue that very little in our universe is not relevant to a subsystem's environment. However, some factors are more relevant than others. If any Wal-Mart store is the focal system, the relevant environment involves other Wal-Mart stores, vendors, media representatives, manufacturers, transportation workers, and dozens of other entities. A single college student named Mike will not be able to handle the deluge.

Subsystems must have sufficient requisite variety to process incoming communications from the relevant environment or the result would be, de facto, a closed system. Such a closed system eventually becomes disabled because of the disorder that results from lack of interaction with its relevant environment and related subsystems. This state of disorder is referred to as "entropy." Since systems theorists hold that organizations (as well as organisms) cannot function without permeable boundaries and input, the desired end for a healthy system is the negative entropy that results from interactions with the environment. A systems orientation precludes entropy or at least retards its development. Negative entropy is a desired result.

Return again to another case introduced in the first chapter. How might a systems theorist analyze this case in terms of

- Identifying subsystems?
- Permeability?
- Requisite variety?
- Avoidance of the silo effect?
- The goal of negative entropy?

> The five-week period beginning Monday, September 15, 2008, is one that investment giants such as Fidelity Investments in Boston are unlikely to forget. Rumors had started the previous weekend that two venerable financial institutions, Lehman Brothers and Merrill Lynch, would soon declare bankruptcy. When on Monday, September 15, these fears were realized and concomitant concerns rocked Wall Street, the stock marketed plummeted 500 points. On Tuesday, the market went down another 400 points. On September 29, the market declined a record 777 points. Throughout the first three weeks in October the stock market bobbed up and plunged down, creating enormous anxiety. Investors in companies such as Fidelity became worried about the security of their funds. Fidelity was *not* a company in jeopardy as Lehman was, but many customers were nervous nonetheless. Would Fidelity go down too? Were investments safe? Billions of dollars were withdrawn from companies like Fidelity to be placed in banks where, ostensibly, money would be more secure.

CULTURAL THEORY

WHAT IS CULTURAL THEORY?

Cultural theory is based on the premise that a phenomenon that can appropriately be labeled "organizational culture" exists. In the same way that ethnicities are said to have distinctive cultures, cultural theory assumes that individual organizations can be said to have distinctive cultures. These cultures are a composite of shared organizational values, customs, and beliefs.

Cultural theorists contend that there is an interdependent relationship between organizational culture and organizational communication. In other words, the culture of an organization can affect how people communicate in it, and the way people communicate in an organization can affect the culture. This relationship extends, of course, to organizational communications pertaining to crises. Researchers such as Edgar Schein, as prominent a writer as there is in this area, argue that "there is now abundant evidence that corporate culture affects corporate performance."[4] Banks, churches, software companies, theater groups, government agencies, universities, BestBuy, Sony, and Charley's Bar and Grill—all have organizational cultures. Terrence Deal and Allan Kennedy's 1982 book *Corporate Cultures* is often identified as the first to discuss the notion that organizational groups, like ethnic groups, can have a culture.[5]

HOW DOES CULTURAL THEORY RELATE TO CRISIS COMMUNICATION?

An organization and/or the individuals belonging to it may genuinely value transparency. A company may support those who behave ethically by celebrating their accomplishments at annual events. It may distribute ethical standards awards and promote those who have the courage to follow the golden rule even in the face of personal and organizational harm. And this company's behavior in the throes of crisis may reflect these underlying values.

However, obviously, an organization can have just the opposite culture. It may be rumored that the company looks the other way when transgressions occur and that the word in the conference room is that you should lie when faced with investigators who wish to explore curious dealings. Some informal communications may suggest that those who are deliberately evasive will be rewarded. A company may seek "team players," which may seem benign as a phrase in and of itself, unless the corporate definition of "team player" is someone who will not expose unethical behavior.

A culture that supports deception may nourish crises. A company motto of "Business is Business" may shelter those who wish to "push the envelope" or employ spurious justifications for illicit behavior that can result in crisis. Tompkins describes the McWane Corporation's slogan of "Disciplined Management Practices" as code for "production come hell or high water" and "an abusive management culture that placed the production of pipe above all else."[6] It is not surprising that the McWane Corporation has suffered many safety accidents at its plant. In the *Informant,* Kurt Eichenwald describes the pervasive culture of deception in the Archer Daniels Midland Corporation (ADM). ADM, the subject of the Eichenwald book and now film, is an example of how a company that condones duplicity—that talks the talk of duplicity—can create a field ripe for price fixing and other types of corporate abuse/misbehavior.[7] A values-driven culture, one that abides by an ethically based mission statement, may default to behaviors that preclude crises and/or are conducive to image restoration.

Chapter 4 addresses the proactive steps that are necessary for effective crisis communication. One of these steps involves creating a crisis communication plan. Organizational culture affects the implementation of that plan. As Francis Marra comments in a *Public Relations Review* piece, "Many practitioners devote significant resources to produce a crisis communication plan that is destined to fail because the technical strategies contained in the plan contradict the dominant and accepted communication philosophies used by their organization. In other words, a great crisis communications plan won't work if 'it's not the way we do things here.'"[8] Culture and cultural theory are important for crisis communicators because they are the source of the foundational DNA that undergirds and directs organizational activity.

Consider a case from Chapter 1. How might cultural theory relate to the evolution, perpetuation, and communications related to this incident?

> Kobe Bryant, a basketball player for the Los Angeles Lakers, was accused of raping a woman he met while attending a conference in Aspen, Colorado. Bryant contended that the 2004 encounter was consensual and pleaded not guilty to the charges, but the accusations lingered and the idea that Bryant had behaved inappropriately gained international attention. Eventually the case ended with a settlement, but Bryant's image was affected well beyond the monetary damage resulting from a loss of endorsements from McDonald's and other companies. Some people contended that the National Basketball Association and the Los Angeles Lakers had also taken a hit in terms of prestige.

WHAT ARE THE PRINCIPLES OF CULTURAL THEORY?

Slogans, rites, rituals, heroes

Al Davis, owner of the Oakland Raiders football team, promulgated two slogans about his club. The more formal slogan was, "Commitment to Excellence." The less formal but equally well-known one was "Just Win Baby." Slogans and other communications, either intentionally or inadvertently communicated, may spread company values. An organization's mission statement may include references to community engagement or fun or punctuality. If notions of the importance of community citizenship, work as play, and timeliness become embedded in the psyche of the workforce then these values may become part of the organization's culture. A ritual of a weekly Friday 4 P.M. social hour may create a sense of friendliness and social support in a company. If after an employee's first month, the executives fete this individual as an initiate, it may become part of an organizational identification process. If the now-retired Shari Davis is regularly acknowledged at company functions as someone who worked indefatigably to seal deals, the fabric of the organizational culture may include a reverence for perseverance and industry.

Functionalists and interpretivists

Some writers, occasionally described as functionalists, assume that the culture of an organization is a direct function of administrative communications. These thinkers suggest that a culture can be engineered by signage, speeches from a CEO, postings on a Web site, and e-mails blasts from vice presidents of human resources. Another group, interpretivists, suggest that the organizational culture is not generated by managerial communications but is the residual of all communications, regardless of how official they may be. Interpretivists interpret the culture of an organization by observing communication patterns, similar to the way an ethnographer studies culture.

They might listen to conversations in the cafeteria, examine both formal and informal e-mails, study the blogs of various personnel, and even linger on the company walking trail in an attempt to understand the culture by observing communication patterns. An interpretivist would argue that Al Davis could create bumper stickers that read "Commitment to Excellence" but, metaphorically, these signs would have to stick. If they did not, if informal communications by players, reporters, and coaches indicated that management was committed to tradition or administrative power, at the expense of performance, these informal communications would create the culture.

Socialization, assimilation, and identification

Newcomers to an organization become socialized to it, in the same way that members of an ethnic group become socialized. Socialization includes anticipatory, encounter, and metamorphosis stages. Anticipatory socialization occurs when someone considers joining an organization: they may read about it informally, then formally discuss the company with members, and visit the organization. Encounter socialization occurs in the early days at a company when one is exposed to rituals, slogans, and rites. If on a first day at a company employees are met with a welcoming banner, it may affect how the culture becomes ingrained in them. At some point an employee changes and becomes part of the organization. This is called the metamorphosis stage because at this point the employee has now become assimilated into the organization. If an employee begins to use phrases such as "this is how we do it here at Charlie's" and becomes proud of the organizational culture to which she or he has been assimilated, it reflects a sense of identification with the company.

Often when companies merge, the clash of cultures is pronounced. In *Journey of a Corporate Whistleblower,* Cooper discusses how WorldCom and MCI clashed and the enduring difficulties that remained when members of each culture were reluctant to relinquish their identification with their premerger company.[9]

Apply the Principles

A tenet of cultural theory is that organizational culture can influence how people in an organization communicate. As it relates to crisis communication, cultural theorists contend that culture can drive behavior that creates crises, and can support or undermine communication efforts during a crisis.

- To what extent can organizational culture
  - Affect precrisis relationships with
    - Internal stakeholders?
    - External stakeholders?
- Select an organization with which you are familiar. It could be your university, a religious organization, a club, or a business you work at during summers or while studying at the university.
  - How would you describe that organization's culture?
  - How do internal communications in that organization reflect its culture?
  - Does the culture of this organization reduce chances for crises to surface?
  - Would the organizational culture undermine chances for
    - Transparency during crisis?
    - Following a golden rule approach to crisis communication?

CLASSICAL THEORY

WHAT IS CLASSICAL THEORY?

Classical theory refers to a collection of theories that were developed in the early part of the twentieth century. The central principle in classical theory is that an organization should be seen as if it were a machine. The best way to maximize efficiency is to consider the most efficient way to structure the machine and control its operations. Classical theorists consider employees to be parts of the machine that is the organization. Just as a tire is part of an automobile and an efficient tire maximizes that automobile's performance, an employee is considered to be part of the machine/organization and the extent to which employees perform tasks correctly maximizes organizational performance.

Frederick Taylor was a leader in the development of classical theory. (Sometimes classical theory is simply called Taylorism.) Taylor believed in scientific management, an assumption that a job can be studied in the same way that a scientist might study biological phenomena. Taylor contended that specific tasks should be examined and management should determine the "one best way" to complete these tasks. Management then has the responsibility to communicate to employees so that employees know how to do what is required and how they will be compensated for working efficiently (or penalized for not doing so).

Classical theorists contended that leaders in organizations derive their authority by rules established by the organization that imbue leaders with this authority. These rules have to be clearly communicated not only to ensure an understanding of how the organization functions but also to explain who has authority and who does not. Another key principle of classical theory is that people work primarily for compensation and not for any inherent pleasure derived from working or being associated with an organization and colleagues.

HOW IS CLASSICAL THEORY RELEVANT TO CRISIS COMMUNICATION?

Classical management theory has certainly been supplanted by more enlightened approaches. However, at least two principles of classical theory are important to consider for those who study crisis communication.

Let us consider the "one best way" principle of scientific management. Assume that there is in fact one best way to do a job or at least that there are good ways and flawed ways to complete a job. If this is the case, employers have a responsibility to explain this best way to employees. Classical theorists argue that employees must be aware of specific job tasks, be familiar with the protocols for completing these tasks, and be rewarded for completing these tasks in the prescribed ways. When people interview for positions, they should be given a clear job description, told how work should be completed, and be informed of the compensation for efficient work. Readers may be surprised to discover how often this basic principle of classical theory is not addressed. Employees often complain of unclear or inaccurate job descriptions. Workers contend that they are unsure of organizational procedures because they were never explained adequately or, in some instances, the protocol simply does not exist. The sad fact is that many readers will *not* be surprised by this because so often it is the case that people complain that at work what to do, and how to do it, is vaguely communicated at best.

One can easily see how ignorance of policies, for example those related to safety, can lead to crises. Employees who are confused about what their jobs are and how to do them are not likely to do their jobs well. The cumulative effect of employees not doing their jobs well can be crises. So while classical theory may be flawed in some ways, the essential idea that organizations are obliged to explain how to work to employees is not flawed.

Similarly important in crisis communication is the idea that rules must be articulated to identify who in an organization is responsible for which roles. In both proactive and reactive stages of crisis communication planning, it is essential to know who does what and who should know what. A stunning and frightening example of ignorance during crisis occurred on the day in 1981 when President Ronald Reagan was shot. During the hectic hours after the shooting, bureaucrats in Washington gathered to discuss how to proceed as the president was being treated for the gunshot wounds. Alexander Haig, then secretary of state, came into a conference and told all that he was in charge. "Read your constitution," he said. Fortunately, there is a constitution and some have read it. The constitution clearly indicates the chain of command during such crises. The secretary of state is fourth in line after the vice president, Speaker of the House, and president pro-tempore of the Senate.

Not all organizations have such an explicit constitution. Classical theorists would be delighted to argue that without rules, and the documents that serve as repositories for them, the result may be chaos during times of crisis.

Consider the following case from Chapter 1. How might this case be analyzed from the perspective of classical theory?

> Virginia Tech University and all of its students, staff, alumni, and faculty were devastated on April 16, 2006, when a crazed gunman indiscriminately killed students and professors on the Blacksburg, Virginia, campus. In the early hours of that horrible day the deranged killer, a student himself, shot students in a dormitory, and then returned to his own room. Two hours later he burst into several classrooms, murdering professors, more students, and then himself. Subsequently, the review board chastised the university for "failing to take action that might have reduced the number of casualties, failing to take note of certain 'red flags.'"[10] The shooter had a history of psychological problems and had previously been asked to leave a class because of inappropriate behavior.

WHAT ARE THE KEY PRINCIPLES OF CLASSICAL THEORY?

Natural and systematic soldiering

Frederick Taylor believed that employees were inherently lazy. "There is no question" he wrote "that the tendency of the average [employee] is toward working at a slow easy gait."[11] He discussed two phenomena related to this contention, which he called natural and systematic soldiering.

By natural soldiering, Taylor meant that employees tend to work slowly. He believed that employees were like soldiers just following orders at a predictably slow pace. Systematic soldiering occurred when an employee was "trained" to work slowly by a veteran employee. The veteran would deliberately discourage industrious behavior because fast workers could be "rate busters." You may have observed this experience yourself. A newcomer at work might be ridiculed or discouraged from working expeditiously or even efficiently. A veteran might suggest that the newcomer is "making us look bad." Taylor contended that veterans feared that ambitious workers would be "rate busters." If jobs could be done in thirty minutes instead of an hour, management might see that a job they thought was worth $10 should be worth only half the original compensation. It was wise, thought Taylor, to eliminate the practice of systematic soldiering. This could be done by management rigidly identifying and enforcing protocol.

Scalar chain/downward communication

Classical theorists believe in centralized authority and a hierarchical chain of command. "The line of authority is the route followed—via every link in the chain by all communications which start from or go to the ultimate authority. . . . It is an error to depart needlessly from the line of authority."[12]

This perspective affects how organizations communicate. While the excerpted quotation states that communications "start from or go to the ultimate authority," classical theorists considered that almost all communication travels downward from the ultimate authority to subordinates. Many organizations today continue to operate using this scalar chain, primarily if not wholly, as a vehicle for downward communication. It is likely obvious to the reader that in the absence of a scalar chain allowing information to go upward, information at lower levels that could eliminate crises remains at these lower levels.

Apply the Principles

In Chapter 2 we discussed the following terms related to crisis communication.

- Relationships,
- Stakeholder theory,
- Counterfactuals,
- Supporting behavior,
- Honoring the account,
- Rhetorical sensitivity, and
- Instructing information.
  - As it pertains to internal stakeholders, how might a classical orientation affect each of the items on this list?
  - How can a classical management style affect organizational culture?
  - How might the resulting organizational culture affect the crisis communication efforts of both internal and external stakeholders?

HUMAN RESOURCES THEORY

WHAT IS HUMAN RESOURCES THEORY?

Human resources theory emerged in response to a number of realizations and at least one failure. A famous series of studies called the "Hawthorne Studies" was the source of the realizations. The attempt to implement something called "human relations theory" was the failure.

Human resource theorists believe that employees are not inherently lazy and that under the right conditions they will enjoy work. These theorists argue that employees seek responsibility and wish to have their voices respected and not suppressed during decision making. In addition, human resource theorists believe, as the title of the theory suggests, that employees are in fact organizational resources.

HOW IS HUMAN RESOURCES THEORY RELATED TO CRISIS COMMUNICATION?

Human resources theorists argue that employees want to participate and can be resources. They also argue that employees need to be respected. This theory does not suggest that employers be compelled to do what employees might suggest, but rather that employers credibly solicit input from and offer respect to employees. Input from employees might provide information that can preclude crises and be helpful during crisis communication efforts. Sources of organizational crisis are often based on respect issues.

No one likes to be "dissed." The pervasive nature of that slang verb indicates how central respect is to our human needs. Should people endure disrespect? Should they be able to work through any intentional or inadvertent communications of disrespect? Should employees be willing—in the vernacular—to just "suck it up?" Perhaps, but this could be a meaningless debate point. What cannot be disputed is how often people leave jobs because of feelings that they are not appreciated, how often people underperform because they feel that they are underappreciated, and how often the source of bizarre behavior is a lack of recognition.

There can be no logical accounting or condoning of mad shootings at post offices or at universities. Crazed killers are known to have claimed that they were disrespected and that is why they behaved as they did. Insane people are likely to be implacable and may under the best of conditions behave unconscionably. However, more stable individuals may become disgruntled and undermine an organization's effectiveness simply because management has failed to recognize that employees are not cogs in a machine and that they have human needs. Strikes, attrition, and violent protests may be obviated by the credible recognition of human resource principles.

WHAT ARE THE KEY PRINCIPLES OF HUMAN RESOURCE THEORY?

The Hawthorne Effect

The Hawthorne Studies were a series of studies conducted in the 1930s and 1940s. Researchers examined employees and how they reacted to certain changes, opportunities, and observation by supervisors. The researchers drew three main conclusions on the basis of these studies. The first is that employees are motivated not only by financial incentives but by recognition. The communication implication of this finding was that organizations had to communicate not only policies and job tasks to employees. Employers had to communicate their assessments of employee performance and also needed to communicate their inherent respect for employees as individuals beyond efficient cogs in the machine that is the organization. The second conclusion was that employees desired opportunities to voice their opinion to management. A part of the Hawthorne Studies revealed that employees wanted an opportunity to vent. The third conclusion of the studies was that while organizations might declare formal routes for communication, in actuality the informal networks were active and may be more credible than the formal networks. The "Hawthorne Effect" is a general phrase used to describe how observation and recognition can affect organizational performance.

Take a moment to review a case from Chapter 1. Consider the possibility that information about this case was available in informal networks. Could an understanding of human resources theory have prevented this crisis?

> On July 1, 2002, officials at America West were dumbfounded and dazed by the news that two of their pilots were detained at the Miami airport. The pilots had been scheduled to fly 124 passengers across the country to Phoenix, Arizona. However, security personnel thought these pilots might be inebriated. The aircraft was taxiing on the runway, when it was called back. The pilots were pulled off the plane and examined. Both failed Breathalyzer tests. America West's image, of course, was damaged. The company was embarrassed. Subsequently, the airline was further humiliated when it was revealed that at least one of the pilots had a history of alcohol abuse.

Jackass fallacy

The jackass fallacy is the assumption that employees are fools, not willing to do much other than collect their salaries. This notion—ridiculed in a *Harvard Business Review* article titled "Asinine Attitudes Towards Management"—contends that employees are, essentially like mules, jackasses that have to be pushed, manipulated, and prodded to do their work.[13] This conceptualization has been called the "jackass *fallacy*" because it represents flawed reasoning. Employees can contribute to the qualitative growth of an organization and often desire to do so. When employees choose to leave their jobs, the reason most often cited is a lack of recognition and inadequate respect for their potential contributions. In other words, salary does not drive people away from an organization as much as discontent regarding perceptions of their worth.

Employees often have expertise in areas that administrators may not. They can be aware of problems and issues related to daily operations about which administrators, by virtue of their other responsibilities, are not aware. Employees can make suggestions for improvement that can save an organization time and money. Not thinking of employees as resources preempts their ability to be sources of information that can avert crises and disengages them from the process of communicating, making them external stakeholders during crises. Just as significantly, thinking of employees as jackasses does nothing to improve the morale of the workforce. A defensive climate and disgruntled employees can create soil ripe for crises.

Informal networks

The research by Keith Davis on informal networks conducted in the 1950s is supported by later studies. The informal network is natural, resilient, and often accurate. Significantly, it is viewed by organizational men and women as more credible than the formal network. That is, people tend to check the veracity of messages disseminated on the formal network by their sources on the informal network. When a formal message from an executive relays that a member of the management team has suddenly decided to step down, the informal network is energized to discover the real data concerning the sudden change. Not respecting the value of the informal network is to ignore sources of information that may preclude crises. When the Peanut Corporation of America contends it was unaware of salmonella poisoning, the grapevine becomes active in trying to discover who knew what when.

Organizational credibility

Because of the Hawthorne Studies an antidote to classical theory was needed and that antidote took the shape of what has been called the "human relations theory of management." This theory countered the tenets of classical theory by incorporating the Hawthorne Study findings. Employees needed to be recognized. Organizations needed to create upward channels for communication, and develop respect for informal networks. However, as Robert Miles pointed out in his often-cited article, "Human Relations or Human Resources?" most managers who attempted to implement human relations theory did so superficially.[14] Often these administrators had been immersed in classical theory and the exposure to human relations principles was taken in only superficially. Miles argued for a more credible application of human relations theory, which he called "human resources" theory.

In contrast to classical theory and the superficial treatment of human relations theory, in human resources theory organizations were encouraged to view employees as legitimate resources who could be tapped to enhance the chances of organizational success. As such, their contributions during meetings were genuinely solicited and expressions of gratitude for industry and success were heartfelt.

Apply the Principles

- How might applications of human resources theory affect legitimacy with
  - External stakeholders?
  - Internal stakeholders?
  - Attribution theory?
  - Halo effect?
- In the case that begins this chapter, "A New Superstar,"
  - How might applications of human resources theory affect
    - Responsibility?
    - Response?

CHAOS THEORY

WHAT IS CHAOS THEORY?

Chaos theory has an unfortunate name. It means the opposite of what it seems to mean. The theory has been attributed to the late Edward Lorenz, who was a professor at the Massachusetts Institute of Technology. Essentially, the theory posits that what may appear to be unrelated phenomena—which collectively seem to constitute chaos—are, in fact, not unrelated and not disparate. While we may not be able to compute how or why, chaos theory argues that these apparently disparate events are part of some larger composite.

In essence, chaos theory argues that the appearance of random chaos is illusory. No action is inconsequential and all actions have some consequence. The theory is sometimes called the "butterfly effect" (with some degree of derision) because it suggests that even the actions of a butterfly cannot be disconnected from other phenomena. The nickname for the theory originated when Lorenz delivered a 1972 paper titled, "Predictability: Does the Flap of a Butterfly's Wings in Brazil Set Off a Tornado in Texas?"[15] The professor's answer was "yes."

How does chaos theory apply to crisis communication?

Chaos theory may seem wild to those first reading about it, but for those who study crisis communication the basic principle is not insignificant and is worth considering. All activity in an organization has the potential to affect all other activity. An action that can seem relatively innocuous and isolated—such as not responding to a voice-mail message—can have the potential to escalate into something catastrophic. It is, of course, not likely that such a thing will result in catastrophe, but it is worth considering that all activity has an effect, and therefore all activity within an organization should focus on the value-driven goals of that organization. All activities that are counter to those goals serve to erode and corrode the DNA of the organization and consequently can create crises.

There is another application of chaos theory to crisis communication. In an examination of the Red River Flood crisis, researchers concluded that "Chaos theory suggests that crisis may be a necessary cyclical state in a process leading to organization and renewal."[16] This suggests that chaos theory provides the foundation for conceptualizing crisis not as an aberration, but as a normal event in a process of rediscovery, reformation, and rebirth. This can be an ethereal and elusive concept to grasp if you are Lehman Brothers charged with embezzling funds and about to declare bankruptcy because of irresponsible corporate conduct. However, it may be at least interesting to consider that the state of crisis allows organizations to reconfigure and evolve more efficiently.

How might chaos theorists argue that the crisis described in Case 3.1, "A New Superstar," could have a salubrious outcome?

Consider the following two cases from Chapter 1. Explain how a chaos theorist would analyze these cases.

On Valentine's Day 2008, JetBlue, an airline that had become the darling of the low-cost flight industry, experienced disaster when a snowstorm forced excruciating delays. As planes sat on the runway for several hours, passengers awaiting takeoff were trapped unable to use toilet facilities as they stewed on board, essentially imprisoned on the stuck vessel. The national press that reported the incident was excoriating in its criticism. JetBlue employees began to refer to the event as 2/14 in the same way that Americans would refer to the bin Laden attacks as 9/11. For JetBlue the experience was, as the CEO subsequently said, "pretty humiliating."[17]

Shortly after the 2008 summer Olympics, Michael Phelps, a swimming champion, was pictured on the cover of *Sports Illustrated* magazine with his record-breaking eight Olympic gold medals draped around his neck. By February 2009, Phelps had secured endorsement contracts from several companies to help peddle their products and sweeten the swimmer's personal treasury. It was therefore calamitous for both Phelps and these companies when a British tabloid, *News of the World,* published a photograph of Phelps at a party. The photo captured the eight-time gold medalist smoking marijuana from a bong pipe. The picture, which appeared in early 2009, was taken in November 2008, a few months after the Olympic and Olympian achievements. Phelps was able to retain his endorsement contract with Subway, the sandwich chain, but lost contracts with other organizations.

CRITICAL THEORY

WHAT IS CRITICAL THEORY?

Critical theory refers to assumptions about the misuse of power in organizations. Critical organizational communication theorists assume that communication can be used as a tool for abuse. Employees who are excluded from committee meetings or invited to attend but not allowed to contribute can become marginalized. Rearranging the bureaucratic structure so that the scalar chain requires a vice president to report to two new intermediaries may reduce the authority of a vice president who formerly had easy access to the president. Critical theorists believe that it is the responsibility of individuals to identify abuses that subjugate employees and also to work to eliminate these abuses. Critical theorists argue that the abuse of communication for the purposes of maintaining power ultimately, if not continuously, compromises the qualitative growth of an organization.

Critical theorists use the word *ideology* to describe beliefs that employers consider normal and natural, which constitute an ideological framework that those in power wish employees to consider standard, foundational, and perhaps even sacred. For example, most people take for granted that managers have authority over employees and are more powerful players in the organization. Critical theorists would consider this problematic. They would argue that belief in the importance of disproportionate power reflects acceptance of an ideology that is inherently oppressive, and by extension conducive to crisis. In other words, accepting the concept of managerial authority as a given will inevitably subjugate employees because they will have bought into the ideology maintaining that organizations must function by preserving positions of relative power. This, claim critical theorists, is insidious and will inevitability create some crisis.

The phrase *manufactured consent* is used by critical theorists to describe the phenomenon of buying into subjugating ideologies. It occurs when employees adopt and may enforce philosophies that could, in fact, be unhealthy for them. Communication patterns in the organization reinforce the ideologies, and, consequently, the organization actually manufactures the buy-in from employees. A critical theorist might suggest that corporeal punishment common in public schools in the 1950s existed because parents and students had bought into the ideology that this was necessary for discipline. Their consent to a behavior that might otherwise be considered reprehensible had been manufactured by educators. One could make the case that such consent was foundational to abuses that created crises for some educational organizations.

HOW DOES CRITICAL THEORY RELATE TO CRISIS COMMUNICATION?

A recent article in the *Journal of Applied Communication Behavior* discusses bullying behavior by managers. Employees described to researchers how they were berated because of minor offenses. Employees had, in these instances, grown accustomed to the normalcy of the bullying behavior.

Consider the following example, which is excerpted from the article:

> The actual office environment was all glass, so he could see into all of the offices. Constant surveillance was deliberate and apparently part of his strategy of control. He could see through every office. . . . He'd scream and yell every day. Veins would pop out of his head; he'd spit, he'd point, he'd threaten daily, all day long to anyone in his way, every day that I was there. Every single day. Oh, yelling! . . . [From my office,] I could see his eyes bulging, his veins and everything, spitting, and pointing his finger. . . . That was daily, with many people, all the time. He would yell in the speakerphone at his general managers. He'd swear profusely, "You [expletive], you don't know anything. You [expletive] idiot! You couldn't run a [expletive] peanut stand."[18]

This might seem to be an isolated example to most readers, but it is likely that some students in your class can describe a similar incident in their organizational experience.

In a famous crisis communication case, Texaco executives had apparently used racist language with impunity and it had been accepted as a matter of course until a taped conversation replete with epithets was made public. This created a crisis for Texaco as they attempted to explain how such abnormal behavior could have become commonplace and accepted. (See case 6.1 for a more detailed discussion of this crisis).

November 18, 2008, marks the thirtieth anniversary of a religious splinter group that bought into the subjugating ideology of a spiritual leader and committed mass suicide at the instructions of an oppressor who had manufactured their consent to the ultimate self-destructive behavior.

While critical theorists have their detractors—and it would be inappropriate for a theory that advocates for relentless criticism not to be so examined—crisis communication scholars should consider the basic tenet of critical theory. Organizations can be sites of domination and abuse. Once detected, abuses that have long remained undetected in the relevant environment can create significant problems for crisis communicators. Examining the organization for festering abuses and purging them before the infection is magnified is an essential responsibility of organizational communicators and an important benefit of critical theory.

KEY CONCEPTS IN CRITICAL THEORY

Multiple stakeholder theory, workplace democracy, concertive control

Stanley Deetz has written about what has been called *multiple stakeholder theory*.[19] He argues that an organization should reconfigure its perspectives of essential stakeholders to include both employees and shareholders as stakeholders. He argues that it is the objective of an organization to create a workplace democracy where all members of an organization think and act like an owner or at least an associate. George Cheney has written that workplace democracy encourages "individual contributions to important organizational choices, and . . . allows for the ongoing modification of the organization's activities and policies by [members of] the group."[20]

It is commonplace in stores such as Wal-Mart and Target to observe that employees are no longer called "employees" but rather "associates." A major university recently held a series of meetings with administrators where the agenda centered on "ownership." That is, individual units were encouraged to think of themselves as owners and to assume responsibility like an owner. Doing so, management claimed, would result in reaping the same type of benefits ownership enjoys. The key variable, of course, in workplace democracy and multiple stakeholder theory is credibility. That is, if an organization credibly reconfigures itself to render itself a participatory democracy then the idea of multiple stakeholder theory can take hold. Naturally, it will have limited value if those declared owners discover that their labels were misleading and little more than a ruse.

The residual of genuine application of multiple stakeholder theory can be what Phillip Tompkins and George Cheney have referred to as "concertive control."[21] Concertive control assumes that members of organizations are not subjugated but work collectively as a team toward the health of the organization. The control is not hierarchical, but rather derives its power and influence from the collection of workers committed to the enterprise.

Apply the Principles

How would critical theorists analyze the following two cases from Chapter 1?

Food Lion, a grocery-store chain, was mortified after an ABC segment on *Primetime Live* suggested that the company employed unsanitary practices in its preparation of products. The program that aired on November 5, 1992, suggested that the company not only sold products that had been tainted, it deliberately attempted to mask the flaws in the foods to be able to sell the products as if they were not damaged. Not only was Food Lion's image tarnished, but the ABC network's behavior was also called into question. The network was accused of employing unethical journalistic techniques to gather information about Food Lion. Both the object of the investigation, Food Lion, and the journalists/network describing the offense were tainted by the allegations.

On December 5, 2002, at the hundredth birthday celebration for retiring Senator Strom Thurmond, Senator Trent Lott of Mississippi made a comment that created a firestorm. In 1948, Thurmond had been the presidential nominee of the Dixiecrat party. In 1948, the Dixiecrats had broken away from the Democrats to run on a segregation platform. At the ceremony for Thurmond, Lott reminded all that the state of Mississippi had voted for the Dixiecrat candidate in 1948. Lott commented, "We're proud of it. And if the rest of the country had followed our lead, we wouldn't have had all these problems over all these years, either."[22] After the ceremony, Lott was chastised for what appeared to be a clearly racist remark. Ironically, six months later when Thurmond passed away, a woman named Essie Mae Washington-Williams surfaced. Soon it was revealed that Washington-Williams was Thurmond's illegitimate African-American daughter. Thurmond, a staunch segregationist during his political career, never acknowledged Washington-Williams when he was alive, but supported her financially throughout his life.

COMMUNICATION THEORY

WHAT IS COMMUNICATION THEORY? TRANSMISSION AND CONSTITUTIVE DEFINITIONS

Ironically, "communication" is a misunderstood word.

Some people think of communication as synonymous with understanding. For example, people say, "We're not communicating" or "we have a communication problem." Both of these statements typically mean that the people involved do not understand one another. Communication is not synonymous with understanding. Some people think of communication in terms of new technology. Effective communication in this meaning may refer to sophisticated computers, personal digital assistants (PDAs—better known as Blackberries), or voice-mail capabilities. These tools can improve the quality of communication in organizations, but the meaning of communication transcends what is conjured up when one considers communication technology. For the purposes of this book it is important to understand clearly what is meant by communication and to be familiar with some basic theory germane to communication study.

Communication can be understood from both a transmission perspective and a constitutive perspective. It is wise for students of crisis communication to consider communication from both of these vantage points. The transmission perspective likens communication to the act of transporting a bucket of water from one person to another. Person A has a message she wants to convey to person B. She fills the bucket with her message and attempts to get it to B. The extent to which B gets the message—sometimes called "message fidelity" in the literature of organizational communication—determines efficiency. In the organizational context, communication as transmission relates to communicating policies, tasks, evaluations, recommendations, innovations, anything germane to the organization's functioning. Person A puts the policy in the bucket and relays it to B efficiently. This perspective is important for crisis communicators because the receipt of information is vital to reducing the chances of crisis and to addressing crises in the event they occur.

The constitutive notion of communication provides a different if complementary perspective. The constitutive notion suggests that one examine communication not primarily as a transmission phenomenon that occurs within the organization, but rather as behavior that shapes or constitutes the organization. Consider the organization to be some sort of container. Inside the container are employees. As we have discussed, the transmission perspective conceives of communication as events that take place within the container—which is the organization—that help the organization's functioning. I tell a coworker to wear safety goggles when she operates the lathe and this helps the container/organization to operate efficiently. The constitutive perspective suggests that communication takes place within a container/organization, but more significantly, because of the nature of communications the size, shape, orientation, and even the goals of the organization are affected. In short, communication creates the evolving container. The process of communication forms and reforms the entity that is the organization.

For illustration, consider a meeting of executives in an organization. Assume that the meeting has a set agenda that is rigidly adhered to. Assume that the protocol at the meeting is for members to regularly challenge the positions taken by others. That is, the protocol is for the participants to generate disagreements in order to refine ideas. Given this scenario, people who are adept at articulating, persuading, defending, and criticizing ideas will be valued and those who are shy and reticent are unlikely to be similarly valued. It is possible that people who are verbose, aggressive, and loud may be promoted to powerful positions because they demonstrate, at least superficially, that they communicate effectively. If this occurs, the formation of the organization—who is in charge, who reports to whom, who is delegated as a decision maker, and who is marginalized—is a function of how people interact in the meeting. Now assume that the meetings are run differently. Instead of debate, each department head presents a document that describes the work of a department. That document is distributed to all and a short presentation is made at the weekly meeting. It is standard protocol in this scenario for PowerPoint slides to accompany the presentation. Other attendees ask polite clarifying questions at the conclusion of the talks. In this example, the most valued member of the committee is the person with the best PowerPoint slides, the most attractive documents, the most thorough report, the most digestible writing style, and the most mellifluous voice. A person with these traits is the one promoted and the one who hires assistants with similar skills and marginalizes contentious others in the organization. Communication as a constitutive phenomenon suggests that the ways in which people communicate and are allowed to communicate form the organization.

HOW DOES BASIC COMMUNICATION THEORY RELATE TO CRISIS COMMUNICATION?

Communication theory is relevant to crisis communication in at least two ways. First, from a transmission perspective, information must go from the organization to stakeholders and stakeholders must have an opportunity to respond. Second, from a constitutive perspective, the manner of communication in an organization can affect the nature of the organization such that its structure, power relationships, and communication styles either act to preempt or fuel organizational crisis. Additional relationships of communication theory to crisis communication are explained in the following sections.

KEY CONCEPTS IN BASIC COMMUNICATION THEORY

Communication is receiver centered and nonlinear

Communication is a receiver-centered phenomenon. This means that a message is not communicated by virtue of its being sent, but rather by virtue of its receipt. A message has been communicated when it has been received. Using the bucket metaphor, giving the water to an emissary to take to B does not constitute communication and would not unless B receives and acknowledges, if not understands, the entirety of the message. Communication is also a nonlinear process. This means that communication does not simply go one way from A to B, but recognizes that B may respond to A to gain clarity, additional information, or controvert the message that was initially received. Someone sends you an e-mail telling you to wear goggles when you work the lathe. You never receive it. Communication has not taken place. Assume you do receive it and you ignore it. A supervisor asks you why you are not wearing the goggles. You explain why. The two of you go back and forth on the issue. Finally, you explain your logic and this back and forth is persuasive to the supervisor to the extent that she decides to allow you to sit on safety committee meetings in the future.

The case of a psychotherapist officer in South Boston represents a stunning example of the receiver-oriented nature of communication. The therapists were having their weekly meeting when a bomb threat was phoned into the building. The therapists were meeting in a room without computers at a time when PDA use was not yet prevalent. No therapist in the room had access to e-mail. An electronic note was sent telling everyone to leave the building. Only people who had access to a computer exited, which did not include the therapists. Fortunately, the threat was a hoax.

Communication is irreversible

Once a message has been received it cannot be eradicated. A single message sent inadvertently or otherwise can create a crisis that is impossible to eliminate simply by retrieving the message. An executive who uses a racial epithet in a speech cannot simply say, "I take that back" and avert the crisis. Consider the case from Chapter 1.

> On January 19, 2004 Howard Dean, a presidential aspirant, reacted wildly, almost insanely to his loss in the Iowa caucuses. Dean appeared to be just a notch short of crazed as he asserted how he would fight on, sounding less like a resilient campaigner and more like a distraught, dispirited, if not demented loser. Dean's rant was captured on television and played regularly on news reports. The videotape portrayed the candidate as someone who had less than the requisite equanimity to lead a nation. Once the front-runner in the primaries, Dean subsequently had to battle a tarnished image because of what became known as the "Dean Scream." Eventually, Dean's candidacy lost traction, and John Kerry became the Democratic candidate for president.

Could Howard Dean meaningfully retrieve the message and eliminate the crisis? Recently, I received two e-mails from a former student informing me (and several others on her broadcasted list) that she feared she would be fired from her job. Then I received a third message telling me (and the others) to disregard the previous messages. It seemed as if all would work out after all. If someone were to ask me about this student I would probably think—though might not say aloud—that things were not particularly secure at her present job. She could not eradicate the first message.

An employer who says, "Don't think. I'll think. You just do," will leave an indelible impression that is likely to be perceived as disrespectful. Later, if your opinion is solicited, you will probably retrieve the tape of the previous conversation and doubt the veracity of the request.

Communication can be verbal or nonverbal

Communication can involve verbal and/or nonverbal messages. A verbal message is one that uses words to convey meaning. The sentences in this book are primarily verbal messages.

Gestures, timing, eye contact, esthetics (e.g., fonts on invitations, quality of paper, attractiveness of Web sites), and other nonverbal factors complement verbal symbols used to transmit the message. For example, a crisis spokesperson whose words have been selected carefully can undermine the organization by delivering the message in a monotone, or worse, in a condescending tone. Similarly, a spokesperson who sounds alert, is dressed professionally, maintains eye contact with stakeholders, and complements the spoken word with meaningful graphics can enhance the inherent quality of a company's statement to the stakeholders.

Point/Counterpoint

In this exercise, two positions are presented. The first is consistent with a point made in the chapter. The second is a counterargument. Consider the counsel and counterargument. Then write a one-page position paper identifying your position on the issue.

- Counsel—Organizations that operate with an understanding of systems theory tenets such as requisite variety and permeability will preclude the emergence of crisis.
- Counterargument—This may happen in some instances, but most crises will surface regardless of how efficiently an organization employs a systems approach. Elliot Spitzer's problem was not that his government's walls were impermeable. He just had a human problem. Procter and Gamble were actually victims of people who like to gossip. Crises are crises. You do not know when they will spring up to bite you. Employ all of the preemptive theories you want. Would they have stopped Katrina? No.

Summary: A Toolbox

Various theories provide foundational planks for those who study crisis communication.

- Systems theory tenets explain how all units of an organization are linked and how it is imperative for personnel to understand the systemic nature of organizations in order to reduce the chances of crises and to enhance communication efforts when confronted with crisis.
- Cultural theory explains how organizations have identifiable cultures and how these can reduce or increase the chances of crisis and success in addressing crisis.
- Classical theories of management explain the importance of relaying tasks and policies to

- employees in order to reduce chances of misunderstanding about responsibilities leading to crisis.
- Human resources theory explains the value of thinking of employees as potential sources of information who can participate in the success of the organization and may act as supporters of the organization in times of crisis.
- Critical theory argues that organizations can be sites of domination and that employees occasionally buy into their own domination. Crisis communicators explore these potential sources of crisis.
- Chaos theory is worth considering if for no other reason than to keep in mind how interrelated all behavior is and how likely even the seemingly most innocuous act may affect an organization in some form or other. The chaos of crisis is also worth considering as an inevitable step in the rebirth, regeneration, and development of organizations.
- Understanding basic principles of communication helps crisis communicators understand that communication is both a transmission and constitutional process. As a transmission process it needs to be studied to examine variables that can impede the successful receipt of information. As a constitutive function it can be studied to see how communication either appropriately or inappropriately shapes the evolving organization.

Exercises and Discussion Questions

1. Are there any organizations that would benefit from a classical management approach as opposed to a human resources approach?
2. Can problems such as the A-Rod case be preempted by the application of any of the theories described in this chapter?
3. How might understanding of a constitutive perspective on communication be beneficial to crisis communicators in the throes of a crisis such as the PCA crisis described in Chapter 2?
4. How do permeability and requisite variety function to facilitate image restoration and perceptions of legitimacy?
5. In your experience, which of the theories presented in this chapter are most relevant to understanding crises you have faced working in organizations?
6. Which of the theories presented in this chapter are most relevant to your experience as an external stakeholder during a crisis?

PRACTITIONER PERSPECTIVE: JULIE HALL

Julie Hall has over twenty years experience in the communications field. She has worked in government, as senior media adviser to Prime Minister Tony Blair's Active Community Unit, in opposition, as press secretary to the Rt. Hon. Neil Kinnock MP, leader of the British Labour Party, and in broadcasting as a network TV political correspondent.

Especially in an era of 24/7 newscasts, it is essential for those who face crises to get all relevant information out and to be transparent. You do not want a crisis to linger. Not being transparent and/or not providing all information is likely to fuel the crisis, not extinguish it. Some people when faced with crisis adopt a counterproductive bunker mentality. There are pressures on politicians during crises that might make a bunker seem to be attractive, but hiding or prevaricating is shortsighted, especially again, given contemporary instantaneous and continuous media reporting.

Teams are vital to the communication effort during a crisis for a related reason.

Individuals at the center of the crisis and even the inner circle of associates may have difficulty looking at a crisis from every perspective. The key players may also be overly invested in achieving certain outcomes, which can sometimes impair sound judgment. The wider the circle of team members, the greater the chance for dispassionate and well-reasoned solutions. Not only do numbers expand the vision, but these very people may be asked subsequently about the crisis and crisis communication. By expanding the circle more people who will be called upon for comments will be aware of the approaches taken to the crisis and can comment confidently and intelligently.

Politicians can definitely prepare for and even preempt crises. Policies that are established by leaders need to be carefully vetted before they are communicated. By examining all facets of policy, risks can be identified that otherwise could become infections and evolve into crises. For example, a politician has to be careful about announcing dates by which certain policy targets will be achieved. While there are some benefits to establishing target dates, the leader has to be prepared to respond if events make reaching the goal impossible. To assert that an objective will be met by October or November is not innately foolish; however, it is foolish not to be prepared to communicate in the event that something unforeseen affects the progress towards a publicly specified goal.

When faced with the decision to apologize, a leader has to consider the damages related to avoidance. Politicians can do considerable harm to their reputations and subsequent campaigns by equivocating. If there is something for which one should apologize, it is wise to fully consider the ramifications of not apologizing. A politician has to weigh the pros and cons in these situations and the cons of avoiding and prevaricating are significant. Politicians—and everyone else—make a big mistake when they underestimate the public.

NOTES

1. William Egelhoff and Sen Falguni, "An Information Processing Model of Crisis Management," *Management Communication Quarterly* 5, no. 4 (May 1992): 443–84.

2. Timothy L. Sellnow and Matthew Seeger, "Exploring the Boundaries of Crisis Communication: The Case of the 1997 Red River Valley Flood," *Communication Studies* 32, no. 2 (Summer 2001). From K.E. Weick, "Enacted Sensemaking in a Crisis Situation," *Journal of Management Studies* 25: 1988 305–17.

3. The sequel is Phillip Tompkins, *Apollo, Challenger, and Columbia. The Decline of the Space Program. A Study in Organizational Communication* (Los Angeles: Roxbury, 2005).

4. Edgar Schein, *The Corporate Culture Survival Guide: Sense and Nonsense About Cultural Change* (San Francisco: Jossey–Bass, 1999), p. xiv.

5. Terrence Deal and Allan Kennedy, *Corporate Cultures: The Rites and Rituals of Corporate Life* (Reading, MA: Addison Wesley, 1982).

6. Tompkins, *Apollo, Challenger, and Columbia*, p. 207.

7. Kurt Eichenwald, *The Informant* (New York: Broadway Books, 2000).

8. Francis Marra, "Crisis Communication Plans: Poor Predictors of Excellent Crisis Public Relations," *Public Relations Review* 24, no. 4 (Winter 1998): 46.

9. Cynthia Cooper, *Extraordinary Circumstances: Journey of a Corporate Whistleblower* (Hoboken, NJ: John Wiley and Sons, 2008), pp. 160–162.

10. http://vtap.com/wikitap/detail/Vt_massacre/WIKI10705678, accessed July 22, 2009.

11. Frederick Taylor, *The Principles of Scientific Management* (New York and London: Harper, 1923), p. 19.

12. Henri Fayol, *General and Industrial Management,* trans. Constance Storrs (New York: Pitman, 1949), p. 34.

13. Harold Levinson. "Asinine Attitudes Towards Motivation," *Harvard Business Review* (January 1973): 72–76.

14. Raymond Miles, "Human Relations or Human Resources," *Harvard Business Review* (July–August 1965): 148–63.

15. Edward Lorenz, "Predicability: Does the flap of a butterfly's wings in Brazil set off a tornado in Texas?" Paper presented at the American Academy for the Advancement of Science Meetings, Washington, D.C., 1972.

16. Sellnow and Seeger, "Exploring the Boundaries of Crisis Communication."

17. Micheline Maynard, "At JetBlue Growing Up Is Hard to Do," *New York Times,* October 6, 2008, Business section, pp. 1, 12.

18. Pamela Lutgen-Sandvik, "Take This Job and . . . : Quitting and Other Forms of Resistance to Workplace Bullying." *Communication Monographs* 73, no. 4 (December 2006): 406–33.

19. Deetz has written quite a bit about this theory. One of his earlier writings on this and democracy in the workplace in general appears in Stanley Deetz, *Democracy in an age of corporate colonization: Developments in communication and the politics of everyday life* (Albany: State University of New York Press, 1992). Another book, *Transforming communication, transforming business* (Cresskill: Hampton Press, 1995), discusses this idea of multiple stakeholder theory as well.

20. George Cheney, "Democracy in the Workplace: Theory and Practice from the Perspective of Communication," *Journal of Applied Communications Research* (August 1995): 167–200.

21. Philip Tompkins and George Cheney, "Communication and Unobtrusive Control in Contemporary Organizations." *Organizational Communication: Traditional Themes and New Directions,* ed. R.D. McPhee and P. Tompkins (Newbury Park, CA: Sage, 1985), pp. 170–210.

22. http://www.cspanarchives.org/library/index.php?main_page=product_video_info&products_id=174100-1, accessed July 23, 2009.

4 Planning for Crises

Chapter in a Nutshell

Researchers and practitioners in crisis communication argue that crises can be addressed proactively. One author on the subject titled his book, *Managing Crises Before They Happen.*[1] Another subtitled his work "Planning for the Inevitable."[2] The counsel is consistent. Organizations can and should prepare for crises. This chapter reviews recurring advice regarding how to prepare for inevitable crises.

Specifically, at the end of this chapter, readers will be able to

- Explain why proactive planning is necessary.
- Identify common denial arguments used by organizations that undermine crisis planning.
- Discuss the importance of social legitimacy and organizational ethos for proactive efforts.
- Explain how an organization can improve its communication infrastructure to prevent crises.
- Describe the relevance of stakeholder theory to proactive planning.
- Discuss the significance of globalization as it relates to proactive planning.
- Describe a step-by-step procedure for crisis preparation.

CASE 4.1: THERE MUST BE SOME MISTAKE

Note: The name of the central figure in this case and the location of the organization described have been changed.

A large public university in a "red" Midwest state boasted and had earned an excellent reputation. Admissions requirements at the school were very high and the quality of the student body was exceptional. The graduate programs were among those in the top 5 percent in the nation. The faculty, for the most part, was very active not only as researchers, but as members of the small community within which the university is set. Unlike similar schools that have a heavy publication requirement, this university also demanded outstanding teaching from its instructors. The school would not grant tenure or promote faculty members who did not meet the excellence in teaching criterion. No one could earn tenure without being considered a good citizen of both the university and the community in terms of service to both.

No professor exemplified the qualities of the outstanding faculty more than John

Worthington. With his high-school sweetheart and now spouse, Worthington had moved to the Midwest from Georgia twenty-five years earlier to take the post of assistant professor at the university. He and his wife had immediately purchased a home, quickly acclimated to the region, and in time raised their three children in the university community.

Worthington was an excellent researcher, having published several well-received books in his field of economics. Within ten years of his arrival he had been promoted to full professor at the school. His classes were nearly always oversubscribed because of the dynamic nature of his lectures. Known affectionately as Dr. W., he was considered brilliant and personable, as well as able to mix with colleagues and students seemingly effortlessly. Twice he had been elected to and served as president of the faculty senate. He was the faculty adviser for years to one of the men's fraternities. Outside the university, Worthington was a regular after-dinner speaker for community groups and a generous benefactor and member of the religious congregation where he and his family worshipped.

In addition to his work in the university and community, Worthington was a nationally known economics consultant. He had a looming presence in the community as an expert, owned his own lucrative consulting business, and was regularly interviewed on television and radio for his comments regarding the state of the economy. Beyond gifts he made to his university and congregation, Worthington generously donated moneys to the colleges that his two daughters and one son attended after they graduated from high school.

It was therefore flabbergasting to read a wire service report that appeared in the local and then national newspapers. The story reported that revered Professor John Worthington had been arrested in Europe for possession of illegal drugs. Equally devastating was the news that Worthington had been found in the company of three graduate students who were similarly indulging. According to the story, Worthington's wife was not present. Further, the news report suggested that the nature of the interactions between the professor and the students had been intimate. This implication was not made explicit, but was suggested when the media story identified the drug as one typically taken to heighten physical desire. Finally, since the college was set in a conservative state, the story was especially damaging because the report identified the graduate students as males.

This story was simply inconceivable. To everyone who knew John Worthington, knew of his family, knew of his spiritual foundation, the story had to be false. The same comment could be heard over and over throughout the university and community the day after the story broke: There must be some mistake.

But apparently there was not. At least no refutation of it appeared the next day or the next in any media publication or university press release. Despite Worthington's reputation, suddenly questions from prospective students' parents began to filter into the Admissions Office. Similarly, university donors wanted to know the details of the situation. The Graduate Student Association requested a meeting with the dean of the graduate faculty and there were rumblings through the grapevine that the parents of the three graduate students had already made an unscheduled appearance in the President's Office. The student newspaper's next edition featured a banner headline, containing only two words: "Dr. Whoa!" Still, the story seemed impossible. Faculty members, most students, and members of the community continued to mutter the same refrain like a mantra. There Must Be Some Mistake.

- Assume you work for the university.
  - If you discovered that the story was false
    - Who would be your primary stakeholders?
    - What messages would you relay?
    - What methods would you employ to communicate the messages?
  - If you discovered the story was true
    - Who would be your primary stakeholders?
    - What messages would you relay?
    - What methods would you employ?
- What other groups need to communicate regarding this incident?
  - Faculty senate?
  - Religious congregation?
  - Consulting business?
  - Fraternity?
  - Any other?
    - For each group identified
      - To what extent has legitimacy been damaged by the event?
      - To what extent do any of the four "Rs" affect these groups' communication efforts?
- If you were John Worthington and you knew you were innocent
  - Of all charges
    - To whom would you communicate?
    - What would you communicate?
    - Of any allegations of sexual improprieties despite acknowledging that you had the illegal drugs,
  - To whom would you communicate?
  - What would you communicate?
- How would the following types of theorists analyze this case?
  - Systems
  - Cultural
  - Human resources

INTRODUCTION—TIME TO FIX THE ROOF

In Chapter 2, you read the interview with practitioner Ed Klotzbier, former director of university communications at Northeastern University. Klotzbier commented metaphorically about crisis management and said that the time to fix the roof of your home is not when it is raining, but when the sun is shining. Ian Mitroff, a professor at the University of Southern California, has written several books on crisis communication. He made a point similar to Klotzbier's when he titled one of his books, *Managing Crises Before They Happen.*

The regular counsel of both practitioners and academics is similar: Plan ahead. Such planning can (1) reduce the chances of crisis, (2) in the event a crisis does occur, make communicating during and after the crisis easier, and (3) limit the damage to the organization that might otherwise be caused by crisis conditions.

Unfortunately, many organizations do not heed the advice to plan ahead. Elizabeth More reports results of studies indicating that only a small percentage of companies are prepared for crisis.[3] She refers to a 1989 study that proved that less than half of Fortune 1000 companies had "any type of crisis management plan in place." She cites a 1992 work indicating that less than 15 percent of companies have a plan. In addition, she reports that most organizations do not believe a crisis can happen to them and two-thirds of companies surveyed believed that their organization would have to be in the throes of a crisis for them to initiate crisis planning.[4]

Fast-forward twenty years and not much has changed significantly. In 2006, Holland and Gill published an article in the practitioner journal, *Communication World,* reporting that one-third of the companies they studied after the hurricane Katrina disaster indicated that they had no formal crisis communication plan in place.[5] Also in 2006, Cloudman and Hallahan reported that 25 percent of the companies that they examined did not have a written crisis communication plan.[6] The proportion of prepared companies has risen somewhat, but a good many organizations are still unprepared for crisis.

Seeger, Sellnow, and Ulmer write unequivocally that "of the various strategic activities organizations can undertake to deal with crisis, planning is the most critical."[7] In the following pages, we discuss how to plan for organizational crisis. Specifically, we discuss the following stages in crisis communication planning:

- Foundations: Avoiding denial; Ethos and legitimacy
- Establishing an internal communication structure
- Nourishing a supportive culture
- Applying stakeholder theory
- Acknowledging globalization
- A step-by-step proactive procedure

FOUNDATIONS: AVOIDING DENIAL; ETHOS AND LEGITIMACY

AVOIDING DENIAL

There are several reasons why organizations do not plan for crisis. A primary one is the tendency for companies to deny the possibility that they will ever face difficulty.

It is sobering to consider that Bernie Ebbers, the former CEO of WorldCom, is now serving a twenty-five-year sentence for a crisis his company endured. Students of the WorldCom crisis may believe that, given the culture of this organization, crisis and subsequent prosecution might have been inevitable. Perhaps the incredible success of WorldCom and the entrepreneurial skill of Ebbers in the company's early days simply went to the heads of the company's leaders. Ebbers may never have considered what he might do if the telecom bubble burst because, given his successes, failure was, literally, inconceivable. Perhaps this sense of invulnerability seeped out of the CEO's office and permeated most, but not all, of the offices at WorldCom. The residual effect was a blind, smug culture and a workforce that believed, "Nothing can happen to us." As Sherman McCoy felt in the novel *The Bonfire of the Vanities,* Ebbers and WorldCom may have sensed they were "masters of the universe."[8] Why plan for crisis? Enjoy the ride.

The themes of many books—both fiction and nonfiction—relate to the sense triumphant characters have that personal or professional crises cannot happen to them. Interested students may enjoy viewing the film or reading the Rudyard Kipling story titled, "The Man Who Would Be King." The story makes clear the potential repercussions of self-deception. Bertrand Russell is credited with having said, "In all affairs, it's a healthy thing to hang a question mark on the things you have long taken for granted."[9] For all those who have assumed their own or their company's invulnerability, an initial step in crisis management is to reexamine this illusory sense of security.

Mitroff identified several aspects of denial as it relates to crisis:

- Outright denial. This simply cannot happen to our organization.
- Minimization. Crises may occur, but their effects are minimal and we can endure what they might be.
- Idealization. Crises are what happens to poorly run organizations. We are well-run and we will therefore avoid the calamities that beset others.
- Power. We are too big and too well-connected to be affected by crisis. Our power and influence will deflect what might come our way.
- Projection. If we do have a problem it will not be our fault. Someone, the media for example, will be out to get us. It will not occur because of something we have done. We will identify the source and be exonerated.
- Intellectualization. While we might have a crisis, the chances are tiny. To invest time and money is foolish in the same way it would be foolish to bet that a highly unlikely scenario would occur. It would be a waste of resources.
- Compartmentalization. We are a multifaceted industry. If something occurs it will not hurt us centrally, it will be located in an area where we can isolate it, address it, and purge it like a cancer that has not yet infected the entire organization.[10]

A RHETORICAL METAPHOR

Rhetoric scholars examine the benefits of different styles of oral presentations. For example, a speaker can deliver an extemporaneous presentation—one delivered from notes—or a manuscript talk—one written out word for word. A speaker might also choose to use a memorized style—committing a manuscript talk to memory. For different types of presentations, one or the other of these approaches may be appropriate.

Some amateur speakers, because of arrogance, ignorance, or laziness, choose none of these approaches. They use what is called an impromptu format. This means, essentially, that they are "winging it." These persons assume that their expertise, facility with words, or general equanimity will allow them to speak eloquently without any preparation whatsoever.

An impromptu format is always a foolish choice. Speech coaches forcefully argue that if one has an option one should take the time to prepare for any presentation. It is true that some people are indeed skilled at delivering impromptu presentations, but no one should be under the illusion that it is wiser to speak without preparation when they have the opportunity to consider and practice what they wish to communicate. Nevertheless, despite coaching, some people decide not to take the time to think about a message, and instead to wing it when they are obliged to speak publicly.

Similarly, ignoring the reality that crises are inevitable, or assuming that when they surface your company will be able to easily address them, reflects foolish arrogance. Intelligence, a work ethic, eloquence, and a sense of moral virtue are not sufficient. An American politician once commented, "More than once I have heard good people come out second best in argument to demagogues because they have depended on their righteous indignation and neglected their homework."[11] Not preparing for crisis communication is "neglecting to do your homework" and the result is that you might come out "second best" to what you could become.

LEGITIMACY AND ORGANIZATIONAL ETHOS

As discussed in Chapter 2, legitimacy is based on stakeholder perceptions. If an organization does not behave appropriately, it loses legitimacy. If it does behave appropriately, it earns legitimacy, and perhaps a halo that is enduring and helpful during the throes of crisis. Image restoration theory refers to the postcrisis approaches an organization may take to restore damaged perceptions of legitimacy. Precrisis, it is important to consider how an organization can establish strong perceptions of legitimacy.

To clarify this point, again consider a comparison to a rhetorical principle. In communication studies, the word "ethos" is used to describe the perceptions audience members attribute to speakers. Ethos was identified by Aristotle in the *Rhetoric* as a crucial factor that could determine the success of a presentation, especially if the objective of a presentation is explicitly, or even implicitly, persuasive. Aristotle identified three categories of ethos—initial, intermediate, and terminal. Initial ethos refers to the perception audience members attribute to speakers prior to the start of a presentation; intermediate ethos refers to the perceptions that fluctuate during the course of a presentation; and terminal ethos refers to the lingering perceptions after a presentation. Terminal ethos is important for speakers not only because of their desire for audiences to perceive them positively at the conclusion but also because of the direct effect it has on initial ethos in subsequent presentations.

Similarly, organizations can be said to have an ethos: that is, a perception attributed to them by stakeholders. Organizational ethos is based on a number of variables, but in essence—like speaker ethos—organizational ethos is based on the reputation it has earned and is earning.

Lyon and Cameron in the *Journal of Public Relations Research* comment that "A good reputation is created and destroyed by everything a company does, from the way it manages employees to the way it handles complaints." Their article speaks specifically to the importance of organizational reputation in determining the value of communicating apologies after a crisis. Predictably, the authors find that reputation is an important factor. They comment further that reputation, like ethos, "is an ongoing index of previous responses to situations, making the most immediate response strategy a key element of that index, but also a response that should be made in light of current reputation."[12] A company's terminal ethos, the cumulative "index of previous responses to situations" is something to nourish and nurture.

Aristotle claimed that ethos was the most effective means of persuasion. More specifically, he wrote that "there are three things which inspire confidence in the orator's own character—the three namely, that induce us to believe a thing *apart from any proof of it;* good sense, good moral character, and goodwill" (emphasis added).[13] Organizations must also prove they have good sense, good character, and good will because "apart from any proof" this will influence if not determine the success of their crisis communication efforts. It will induce "stakeholders to believe a thing" apart from any proof of it. The inverse is also true: illogical decisions, immoral character, and indifference to the needs of others will "apart from any proof of it" damage crisis communication efforts.

Organizations should work to earn this ethos. Or, in the language of crisis communication, organizations should work to preserve the perceptions of legitimacy.

PROACTIVE PLANNING: COMMUNICATION INFRASTRUCTURE

INFRASTRUCTURE—CULTIVATING NETWORKS

The review of theory in Chapter 3 made clear the importance of internal communication for crisis communication efforts. Internal communication can reduce the chances that problems will fester and become crises, and internal communication can help organizations make informed choices when in the throes of crisis. An important feature of effective internal communication is efficient networking.

A communication network is similar to a highway. It is a channel that facilitates the transportation of information. Communication networks allow information to travel between and within subsystems.

UPWARD NETWORKS AND CRISIS COMMUNICATION PLANNING

One type of network that is often underutilized and sometimes barely engineered is the upward network. Upward networks are very important conduits for proactive crisis communication planning. Most organizations are adept at relaying information downward. An organization typically creates an organizational chart depicting who reports to whom and how information should travel from superior to subordinate. Organizations are not as adept at communicating upward or horizontally, or acknowledging the value of the informal network. Upward networks are very valuable to organizations, in allowing management to receive feedback from previous messages they have sent to subordinates, discover where there are problems, and to obtain ideas that they may never have considered. Horizontal networks eliminate silos because they allow the sharing of information interdepartmentally. Informal networks are important because they are considered credible and they carry information quickly throughout an organization. A grapevine out of control can undermine a crisis communication effort or create a crisis when there is none. The British politician James Callaghan is credited with having quipped that "a lie can be halfway around the world before the truth has its boots on."[14]

CLOGGED NETWORKS

Organizations have to develop upward and horizontal networks and respect the power of informal networks. The importance of these networks and the effect of their absence on organizational crises was revealed in two stunning experiments conducted during the Rogers Commission Hearings after the space shuttle Challenger exploded.

The late physicist Richard Feynman, a member of the Rogers Commission, discovered something that he found very troubling. Apparently, the cause of the Challenger explosion was related to a piece of equipment called an O-ring. Under certain temperatures, the O-rings proved not to be sufficiently resilient. What happened on that January morning was that the cold temperatures that day prevented the O-rings from returning to their natural state.

Feynman conducted a simple and now famous experiment in front of all members of the Rogers commission. He placed a piece of the 0-ring in a glass of ice water, thus demonstrating that the O-ring was not resilient. Clearly, when he removed the O-ring from the ice water, it did not return to its former state.

The lack of resiliency of the O-ring was *not* what was perplexing to Feynman. What was perplexing was how in the world the rocket scientists could not have known this? Clearly, if they had, this terrible crisis would have been averted. Feynman conducted a second experiment. He asked three engineers at the Marshall Space Flight Center to estimate the probability of rocket failure. He also asked a manager to estimate the probability of rocket failure. Instead of asking the engineers to give their estimates verbally, Feynman asked each of the engineers and the manager to write down their estimations.

One engineer wrote that the chance of failure was one in 200. Another wrote that the estimate was one in 300. A third engineer wrote that the chances were one in 200. But the manager's estimate astounded both Feynman and the other engineers. The manager wrote that he believed the chance of failure was one in 100,000.

FEYNMAN'S THEORY

How was this possible? How could the rocket scientists and the managers have such completely disparate perceptions of reality? To answer his own questions, Feynman developed a theory related to crisis communication, which he explained in an article he published in *Physics Today*.[15] Feynman argued that information available at the bottom of an organization often does not rise to the top of the organization. He contended that the reason for this was that the upward networks that are conduits for this information are typically clogged. Moreover, he argued that the upward networks were clogged because there was implicit discouragement of messages that would be sent using these networks.

Feynman suggested that managers tend to exaggerate accomplishments of their units when they communicate with superiors. Management may do this for reasons related to pride or resources. Several managers may be competing for funding in a zero-sum game and, consequently, unit heads may embellish what their department is doing to assure that projects will continue and funding will remain with the unit. Consequently, Feynman contends that managers are unwilling to listen to subordinates who desire to disabuse their supervisors of the exaggerated claims. To listen to contradictory information may require that a manager rescind requests for resources that were based on the exaggerated claims. To eliminate the need to rescind these claims, Feynman argued that many supervisors deliberately discourage information that would compel them to rescind the claims. Without information to the contrary, a manager can claim a simple lack of knowledge that they just did not know that a problem existed. With the information, a manager would not have the same plausible deniability.

Feynman asserted that because of this phenomenon, while an organization might have a prescribed upward network, this channel might be illusory, or more likely, just clogged. Information on the informal network would carry the word that the manager did not want to hear news that was antithetical to articulated positions. And therefore nobody would send contrary information up the line.

The crisis implications of this theory were and are enormous. What happens when subordinates know of impending disaster, but do not relay the information because of clogged or nonexistent networks? Problems that could be addressed are not addressed before they lather and become crises.

- An employee who knows of several bad loans may not tell a superior who has just boasted about successful loan activity in her division.
- A brilliant, but eccentric colleague, who acts out, sometimes violently, may not be reported to a top manager who has intimated that "I pay my managers to take care of the Mickey Mouse stuff."
- Several workers may notice that a person on an assembly line typically does shoddy work, but these workers may feel that the "open door" policy is only open for good news.
- An awareness of recurring sexual harassment may remain on the informal network if executives tend to react in exasperation when such information is brought to their attention.

If the upward network is clogged, financial companies can "suddenly" collapse; lunatics may "unpredictably" injure colleagues; automobile parts may "inexplicably" be defective; sexual predators may be "discovered" after complaints damage the integrity of an organization. Clogged upward networks can create crises. Open upward networks characterize a communication infrastructure that retards the development of crises. Information simply gets to people who can take action to stop a developing crisis.

HORIZONTAL NETWORK INFRASTRUCTURE

Similarly, clogged horizontal networks can create crises and open horizontal networks can reduce the chances that crises will develop. Consider the following case that describes how a crisis evolved because of a breached horizontal network.

Sell-sell-sell-party-party-party

A software company located in the United States was acquired by a larger foreign organization. Prior to the acquisition the sales force at the software firm was a play-hard/work-hard bunch whose motto was "sell-sell-sell-party-party-party." Members of the sales team were paid on commission. They sold aggressively and reveled in the rewards of their hard selling. One of the problems the firm had prior to the acquisition was that customers occasionally complained that when they purchased a product they had received vague assurances of technical support, but that technical support was often delayed. These complaints were like water off a duck's back to the sales force. They kept selling, kept earning their commissions, and decided that the information technology (IT) team and the big shots should figure out the problems with tech support.

The acquiring organization had been made aware of the customer complaints about tech support when they acquired the company. To address this they imposed a new policy. The new policy was that no product could be sold until and unless the IT group was able to schedule an installation and training session with the customer. Customers could thus be assured that the sale would be quickly accompanied by technological support. Any sale would be predicated on communication between sales and IT that confirmed a date for installation and tech support. No new channels, however, were established to facilitate interactions between sales and IT.

Members of the IT team were paid on salary. They took the new rule seriously. Members of the sales team were paid on commission. When they made a sale, the IT staff would delay the sale (and the commission) until they could comfortably schedule a training session. The delay did not affect the income of IT staff because they were not paid on commission. Of course, unreasonable delays in accommodating customers would be reflected in performance reviews and that could affect salaries. But as long as there were no serious delays or customer complaints, there would be no monetary losses for the IT personnel.

The sales force was livid. This new policy and the IT department's ability to delay sales affected their income. Their income was dependent on the pace of the IT trainers. The result was predictable. Some members of the sales group decided to circumvent IT and the policy. They ceased to communicate with the IT team about the installation dates. These salespeople continued to submit their sales reports to the acquiring overseas organization indicating on the statements a date for IT service that was within what they considered to be a reasonable time for IT to do its work. The sales people thus implied, disingenuously, that the tech support schedule had been agreed to by IT. It had not. In order for the subterfuge to work, not only did the IT people not approve the installation schedule, they could not even know of the sales.

Subsequently, IT received calls from customers angry that the installation was late. IT was beyond flabbergasted. They were being reprimanded by angry customers. They told the customers that as far as they knew there had been no sale. Customers complained to the home office. Customers contacted watchdog agencies. A public investigation of the company was announced. The acquiring organization was terribly embarrassed.

Letters had to be generated to consumers. Prospective customers were contacted assuring them that the noise they heard reflected an aberration. Emergency teleconferences were held with sales and IT staff. An advertisement was taken out in trade magazines apologizing for the problems. Significantly, resentments lingered between the two groups for years. A crisis developed because horizontal networks were not constructed and those that existed informally were not used.

Detecting and deflecting crises

At the Marshall Space Flight Center, years before the Challenger exploded, the organization had a very sophisticated approach to upward and horizontal networks. This approach deflected crises. The head of the center Dr. Wernher von Braun, was years ahead of his time in terms of respecting the importance of communication. Von Braun commented that he was in the "earthquake prediction business." In other words, he was in the business of detecting potential problems and purging them before they became crises.

Von Braun employed a regular communication process called "Monday Notes." Each Monday a series of departmental reports were generated by unit heads and distributed to von Braun. Von Braun would read the notes, make comments in the margins, and then distribute all of the Monday Notes to each department head. The system worked well. Von Braun wrote meaningful comments on the reports. The department heads sensed that the objective of the report was to share information and not to assess performance. Each department head found that the information about other units was meaningful. The value of these notes was so great that employees within departments would generate a set of Friday Notes prior to Monday so that the composers of the Monday Notes would have sufficient information to comprehensively create their Monday Notes. The protocol allowed units to detect earthquake tremors and avoid earthquakes.

Von Braun identified the difficulties of being in the earthquake-prediction business: one has to decide which tremors are legitimate and which are invalid, otherwise one might react often and prematurely. However, it is worth the effort to create the networks. Indeed an analysis of NASA's subsequent crisis problems—after von Braun left the Marshall Space Flight Center—suggest that their crises surfaced precisely because such networks were lacking.

LEARNING ORGANIZATIONS

A learning organization, as the name suggests, is one dedicated to sharing information. A learning organization gathers information and evolves qualitatively because of what it has learned from sharing information. Peter Senge is the author most closely affiliated with the concept of learning organizations. In books such as *The Fifth Discipline: The Art and Practice of the Learning Organization,* he articulates the importance of conceptualizing an organization as one that advances because of what it understands.[16] Senge also writes about organizations that have "learning disabilities." These organizations are incapable of learning, or—just as often—lack the desire to learn, as a recalcitrant underachieving high schooler does. And also like the recalcitrant high schooler, organizations that deliberately avoid information and communication regularly get into trouble.

PROACTIVE PLANNING: APPLY STAKEHOLDER THEORY

In his article "Planning for the Inevitable," John Aspery writes, "Crisis communications built on well-established relationships with key audiences stand a better chance of protecting, even enhancing company reputations in times of difficulty. The real success stories are told by organizations to whom effective corporate communications is an intrinsic part of their day-to-day business activities."[17]

Stakeholder theorists posit that every organization has multiple stakeholders. A key to effective crisis communication is to identify all of its external and internal stakeholders and, in the throes of crisis, communicate with each distinct population by generating relevant messages to every group. However, stakeholder theory applies prior to crises as well. According to a study done by Wan and Pfau, reputation management is a key to effective crisis communication.[18] Reputation management involves creating positive relationships with stakeholders before any crisis so that they will be more sympathetic to the organization during crises.

Considerate people in organizations are likely to establish positive relationships with stakeholders as a matter of course. However, some organizations need to be reminded of how important all audiences are regardless of how immediately these persons can affect a company's bottom line.

A school system, of course, must be aware of parents, students, teachers, and local government officials. Any school administrator knows this intuitively. But will all central administrators be aware of other audiences such as police officers, fire officials, sanitation workers, highway maintenance personnel, neighboring homeowners, storeowners, or the manager of local radio stations? All of these are external stakeholders. Are there internal stakeholders that a school superintendent might overlook? Establishing relationships with the teachers union is certainly important, but what about the student newspaper staff, head of the counterculture magazine, athletic departments, guidance counselors, nurses, and psychologists?

MALDEN MILLS

The Malden Mills crisis case is a good one to review in terms of the value of applying stakeholder theory as a proactive crisis communication activity. As Robert Ulmer asserts in his *Management Communication Quarterly* article about Malden Mills "The analysis [of this case] demonstrates the importance of establishing strong communication channels and positive value positions with stakeholders well before crises erupt."[19]

Malden Mills is a textile company located, despite its name, in Lawrence not Malden, Massachusetts (both towns are suburbs of Boston). In December 1995, the plant burst into flames, workers were injured, and the plant was forced to shut down. Despite the tragedy, Aaron Feuerstein, the CEO of Malden Mills, became a local and national hero. Then President Clinton even introduced and lauded Feuerstein during the 1996 State of the Union address. Townspeople in Lawrence referred to Feuerstein in terms just short of reverence if not deification.

Ulmer makes the case that the success of the Malden Mills crisis communication effort was due to precrisis relationships with employees and community members. These relationships had developed largely through the CEO Feuerstein's efforts. It is possible if not likely that what Feuerstein did in establishing these relationships was less a function of strategy and more related to his ethical DNA, but regardless of the reason, Feuerstein and Malden Mills are often cited as an example of a company that did it right. Feuerstein had developed a reservoir of good will with his employees and the community "through consistent communication [of] value positions of trust, reciprocity, and loyalty."[20] After the fire, stakeholders not only believed and appreciated Feuerstein's postcrisis statements of support, *they acted as communication agents of the company speaking positively about it* exhibiting what is called "supportive behavior." In the language of crisis communication discussed in Chapter 2, internal and external stakeholders "honored the account" and exhibited "supporting behavior."

Not all situations similar to Feuerstein's have such a happy ending. In part, his success can be attributed to the fact that the crisis was the result of an accident. Nevertheless, what happened in Lawrence with Malden Mills illustrates how stakeholder theory can work with internal and community stakeholders.

Ulmer writes what we probably all know intuitively, "Critical to the understanding of organizational values is that they are developed over time through consistent communication behavior."[21] While we may all know this intuitively, we may not take the time to establish relationships through consistent communication behavior that reflects our values.

Many readers have seen or heard the quip, "When you're up to your neck in alligators it is difficult to remember that your original intention was to drain the swamp." Being "up to your neck in alligators" is not what we have been referring to as crisis. It is about the daily chaos of our work world. We all tend to have many things going on. Given our full days, we may assume that establishing relationships is something to be done when we have time. The problem is that we never have time for activities unless we make time for them.

Stakeholder theory as applied to crisis communication suggests that we need to make time to establish relationships. Establishing these relationships is not something to do after priorities have been addressed. This is a priority. Feuerstein's stakeholders saw him as legitimate because ongoing communications had developed relationships that earned him that legitimacy. They did not just like him. When faced with a crisis, his stakeholders worked for him.

INOCULATION THEORY

Inoculation theory assumes that one can prevent attitude changes by subjecting receivers to a counter-attitudinal argument and rebutting that argument proactively.

Originally developed by William McGuire in the early 1960s, inoculation theory is so labeled because the platform on which it rests is the same as the one that supports medical inoculations.

When people are inoculated against diseases, the procedure works by exposing the patient to the illness in small doses. The inoculation has the effect that one builds up antibodies to combat the illness if one is exposed to it. Inoculation theory as applied to crisis communication is similar. Stakeholders are exposed to a counter-attitudinal attack and then provided with rebuttals to that attack. Thus, the stakeholder has been given antibodies to combat counter-attitudinal attack.

Inoculation researchers speak about refutational-same pretreatments, and refutational-different pretreatments. Refutational-same pretreatments "contain the very specific counterarguments refuted in the messages that can be anticipated in later real attacks." In other words, receivers who are exposed to refutational-same treatments will see the same counterarguments in subsequent attack messages as those seen in the treatments. Refutational-different messages, on the other hand, are generic in nature.[22]

For clarification, consider this example. Prior to a college super bowl game, officials from an urban university contact community members. They do this because after a home team's victory there tends to be revelry that can be noisy and disruptive. In the past, students have been blamed for being unruly. The university presents to community members the possibility that there may be excessive noise, that some students may be involved, and that students will likely be blamed for property damage.

However, the university's message includes the fact that in the past students who have been disruptive represent less than one percent of the offenders. Moreover, the university explains that it has a harsh policy of expelling any students who are found to be culpable. By doing this, the university attempts to inoculate community members who may be exposed to a counter-attitudinal argument—students are disruptive miscreants—by presenting them with that argument and then refuting it prior to any potential exposure. Thus, the university is attempting to embed antibodies that can fight against any developing illness. A refutational-same argument may be to counter the specific claim that the university had no campus police working the night of the Super Bowl. A refutational-different argument may be that the university has a laissez-faire attitude toward student behavior.

What do you think of inoculation theory as a way of preempting crises?

Apply the Principles: Stakeholder and Inoculation Theory

- Assume you work in the office of corporate communication for
  - John Worthington's university precrisis
  - The National Rifle Association
  - Your bank
  - The governor of your state
  - Google
  - A hospital
- How might you apply inoculation theory with
  - Two groups of internal stakeholders?
  - Two groups of external stakeholders?

Hubble Space Telescope

Earlier in this chapter we discussed problems with NASA and the Challenger crisis. Another NASA case is illustrative here. Instead of using inoculation theory, NASA attempted what amounted to an antithetical approach, which, unfortunately, is not unique. Other organizations have done similar things that, in the final analysis, created crises.

James Kauffman discusses this case in a *Public Relations Review* article, where he examines NASA's crisis with the Hubble Space Telescope.

Prior to launch, NASA exaggerated the telescope's potential. Specifically, NASA described the high quality photographs that would be a product of the experiment and how extraordinary these pictures would be. The problem was that NASA knew the telescope could not do what it claimed. Why NASA would then embellish as it did is confounding. Eventually, the exaggeration would be apparent to any person who viewed the pictures. The Hubble Telescope could not deliver what NASA contended it would.

The pictures from the telescope, predictably, were not as engaging as the exaggerated claims. In addition to the photos' relative blandness compared to the expectations, the photos contained what NASA referred to as a "spherical aberration" that limited the quality of the pictures. The existence of the spherical aberration, of course, was more glaring because of the exaggerated expectations. Not only had NASA not inoculated audiences by suggesting that things could go wrong, they had enhanced the expectations of stakeholders.[23]

"Although the hobbled Hubble could do exciting science, NASA's exaggerations and focus had whetted Congress's and the public's appetite for pictures. Without photographs Hubble was viewed as a failure."[24] To further erode their crisis effort, NASA tried to fault a contractor for the problem, blaming Perkin Elmer for poorly grinding the mirror.

Establishing positive relationships with stakeholders is wise. Myopically promising outcomes that are not deliverable is not wise and will eventually create crises.

GLOBALIZATION AND ETHNOCENTRISM

In 1967, Marshall McLuhan wrote a book called *The Medium Is the Message.* In it (and in some other writings), McLuhan described a phenomenon he referred to as the global village. By this he meant that with advances in transportation and communication technology the entire world would soon resemble a village. Information would be available worldwide instantly in much the same way that people in the past discovered what was "news" by visiting the general store.

We are there.

In a single day in February 2009, I communicated almost instantly with colleagues in St. Louis, California, New York, Nebraska, Florida, and Australia. This day and my situation is not unique. Readers no doubt have similarly interacted with people all over the world in a single day. Today we can find out about skirmishes in the Middle East more rapidly than we can walk to the corner to see what the commotion is about in the local park. This evening, February 12, 2009, a plane crashed in Clarence, New York, and over forty people perished. If you turn on your computer minutes after such a tragedy has occurred, on any continent, you can learn about this accident as quickly, or more quickly, than colleagues of mine who work in Buffalo, fifteen miles from the crash site.

In 2005, some forty years after McLuhan's *The Medium Is the Message,* columnist Thomas Friedman wrote the enormously popular book, *The World Is Flat,* which has a similar global village theme. Organizations are "going global" in part, because the world is flat. American companies that may at one time have been run and almost completely operated in small isolated towns, now have offices in Europe, South America, Africa, Asia, and Australia. If offices are not located overseas, often work is contracted out to other countries. Have a problem with your computer? Have a service contract? Make a phone call and you are speaking to someone in Malaysia who tries to help.

In addition to the cultural diversity that results when organizations have locations all over the world, because of the ease of travel, the workforce in any single location can reflect tremendous diversity. The workforce population of your grandparents' and even your parents' generation was far more homogeneous than yours will be. Within any location, the workforce represents multiple ethnicities, races, religions, and cultures.

Why is this significant for crisis communicators?

Before we begin to answer this question, take a moment to read the following case concerning the Toshiba Corporation.

TOSHIBA CORPORATION

In 1987 a company called the Toshiba Machine Company, a subsidiary of the Toshiba Corporation, engaged in conduct that enraged the United States Congress as well as many of the country's citizens. The Toshiba Machine Company with the help of another company from Norway had illegally sold submarine propeller technology to the then Soviet Union. This technology could help our cold war enemy, the Soviet Union, construct quieter, less detectable submarines. These submarines would be more sophisticated than vessels used by the United States and therefore jeopardized our prior superiority in this military area. It is important to note that the illegal behavior had not been sanctioned by the Toshiba Corporation itself, just by the subsidiary Toshiba Machine Company.

Because of the illegal sale, members of the House of Representatives railed against Toshiba and proposed a five-year ban on the sales of its products in the United States. On one day during the congressional discussion, congressmen took out a sledgehammer and smashed a Toshiba radio and tape-recording product to bits.

The U.S. government and its citizens were important external stakeholders for Toshiba. It was essential that Toshiba attempt to restore legitimacy. Toshiba had to make clear that while they accepted responsibility and were sorry, the parent company was not involved with, nor did it condone, the illegal sale. Another challenge for Toshiba related to addressing what seemed to be a xenophobic congressional reaction. There was concern that the extreme nature of the penalty could be a function of cultural tensions.

To begin the process of image restoration, Toshiba's chairperson, Shoichi Saba, and its president, Sugiichiro Watari, announced their resignations. The new chairperson, Joichi Aoi, said that his most important challenge was "to figure out how to restore the trust in Toshiba that has been damaged by the actions of Toshiba Machine."[25] As is evident in Aoi's remark, Toshiba apologized, but clearly indicated that the Toshiba Machine Company, not Toshiba, had been the transgressor.

The issue of xenophobia was thornier. Was the proposed penalty excessive? The executive director of a human studies institute commented that "It's rather interesting that the Congress didn't smash Norwegian sardine tins, only the Toshiba radio." A press release on behalf of Toshiba of America claimed that, "the sanction on Toshiba is a blatant double standard which can only be perceived by Japan as highly discriminatory." The press release also included a charge from Japan's trade minister, "It seems the measures taken are not only aimed at the trade problem but are also based on racial discrimination against the Japanese."[26]

The Toshiba case was further complicated because not only was Toshiba lobbying to reduce the recommended penalties, but so were U.S. companies like IBM, AT&T, General Electric, and Xerox. These companies were motivated because the ban on Toshiba products would have affected these companies as well in terms of work and jobs.

Eventually the penalties were changed and the sanctions were placed primarily on the Toshiba Machine Company. Penalties on the Toshiba parent company were limited.

Below are some questions to consider regarding this case.

1. Previously in this chapter we discussed several issues related to proactive crisis communication. How are the following related to this case?
    a. Stakeholder theory
    b. Organizational ethos
    c. Communication infrastructure
    d. Feynman's theory
2. Was the congressional attack on the Toshiba Corporation fair since it was a subsidiary, not Toshiba Corporation, which committed the act?
3. Why did the United States not ban Norwegian sardines?
4. Might an understanding of culture and international relationships have affected the development of this crisis?
5. Was this a racial incident? Did it reflect congressional xenophobia?
6. Could international tensions escalate because of something like this incident?

CULTURE AND CRISIS

Organizations can plan for some crises by
- Acknowledging the reality of what has been called globalization,
- Respecting the multiethnic nature of their workforce, and
- Recognizing that ethnocentrism and ignorance can breed crises.

Some classic crisis cases from the past involved marketing U.S. products to other countries. General Motors attempted to sell the Nova to Mexican markets and was mortified when the company became the subject of ridicule. "No va" in Spanish means "does not go." You are unlikely to be able to sell many automobiles that are called "Does not go."

DuPont attempted to sell its paint products in Spanish-speaking markets and simply translated its slogan, "DuPont for years" for their Spanish-speaking consumers. The translation, however—in a stunning display of ethnocentric ignorance—neglected to include the tilde over the "n" in the Spanish word for "years." I will leave it to readers to discover the humiliation that this error caused for DuPont, a conservative company that was championing its products by utilizing what, in translation, became a profane slogan unlikely to convince readers to purchase a DuPont product.

Language is not the only factor that can create crises in our increasingly flat world. Issues related to time, cultural norms, race, religion, politics, and history must be understood to avoid reckless behavior, however inadvertent, that can create crises.

Ethnocentrism, the tendency to see the world from the perspective of one's own ethnicity, is the bane of successful intercultural communication. People who are ethnocentric not only view the world from their own vantage point, but assume that their ethnic perspective is superior to others. For example, persons from a culture that values industry may not see people who are less driven simply as different, but may consider them inferior as well. If your ethnic or corporate culture endorses the credo "the bottom line is the only line," it may be difficult to understand the stakeholders with whom you may have to interact during crisis. It will also be difficult to establish relationships prior to crisis that will make stakeholders willing to honor your accounts of the crisis.

POLITICAL CRISES

Both presidents Jimmy Carter and George W. Bush experienced frustrating problems with political crises, in part because of ethnicity and culture. In *Communication Studies,* Denise Bostdorff writes about the 1979 Iranian hostage crisis and is critical of President Carter's behavior during it. Bostdorff writes that Carter was too much an idealist and too passive and needed to be a pragmatist when dealing with the Iranian students holding the Americans captive for over a year.[27] Bostdorff suggests that the duration of the crisis was in part due to the way President Carter—and most Americans—constructed the universe and perhaps ethnocentrically conceived of power, certainty, and independence. It seems possible, if not likely, that the inability to secure the release of the hostages was related not to the ostensible issue of not returning the Shah, but to America and its leaders' lack of understanding of the culture and values of Khomeini's regime in Iran.

Similarly, the war in Iraq that began in 2003 during George W. Bush's presidency has been criticized because of assumptions about the way Iraqis would respond to their liberation once Saddam Hussein was captured. Imagining the world from a Western perspective leads one to think that liberation would result in universal jubilation. There would be a Munchkin-like celebration of Iraqis crooning about their freedom, a subsequent increase in entrepreneurial activity, civil elections, and the emergence of democracy and capitalism. These were ethnocentric assumptions about how people think and what they would do, on the basis of our cultural orientations.

Understanding your audience should be a preliminary step in all message preparation. Audience analysis is more complex when stakeholders are culturally diverse. Proactive planning for crisis thus requires an acknowledgment of issues germane to ethnocentrism and other variables that affect intercultural interaction.

PERCEPTUAL VARIANCE: THE HOFSTEDE STUDIES

The Hofstede studies are so called because they were conducted by a researcher named Geert Hofstede. The first set of Hofstede experiments was conducted in 1980. In 2000 Hofstede published a second book revealing that his initial research had been supported by subsequent studies. Geert Hofstede identified four distinctive categories of information processing depending on culture and nationality. He called these categories power distance, uncertainty avoidance, masculine versus feminine, and individualism versus collectivism. In recent years, Hofstede has added a fifth category, long-term versus short-term orientation.

Below is a description of three Hofstede categories that are particularly relevant to crisis communication.

Power distance

Power distance refers to the respect attributed to people with authority. Countries that are high power-distance countries attribute respect to supervisors, managers, and administrators because of the status they have as people in authority. Cultures that are categorized as low power distance do not inherently grant leaders respect. A student in a low power-distance country does not automatically respect an instructor. In a high power-distance culture instructors, managers, and superiors are inherently respected. Malaysia, Guatemala, and Panama are identified as high power-distance cultures. Austria, Israel, and Denmark are labeled low power-distance cultures.

How might an ignorance of the different perceptions of power distance create organizational crises?

Individualism versus collectivism

This categorization refers to whether the culture reveres people who act independently or those who respect collective activity. A culture that sees the family unit as sacrosanct differs from a culture that encourages each person to "do his own thing" and rewards maverick behavior. Sammy Davis Jr. sold many records in the United States with his song, "I've Gotta Be Me." Similarly, Frank Sinatra's song, "My Way," was called by the singer the national anthem of the country. Communicators appealing to the sensitivities of stakeholders from different cultural orientations would be wise to be aware that others will not value the same perspectives on collectivism versus individualism. The United States, Australia, and Great Britain are considered countries that greatly respect individualism. Guatemala, Ecuador, Panama, and Venezuela place high values on collectivism.

How might an ignorance of the different perceptions of individualism versus collectivism create organizational crises?

Uncertainty avoidance

Cultures that are called high uncertainty-avoidance cultures require specificity in a way that low uncertainty-avoidance cultures do not. Uncertainty avoidance means the desire to be specific, or in other words, to avoid uncertainty. Low uncertainty avoidance means that it is unnecessary to be specific. A meeting of people with low uncertainty avoidance would not care particularly if the agenda were nebulous. High uncertainty avoidance would want the agenda to be specific. In times of crisis high uncertainty-avoidance cultures need far more specific information than low uncertainty-avoidance cultures. Greece, Portugal, and Guatemala are cited by Hofstede as high uncertainty-avoidance cultures. Singapore, Jamaica, and Denmark are low uncertainty-avoidance cultures.

How might an ignorance of the different perceptions of uncertainty avoidance create organizational crises?

LANGUAGE AND LINGUISTIC RELATIVITY

It is obvious that intercultural communication can be problematic if people do not share the same language. More subtle language problems occur when idiomatic expressions or slang terms are used, which are not easily understood or are literally decoded by receivers. Communication noise can occur even between generations in this way when terms familiar to certain age groups are unfamiliar to others. Expressions like *dis, phat,* and the *bomb,* can be misconstrued by those not familiar with the jargon. Even communication terms like *wikis, blogs,* and *flickr* may be unfamiliar to people of another generation. However, cross culturally, idioms can be wildly misinterpreted, embarrassing, and even comical when used to communicate to audiences that derive different meanings from the terms.

The Sapir-Whorf hypothesis or linguistic relativity is another factor that affects intercultural communication. The assumption behind linguistic relativity is that words drive thought and behavior. Language induces conceptualization and not vice versa. The effect of linguistic relativity on intercultural communication is that people with certain words can think in a way and can conceptualize in a way that those without those or similar words cannot. A person with a sophisticated vocabulary has the potential to conceptualize in ways that someone with a skeletal vocabulary cannot.

How are ethnocentrism, perceptual disparities, and language significant to crisis communication planning? In a world that is getting smaller, organizations need to respect the diversity of stakeholders. To avoid misunderstanding and insults, crisis communicators should be careful when establishing and maintaining relationships to acknowledge the role cultural diversity can have on the process.

STEP-BY-STEP CRISIS PLANNING

As has been suggested in the previous pages, the foundation for crisis communication success involves crisis planning. Organizations must recognize their vulnerability to crisis, establish an effective communication infrastructure, apply stakeholder theory to develop relationships, and be sensitive to diverse cultural orientations. These items require ongoing behavior. An organization cannot tick off "establish stakeholder relationships" after a contact is made and assume that a part of its proactive crisis planning has been addressed.

However, one can take steps that amount to a checklist that can be ticked off as an organization prepares for crises. These are not steps to be done in lieu of what has been previously discussed. These are actions that presume the other activities are ongoing. Below is a step-by-step approach to crisis communication planning.

1. Get commitments. Obtain a pledge from chief administrators to respect the importance of crisis planning and, significantly, to implement developed plans when the organization is confronted with crisis. There have been cases when an organization had a plan for specific crises in place, but when confronted with the crisis the organization would not employ it. An initial step is getting buy-in.

   Crisis practitioners also argue that before developing any plan, all of the architects and executives involved in its development must become committed to creating plans that they are willing to publish. The organization may not actually publish them, but the integrity of the plans is such that nothing in them would embarrass the organization if they were made public.

2. Create a crisis communication team. This should be a cross-functional group. The value of diversity on this team is that persons from different units of the organization provide varied perspectives on solutions. People from different units can also anticipate crises that members from other units may not be as likely to consider.

   There are some variations regarding precisely who should be on the team. Steven Fink contends that the central core of the team should consist of a chief executive, the chief financial officer, the head of corporate communications, and a general counsel.[28] Others suggest including a safety officer and someone from human resources.[29] Seeger, Sellnow, and Ulmer report that the team should have information technology specialists, emergency-response professionals, medical liaison professionals, and family liaison personnel.[30]

   The composition of your team may be unique to your business and the type of crises you are likely to face. The team has to be small enough to be manageable. In Chapter 7, we discuss issues related to team interaction, but the point can be made here that as teams get larger, meaningful interaction becomes more challenging. Some people who might participate in a small group may not do so in a larger group.

   In sum, you need a team. The team should include people from various organization areas. The precise composition will depend on your organization and the crises it may face. The size cannot be such that the group ceases to be manageable.

3. Predict crises. The team should attempt to predict crises that could surface in the organization. The group brainstorms, lists, and records all of these. (Details regarding procedures for brainstorming and other idea-generating techniques appear in Chapter 7.) The team then categorizes crises that are similar.

   For example, crises related to industrial accidents may be in one category, personnel misdeeds in a second, unexpected financial downturn in a third, natural disasters such as blizzards in a fourth, and mergers in a fifth.

4. Identify stakeholders. For each crisis category the group applies stakeholder theory and identifies discrete populations that require distinct messages if crises do occur.

   For example, a restaurant would likely list food poisoning as a crisis category. In this step, the team identifies stakeholders who would need to receive information in the case of food poisoning: waitstaff, cooks, vendors, regular customers, newspapers, culinary critics, trade magazines, stockholders if the company is public, other restaurants, local hospitals, medical personnel, and so on. While the nuances of any case, of course, cannot be predicted, stakeholders can be identified for the crisis categories.

5. Identify nuggets. Earlier we defined nuggets as the units of information contained within any message. For each crisis identified in the prior step, the team should list the nuggets essential for specific stakeholder groups. The details of some nuggets would, of course, be unknown prior to individual crisis, but some nuggets can be generally identified.

Apply the Principles

Assume that you work for a
- Hospital
- Health club
- Automobile dealership
- Grocery story

Identify:
- Three types of crises each group might face;
- Two internal and two external stakeholders for each crisis identified; AND
- The two most important nuggets for each stakeholder group.

---

6. Identify methods. After identifying the nuggets, the team needs to determine the best method for delivering these nuggets.

   Should the message be relayed at a press conference accompanied by a written statement, in an electronic mailing, or posted on a Web site? Should representatives phone afflicted consumers or post a notice in a newspaper? In a world of wikis and Web sites, it is imperative that members of the team be aware of new social networks when deciding what methods are best for communicating with each stakeholder population.

7. Prepare materials ahead of time. Some information cannot be prepared ahead of the actual crisis, but some can.

For example, in the food-poisoning category, the restaurant crisis communication team could prepare the following material before any crisis:

- The restaurant's written policy for maintaining health standards;
- A statement that documents an outstanding record in terms of customer complaints;
- A list of awards from nutritionist organizations;
  - Quotes and commendations from health officials;
  - The company's standard policy for dealing with customer complaints related to illness;
- A list of procedures conducted daily to ensure cleanliness; and
- The history of the restaurant and its successes.

8. Identify a sequence. Some stakeholders may receive more than one communication. All stakeholders will not receive all messages concurrently. In this step, the team determines which stakeholders need to be contacted first, and if messages to a single stakeholder are to be disseminated in stages how these multiple messages should be sequenced.

   For example, in a blast e-mail, regular customers may be told (a) what took place, (b) what they can do if they believe they have been affected, and (c) that on Tuesday there will be clinic hours at St. Joe's Hospital dedicated to this purpose. Those who attend the clinic may receive a printout describing corrective actions taken to preclude this from happening in the future while concurrently all regular customers receive another e-mail identifying the same corrective actions articulated on the handout distributed at the clinic. Those who attend the clinic may be invited to meet with restaurant personnel who are seated at a table labeled "ASK US," on which brochures indicating the impeccable cleanliness record of the restaurant are stacked.

   Communication is a nonlinear phenomenon. Part of this sequencing stage involves predicting how stakeholders will respond to communications and preparing responses to these predicted reactions.

9. Create a center for communications. There should be a designated place that the crisis communicators know is headquarters for the team. These headquarters must be technologically equipped to allow a variety of sources to send and receive communications.

10. Identify and train spokespersons. Excellent plans can be undermined by people who cannot deliver messages eloquently. Stories abound of brilliant executives who are poor communicators.

    I have conducted speaker-training workshops for years and the range of speaking skill is stunningly diverse. High-paid executives have mumbled through talks, used excessive speech fillers, digressed, omitted significant content, been unable to maintain eye contact, seemed unwilling to learn the knowledge base of audience members, been ineffective in responding to questions, used words that did not match the idea or were inappropriate for the occasion, spoken too rapidly for digestion, used visual aids that did not aid or were not visually explanatory, spoke too softly to be heard, and used random hand gestures that created distractions—in short, they have exhibited communication behavior that is inconsistent with the presentation goal.

Spokespersons should be coached in techniques that can facilitate effective transmission. Those who will represent your organization must be trained to speak well and it cannot be assumed that by virtue of their organizational status or intelligence quotient they will be able to do this effectively. Some people may be skilled speakers when discussing plans for a new building, but are not comfortable under pressure. Duress is not easy to simulate, but spokespersons can be trained. In Chapter 8 there is a discussion of techniques for reducing anxiety and delivering oral presentations.

11. Simulate enacting the crisis plan. Every writer on the subject of crisis communication emphasizes the importance of conducting simulations. Crisis communication is not the time for on-the-job training. Simulating press conferences, making presentations to angry stakeholders, and generating instructive information to stakeholders can and should be practiced in simulations.

12. Record your plan. Update periodically. There should be a record of the plans you have constructed. The team should meet regularly to review the plans and revise them if necessary. When confronted with a crisis, the team should be aware that they are to gather in the crisis communication facility, review the crisis plan generated for the particular crisis, and begin enacting the plan.

Apply the Principles

Use the step-by-step method presented in this chapter to establish a crisis communication plan for one of the following:
- College,
- Church or synagogue,
- Fraternity or sorority, OR
- Current place of work.

What are the two biggest obstacles you would face?
- Developing the plan?
- Getting buy-in from others?
- Implementing the plan should a crisis arise?

WHY PLANS FAIL

This step-by-step process would seem to ensure success, but often crisis communication plans are not enacted successfully. Crisis communication practitioners Dezenhall and Weber write that successful crisis communication requires clients who

- Have strong leaders,
- Question conventional public relations wisdom,
- Are flexible,
- Commit significant resources to a project,

- Have a high threshold for pain, realizing that things can get worse before they get better,
- Think in terms of baby steps not grandiose gestures,
- Know themselves and are honest about what kinds of actions their culture can and cannot sustain,
- Believe that corporate defense is an exercise in moral authority, and
- Are lucky.[31]

Apparently, the authors feel that the absence of these characteristics creates an environment where planning for crisis will inevitably fail. Below is a summary of the reasons identified by practitioners and researchers for the failure of crisis communication plans.

Not testing the plan

Authors regularly suggest that organizations practice their crisis plans prior to crises. Not testing the plan prevents the possibility of tweaking it.

Not anticipating reactions to the messages generated

Taking a linear approach to communication will give communicators the illusion that once they send their messages their work is done. Responses to messages from internal and external stakeholders are inevitable. There must be preparation to respond to the reactions.

Nurturing and nourishing a culture that does not prize transparency

As we have discussed previously, a crisis plan that calls for transparency is likely to be ineffective if the organizational culture does not support honesty. If the heroes are liars, and values condone getting it done at all costs, then it will be difficult to complete the communication plan. An absence of commitment to honesty or the assumption that one can finesse crises is at best risky and at worst foolish.

Lack of resources

It can be expensive to implement a communication plan. The organization has to have the money, or have budgeted the money, to allow the plan to work.

No real plan or failure to follow the plan

Fundamentally, crisis efforts can fail because the plans are discarded once a crisis occurs. There might be something that looks like a plan, but it is superficial and the feeling is that "when it happens, we will just know how to react." What will likely occur is the organization, like a speaker "winging it," presents an uncoordinated disjointed effort. Speakers, ostensibly representing the organization, talk without authority but are perceived by stakeholders to be speaking with authority. Contradictory messages confuse stakeholders and damage legitimacy.

Organizations do not follow the wisdom of George Santayana

The famous philosopher George Santayana, once said "Those who cannot remember the past are condemned to repeat it." So many companies have been the victims of counterproductive tendencies. Nevertheless tomorrow's newspaper is likely to include stories of a company that similarly behaved counterproductively. Despite the lessons of history, companies repeatedly put their organizations in jeopardy, by spinning the facts, attempting to dodge responsibility, and/or ignoring the realities of crises.

Point/Counterpoint

In this exercise, two positions are presented. The first is consistent with a point made in the chapter. The second is a counterargument. Consider the counsel and counterargument. Then write a one-page position paper identifying your position on the issue.

- Counsel—A crisis communication team should meet regularly precrisis to prepare for crises. The essential first step in crisis planning is to get a commitment from top management to be honest during crises.
- Counterargument—This counsel may seem to make sense but it does not withstand real-world scrutiny. Using the word "team" makes it seem as if there will be a cohesive unit working on this proactive crisis activity. Any person who has studied groups knows that they are often difficult contexts for communication. Egos collide and people focus on their blackberries instead of paying attention. What is more, in these crisis groups, those on the team have other jobs to do. Their primary responsibility is not the crisis team, but rather some other administrative work. Furthermore, it is foolishly shortsighted to believe that it would mean anything to get precrisis "commitment from top management to be honest" during crises. Even administrators who believe they are genuinely making this commitment will feel differently when the heat is on. If "obtaining commitment" is an essential first step, you might as well forget the entire illusory enterprise of proactive crisis communication.

Summary: A Toolbox

- Proactive planning is crucial for crisis communicators for two reasons:
  - It can help stop crises from developing.
  - It can prepare crisis communicators to be ready when crises surface.
- It is common for organizations to be "in denial" about the potential for crises.
  - Some organizations deny that a crisis may happen to them.
  - Some organizations deny the need to communicate during crises, hoping that the crisis will go away.
- Organizations can create a communication infrastructure to reduce the number of crises an organization may need to endure.
- The Malden Mills case is an example of the importance of precrisis relationships when dealing with crises.
- Awareness of problems related to intercultural communication is essential in this area of globalization in order to avoid crisis.
- A crisis communication team should be assigned well before any crisis occurs to proactively address crisis issues.
  - This team could follow a twelve-point step-by-step plan to prepare for crises.

- Crisis communication efforts often fail for reasons related to proactivity. Specifically, often
  - There is no real plan.
  - The plan is not tested through simulation before a crisis.
  - Insufficient resources are allotted for implementation.
  - The plan does not acknowledge the nonlinear nature of crisis communication. There are no contingencies for any or varied responses.
  - The organization is not committed to implementing any previously developed plan and therefore the plan is not used.
  - The organizational culture undermines the plan.

PRACTITIONER PERSPECTIVE: ALAN BAROCAS

Alan Barocas served as the Senior Vice President for real estate and construction for the Gap, retiring from the company after working there for twenty-five years. As Senior Vice President, Mr. Barocas was responsible for all the real estate, store architecture and construction activities for the 3500-unit retailer, which included Gap, Old Navy, and Banana Republic brands. Mr. Barocas is now the principal of his own retail real estate consulting company, Alan J. Barocas and Associates, a firm that has worked with clothing giants Calvin Klein and UnderArmour among other retailers. His company's mission is "to assist retailers, developers, and investment groups in creating and executing their respective growth and investment strategies."

During times of crisis, an effective communicator must be concerned with four things: First, you have to know and understand your audiences. A different message or a different way of expressing a message may be appropriate for one group of stakeholders and inappropriate for another. Second, the timing of the communication is critical. In times of crisis it is important for any leader to convey a sense of command over the situation. Premature communication may convey panic. Delaying the communication could convey indecisiveness. Third, insure that the content of your communication is thought through and relays an understanding of what the issue is and what steps are being taken to resolve the issue. Finally, you must assign a specific individual or team who will be responsible for communicating the status and progress that is being made in resolving the crisis. This person or group must also act as the repository for questions and concerns. The company has to be aware of the roles in the crisis communication effort.

One of the biggest errors a company can make during a crisis is to develop a "circle the wagons" mentality. That is, during times of crisis there is a tendency to either not acknowledge that there is a crisis or keep whatever crisis plan there may be confined to a very small group of people. Another error that companies make is not developing any plan prior to the crisis. Teams can be effective when preparing for and during crises. A key to team success is for there to be a clear delineation of roles within the team. Otherwise, the potential value of the team can be undermined by confusion and frustrations that could derail the process. The result of these frustrations could be an inferior solution to a crisis problem. Leadership is crucial for organizations and also for any crisis teams. The leaders set a standard and can affect the organizational culture.

Organizations can learn from crises—in this way, a crisis can have some value. How we dealt with the aftermath of 9/11 and Hurricane Katrina forced companies to take a hard look at their abilities to deal with such catastrophes. Organizations are more aware of the potential for unpredictable events that can rock an organization and, in the case of 9/11 and Katrina, affect human life itself. Disaster plans are now part of most big business' DNA. The communication that is involved when implementing these plans is critical to an organization's success.

Exercises and Discussion Questions

1. Does denial seem to be a realistic behavior for those who have a financial stake in the health of the company? Does it make sense that someone who stands to lose personal well-being would still deny the possibility of crisis?
2. Of horizontal networks and upward networks, which are more crucial for preempting crises? In your experience what makes the natural maintenance of these networks possible?
3. Will there be a time in the future when globalization and diversity are so prevalent that concerns about intercultural tension will be unnecessary? That is, will there be a time in the near future when we are all familiar with multiple ethnicities and therefore, communication problems based on lack of familiarity will no longer be common?
4. Assume you are in charge of crisis communication for your academic department. Could you identify stakeholders proactively to address, for example, (a) exposed plagiarism of a faculty member, (b) a student cheating scandal, or (c) a homicide involving a student victim? Would such identification be helpful?
5. Several steps have been identified as necessary for crisis communication teams to be successful. Which of these steps are the most important? Has any organization in which you have been employed conducted such precrisis planning?
6. Of the several reasons why communication plans fail, which cause seems most likely?

NOTES

1. Ian Mitroff with Gus Anagnos, *Managing Crises Before They Happen: What Every Executive and Manager Needs to Know About Crisis Management* (New York: American Management Association, 2001).

2. Steven Fink, *Crisis Management: Planning for the Inevitable* (Cincinnati, OH: Authors Guild, 2002).

3. Elizabeth More, "Crisis Management and Communication in Australian Organisations," *Australian Journal of Communication* 22, no. 1 (1995).

4. Ibid., p. 40.

5. Robert Holland and Katrina Gill, "Ready for disaster?" *Communication World* 23, no. 2 (March/April 2006): 22–24.

6. Reghan Cloudman, "Crisis communications preparedness among U. S. organizations: Activities and assessments by public relations practitioners." *Public Relations Review* 32, no. 4 (November 2006): 367–376.

7. Matthew Seeger, Timothy Sellnow, and Robert Ulmer, *Communication and Organizational Crisis* (Westport, CT: Praeger, 2003), p. 163.

8. Tom Wolfe, *The Bonfire of the Vanities* (New York: Farrar, Straus, & Giroux, 1987), pp. 10–27.

9. http://www.lewrockwell.com/orig9/fein-b3.html, accessed July 21, 2009.

10. Mitroff, *Managing Crises Before They Happen*, 47. Mitroff labeled some of these categories differently. I use "power" for his "grandiosity" and I use "minimization" for his "disavowal."

11. Norman Thomas was born in the late 1800s and was active in the American political arena during the first half of the twentieth century, until his death in 1968. While described at times as an American socialist (and as a six-time presidential nominee of the Socialist Party), Thomas vigorously opposed Communism and was active in the American Civil Liberties Union. This quote varies slightly in some sources. http://books.google.com/books?id=qJnrg1ZYnAkC&lpg=PA14&ots=etHziJyGb7&dq=%22 second%20best%20to%20demagogues%22&pg=PA14.

12. Lisa Lyon and Glen T. Cameron, "A Relational Approach Examining the Interplay of Prior Reputation and Immediate Response to a Crisis," *Journal of Public Relations Research* 16, no. 3 (2004): 213–41; quotes appear on pp. 215 and 218.

13. James McCroskey, *An Introduction to Rhetorical Communication* (Needham Heights, MA: Allyn and Bacon, 2001), pp. 83, 85. As it pertains to the components of ethos, Aristotle's own words are: "There are three things which inspire confidence in the orator's own character—the three namely, that induce us to believe a thing apart from any proof of it; good sense, good moral character, and goodwill." *The Rhetoric of Aristotle,* trans. W. Rhys Roberts (New York: Modern Library, 1954), p. 91.

14. http://www.brainyquote.com/quotes/quotes/j/jamescalla141485.html, accessed July 21, 2009.

15. Richard Feynman, "An Outsider's Inside View of the Challenger Inquiry," *Physics Today* 41, no. 2 (February 1988): 26–37.

16. Peter Senge, *The Fifth Discipline: The Art and Practice of the Learning Organization* (New York: Doubleday Currency, 2006).

17. Quoted in Lyon and Cameron, "A Relational Approach Examining the Interplay of Prior Reputation and Immediate Response to a Crisis," p. 37, originally from John Aspery, in "Planning for the Inevitable." *Management Science* 39, no. 2 (1993): 16–17.

18. Hua-Hsin Wan and Michael Pfau, "The relative effectiveness of inoculation, bolstering, and combined approaches in crisis communication," *Journal of Public Relations Research* 16, no. 3 (2004): 301–328.

19. Robert Ulmer documents the success of Malden Mills and Feurstein in "Effective Crisis Management Through Established Stakeholder Relationships: Malden Mills as a Case Study," *Management Communication Quarterly* 14, no. 4 (May): 590–615. Quote from p. 591.

20. Ibid., p. 609.

21. Ibid., p. 596.

22. Hua-sin wan and and Michael Pfau, "The relative effectiveness of inoculation, bolstering, and combined approaches in crisis communication," *Journal of Public Relations Research* 16, no. 3 (2004): 305.

23. James Kauffman, "NASA in Crisis: The Space Agency's Public Relations Efforts Regarding the Hubble Space Telescope," *Public Relations Review* 23, no. 1 (Spring 1997): 1–10.

24. Ibid.

25. Jeffrey Hobbs, "Treachery by any other name: A case study of the Toshiba public relations crisis," *Management Communications Quarterly* 8, no. 3 (1995): 323–346.

26. Ibid.

27. Denise M. Bostdorff, "Idealism Held Hostage: Jimmy Carter's Rhetoric on the Crisis in Iran," *Communication Studies* 43, no. 1 (Spring 1992): 14–28.

28. Fink, *Crisis Management.*

29. Interview with Ed Klotzbier see page 15.

30. Seeger, Sellnow, and Ulmer, *Communication and Organizational Crisis,* p. 186.

31. Eric Dezenhall and John Weber, *Damage Control: Why Everything You Know about Crisis Management Is Wrong* (New York: Penguin, 2007), pp. 7–8.

5 Responding to Crises

Chapter in a Nutshell

When confronted with a crisis, an organization must respond intelligently in order to restore its image. What are the best ways to do this? Should an organization apologize if it is, in fact, guilty? Should it deny responsibility until faced with a "smoking gun?" Would it be wise to attempt to deflect attention from a particular event by boasting about achievements in other areas? Is it a good idea to trivialize the damage related to the event? This chapter discusses various approaches to communicating with internal and external stakeholders during crisis.

Specifically, at the end of this chapter students, will be able to

- Identify, define, and provide an example for the following image-restoration approaches:
  - Apology
  - Attack
  - Bolstering
  - Compensation
  - Corrective action
  - Defeasibility
  - Differentiation
  - Displacement
  - Ingratiation
  - Intimidation
  - Minimization
  - Mortification
  - Suffering
  - Transcendence
- Describe the recurring counsel about how to respond to crisis.
- Present counterarguments to traditional counsel and debate both sides of the issue.
- Explain why crisis communication often fails.

CASE 5.1: "WHAT WOULD YOU EXPECT THE COMPANY TO DO?"

On its Web site, the Schwan Food Company makes the following claim as part of its mission statement.

> Schwan people do what is right regardless of the cost or consequences. As a company and individually, we have a responsibility to invoke sound judgment, ethical and professional behavior, and honesty with fellow employees, customers, suppliers and the communities in which we live and work.

This credo was put to the test in 1994 when the company endured a crisis. Ice cream produced and sold by Schwan had been tainted by salmonella poisoning. Customers were getting sick from eating Schwan products.

Schwan did not immediately know the specific source of the problem. What they knew, on October 7, 1994, was that there was a large "statistical relationship" between a wide salmonella outbreak, illnesses, and their ice cream. At that time, the Schwan Food Company had not been ordered by any government agency to recall its products. Nevertheless, Alfred Schwan, the president of the company, issued a directive that was to drive decisions related to the looming crisis. He told his employees that all company actions taken in response to this incident should be based on one single and simple question.

If you were a Schwan's customer what would you expect the company to do?[1]

WHAT HAPPENED

Schwan produces and delivers food products door to door. One of their products is ice cream. In this incident, the source of the problem was a mix that was used for Schwan's production of its ice cream. Schwan had hired a trucking company, Cliff Viessman, to deliver ice cream mix to its factories. Prior to a particular delivery to Schwan, Viessman had been hauling raw unpasteurized eggs for another client. Eggs often carry salmonella. The eggs that Viessman had transported were tainted and Viessman did not adequately clean its trucks after delivering the eggs and before transporting the ice cream mix. Therefore, the ice cream mix was affected—the ice cream produced and then delivered door to door by Schwan representatives contained salmonella poisoning, and consumers of the product became very sick.

The crisis that Alfred Schwan and his company faced was the largest of its type. A total of 224,000 people were affected because they had consumed bacteria-tainted ice cream products. In contrast to other companies that faced similar threats, Schwan's approach was all corrective action, all the time—even before they were compelled to take action, even before they were certain about the source of the problem, and even after they realized that a good case could have been made that they were not responsible.

RESPONSE

Before Schwan knew the precise cause of the crisis, the company took the following steps.

- They halted the production and sale of the company's ice cream products and began a public-awareness campaign asking people not to eat any products they had purchased.
- They recalled their products, provided refunds to customers, and issued apologies to customers in the same way they delivered their products—door to door. They did this well before they knew whether the company had actually caused the infection and prior to any government demand for a recall.[2]

Because the product was delivered door to door it was relatively easy for Schwan to identify who might have been infected by which products. The representatives who had delivered the goods were the same people who would issue the apology. As opposed to a grocery store stocking bad cream and not knowing who bought it, Schwan had records not only of who bought what but also who delivered these products to which customers. They could therefore relatively easily recall products, provide refunds to the right people and not to scammers, and deliver focused apologies. In the vernacular of communication studies, they were able to use a rich medium to convey their messages credibly.

- They encouraged customers to see their physicians and agreed to pay for the doctor visits for all those afflicted and for any who wished to be tested to determine whether they were afflicted. A letter was mailed to each customer. The letter included this paragraph:

> If you believe you may have persisting symptoms of salmonella and have eaten any of our ice cream products mentioned, we want to encourage you to see your physician and get the tests necessary to confirm it one way or the other and get the treatment you need. The information on the reverse side of this letter will explain what the symptoms might include and how to go about getting the test. We will pay for the test.

- They created a toll-free hotline operational twenty-four hours a day for customers who had questions about the crisis. Callers did not listen to a taped message containing instructions. The hotline was operated by "live" representatives. The company estimated it received 15,000 calls a day at the peak of the crisis. This was another relatively rich medium that the company employed.
- Once Schwan discovered the source of the problem
  - Schwan purchased its own fleet of trucks for future transportation. No longer would they rely on a contractor who might or might not do an adequate job of cleaning trucks.
  - They began building a repasteurization plant. This facility would repasteurize products delivered to their production facility to ensure that no products would be tainted. Even when trucks owned by Schwan delivered the products, this plant would ensure that any product delivered to Schwan would leave Schwan pasteurized.
  - Until the repasteurization plant could open they created and implemented a "test and hold" policy. Public relations spokesperson David Jennings said that "Each day's products will be tested for salmonella and held from distribution until the results are received."

Schwan's brand of corrective action was extensive and their expressions of apology effective as much for their content as for the method of relaying the content. Because of their behavior in response to the crisis, and despite the enormity of the outbreak and the national press coverage, Schwan maintained its customer base as well as its reputation in the wake of the crisis. Five months after the crisis Schwan was able to return to regular sales levels. After a similar problem at Jack in the Box, when the hamburger company took a different approach to salmonella poisoning, it took three years to return to its sales levels.

Questions for Analysis

- Schwan took several costly actions prior to knowing what the source of the problem might be. Would you have done this?
- Schwan could easily have blamed Viessman for the crisis.
  - Should they have?
- Which of these communication factors were most significant in restoring legitimacy?
  - Delivery of apology using a rich medium
  - Toll-free hotline
  - Communication of intention to adopt a "test and hold" policy
- In hindsight we know that Schwan's approach worked. Their image was restored quickly.
  - Was their image restored because, as it turned out, the crisis was not Schwan's direct fault?
  - Would their image have been restored quickly because of the immediate actions they took, even if it turned out that the company, itself, had been responsible?
- Schwan clearly took a golden rule approach. How significant do you believe the company's prior culture was to the successful implementation of this approach?
  - If the culture had followed a "bottom line is the only line" approach, what would Schwan have communicated when it was told that there was a large "statistical relationship?"
  - What would the company have communicated when it was revealed that Viessman had been the source of the problem?
  - Would a "golden rule" approach automatically work in another country and culture?
- If you were a Schwan's customer who had become ill, would you continue to purchase Schwan products after this incident?
- Would your attitudes toward the company be affected because of the incident?
- What would you have done differently to address the crisis?
- In the previous chapter we discussed proactive crisis planning. If you owned or managed a food operation, what would you do proactively to be able to respond as quickly as possible to problems such as the one Schwan faced?

NOTES

1. Timothy Sellnow, Robert Ulmer, and Michelle Snider, "The Compatibility of Corrective Action in Organizational Crisis Communication," *Communication Quarterly* 56, no. 1 (Winter 1998): 60–74.

2. Ibid.

INTRODUCTION

In the preceding chapters we discussed how to prepare for crises and the importance of legitimacy. We also identified four Rs as being factors in crisis communication: relationships, reputation, responsibility, and response. In this chapter, we examine methods for responding when legitimacy has been affected by crisis. The response most appropriate for image restoration will be largely a function of relationships, reputation, and responsibility.

Consider the following situations. Each of these cases will be discussed later in this chapter. Based on these short descriptions, what is your immediate reaction regarding how the organization should have communicated in response to its crisis? Should they have communicated at all?

- Dow Corning faced charges that the breast implant products it manufactured could have deleterious effects on women's health. Moreover, the company was charged with having been aware, prior to sale, that health hazards were associated with the products.
  - Assuming the charges were true, what should the company have communicated to internal and external stakeholders?
  - Assuming the charges were false, what should the company have communicated to internal and external stakeholders?
- Federal legislation commonly called the Superfund was passed into law in December 1980 to ensure environmental protection in the United States. During the Reagan presidency, which began in January 1981, the administration was attacked when it appeared as if the woman President Reagan had appointed to head the Superfund was a professional colleague of organizations that were known polluters. Accusations were made that instead of protecting the environment, the Superfund was deliberately being used as a ruse to permit unrestricted behavior.
  - Assuming the charges were true, what should the government/president have communicated to internal/external stakeholders?
  - Assuming the charges were false, what should the government/president have communicated to internal and external stakeholders?
- ValuJet faced a horrible crisis when one of its planes crashed in the Florida Everglades. There were accusations that ValuJet was in some ways responsible for the crash because of inadequate preflight servicing of the aircraft.
  - Assuming the charges were true, what should ValuJet have communicated to internal/external stakeholders?
  - Assuming the charges were false, what should ValuJet have communicated to internal and external stakeholders?

IMAGE RESTORATION THEORY

Image restoration theory has been developed by scholars over the past forty years. As has been discussed in Chapter 2, the theory is based on the premise that communication during and after a crisis can reduce the negative effects that the crisis may have on an organization's legitimacy.[1] Simply, communication can limit the damage caused by a crisis.

In the crisis management book *Damage Control,* the authors explain that the title phrase comes from military usage, and originally described how to react when a vessel was torpedoed. "Even if torpedoed, a vessel could sometimes recover and carry out its mission if the crew had the right skill set."[2] The key to military damage control was to minimize the injurious effects of a hit on a vessel. Keep it upright. Keep it functioning, even if teetering, until such time that it could again operate efficiently and safely. Similarly, crisis communicators are responsible for using the right skill sets to minimize the injurious effects of a hit on an organization.

The torpedo analogy is not completely right for crisis communication study because torpedoes attack from outside of the vessel. Many crises in organizations surface because of internal problems: labor strikes, reprehensible executive acts, myopic decisions, or perhaps shoddy production that causes lawsuits. However, regardless of whether the "torpedo" comes from the outside or inside, organizations need the right "skill set" to respond accurately.

A STONE ON THE WINDSHIELD

Consider another metaphor as it relates to damage control, the correct skill sets necessary to control damage, and contemporary communication.

Imagine driving in your car and suddenly some rock or other projectile skips up and hits your windshield. You know that there will be a blemish on the windshield, but the question is to what extent and how rapidly it will spread. We live in an age with very sophisticated communication technology. Now when a stone hits your windshield, it is more important than ever to use the correct skill sets that will contain the spread of damage. Beyond national, city, and even community media, social networking media are exploding. Wikis and blogs and a host of their cousins have made everyone potential mass communicators, who, if they write well, may seem to have a degree of credibility. An organization acts irresponsibly, a politician makes an error in judgment, a piece of equipment proves hazardous—now everyone is a commentator and a journalist. *Moreover, after the organization acts irresponsibly, depending upon how the organization communicates to the public, it will now be grist for robust virtual communications that could shatter the windshield.*

In early 2009, when Brandeis University decided to sell its Rose Museum, it may have anticipated some negative reaction. However, the university did not expect the explosion of criticism on the part of so many who considered this a blatant disrespect of the arts, and who because of new media and social networking were now, immediately, part of the larger conversation. The splintering of the windshield was nearly blinding for Brandeis. Within days, the president was in retreat mode. From Facebook conversations that lathered into e-mail blasts, that exploded into outrage, the shards from the windshield so threatened to raze Brandeis's legitimacy that within three weeks of the decision the president had to recant. He can now see out of the windshield, but for years the vision will be marred by lingering assumptions about how a university was willing to sacrifice the arts.

It is crucial that crisis communicators use skill sets wisely in order to contain damage, particularly in an age of growing media access.

SPINNING REDUX

It is important to remind readers of a point made in Chapter 1. The phrase "image restoration" might seem a euphemistic way of describing spinning. That is, some may assume that image restoration is the art of adjusting reality to create illusions.

Some crisis communicators indeed do use the methods described in the following pages in an attempt to alter reality. As you will see, some of the approaches can even aid those who choose to be disingenuous. Nevertheless, image restoration theory is not synonymous with spinning even if those involved in image restoration choose, myopically, to take that route. The recurring—if not unanimous—counsel from practitioners as well as scholars is that transparency, not deception, is a key to effective image restoration and legitimacy. Take a moment to review the following comments reflecting the perspective of crisis communication practitioners and scholars.

- "Quick and complete disclosure, while damaging in the short run, reduces the risk of rumors, leaks, drawn-out media coverage, and the perception of dishonesty."[3]
- "A candid, prompt, honest, and complete response may also bolster an organization's reputation and integrity in the long run."[4]
- "Maintaining open communication is a fundamental tenet of crisis management."[5]
- "Whether you find yourself in a one-on-one interview or at a press conference, facing friendly media or hostile, *honesty* [emphasis in original] is of paramount importance. Do not for a moment think that any of the communication techniques or verbal sparring described are meant to be, or to promote, dishonesty or chicanery of any sort. Nothing could be farther from the truth."[6]
- "Remember, lack of honesty seriously damages organizational-stakeholder relationships—destroys the organization's reputation—and can lead to massive monetary awards against the organization in future lawsuits."[7]

Image restoration should not be about spinning. With this as prologue, below are the types of image restoration strategies available to crisis communicators.

IMAGE RESTORATION APPROACHES

ATTACK

One way to attempt to restore legitimacy is to attack those who are challenging the organization. Instead of accepting responsibility, a spokesperson can attack the media for poor reporting, clients who are alleging misbehavior, employees who are complaining about working conditions, or any adversary.

When Dow Corning was accused of producing unsafe breast implants, the company's initial response was to attack its accusers—specifically the collective media, and the

Food and Drug Administration (FDA). Media reports had promulgated the claim that documents written and disseminated at Dow Corning proved not only that there was a problem but also that the company was aware of the problem with the implants. The FDA also suggested that the company had been aware of the problem and failed to make the concerns public. In addition, the FDA had questioned the information that Dow Corning was distributing over a "hotline" about the safety of the product.

Dow Corning attacked. Robert Rylee, the chair of the company's health care businesses claimed that the *New York Times*'s attributions were "a total mischaracterization of the facts." Rylee contended that the discourse about the company's conflict with the FDA was not objective but reflected rather "a media circus." He threatened the FDA, saying "if [Corning is] going to have to continue to work under a very hostile environment from the FDA, we may well decide to exit."[8]

It is noteworthy that despite Rylee's attacks, various agents continued to question Dow Corning in the matter of the safety of their silicone breast implants.

Is attack an effective image restoration policy if you feel that your company is being unfairly criticized? Is attack ever an effective image restoration policy if your company is guilty? More about the Dow case is presented later in the chapter.

BOLSTERING

Bolstering occurs when spokespersons identify the achievements of an organization that may be, at best, peripheral to any specific crisis. If toxins are found in a product, an organization might identify its history of cleanliness, lack of any prior crisis akin to this one, its community efforts on behalf of the poor, the profit margin for stockholders, fair pricing for customers, or any other related or unrelated positive attribute about the organization. By bolstering, the organization attempts to restore legitimacy by identifying the company's positive features.

Bolstering was a technique used by President Reagan during the Superfund crisis discussed earlier. Ironically, the Superfund crisis surfaced as a result of another crisis and another image restoration technique. That technique—corrective action—will be examined in detail shortly.

As mentioned, in December 1980, Congress passed the Superfund law designed to protect communities that had been affected and infected by industrial dumping of toxic waste. The catalyst for the legislation was the revelation that Love Canal—a residential area in western New York state—was valueless and dangerous because of toxins embedded in the land. People who lived in Love Canal were at high risk for illness and had to flee their valueless homes.

The Superfund law was created in the wake of this crisis. In 1982 President Reagan appointed Rita Lavelle to administer the Superfund. This was a controversial appointment because Lavelle had industry experience with companies identified as polluters. There were assertions that her prior industry relationships precluded her ability to legislate effectively. In 1986, her adversaries claimed there was evidence that Lavelle was not doing her job and the fund was not doing what it was designed to do. It was suggested that Lavelle was, essentially, the fox guarding the henhouse. Reagan was criticized for appointing Lavelle to this position.

Reagan addressed the crisis by employing a number of image restoration strategies. One was bolstering. In two speeches where he directly addressed this issue and in press conferences when queried about the matter, he identified his commitment to the environment when he was governor of California, praised the Environmental Protection Agency, asserted that progress had been made in settling conflicts with industry, and lamented that the agency's accomplishments had been diminished because of the "flurry of accusations."[9] These are all examples of bolstering, an attempt to reduce image damage by identifying other or peripheral positive aspects of the organization when allegedly addressing the crisis. (The president accepted Lavelle's resignation.)

Is bolstering a wise strategy when a company can legitimately boast about a real accomplishment however peripheral that accomplishment may be to the existing crisis?

COMPASSION

Compassion is an approach that attempts to restore legitimacy by expressing concern, consideration, and sympathy for those affected by the crisis.

If an insane employee commits horrific crimes against coworkers an organization is wise to express compassion for the victims. This is particularly important if there are intimations that the organization should have been more diligent when vetting this person in the hiring process. The success of compassion is based at least in part on the stability and reputation of the organization. Recall from Chapter 2, that "stability" is a term used in crisis communication to refer to the frequency of crises. If an organization regularly experiences crises, then expressions of compassion are not likely to be effective because stakeholders may attribute responsibility to the organization because of the history.

The film *The Queen* illustrates how the newly elected prime minister, Tony Blair, attempted to defuse a developing crisis for the monarchy in Great Britain. In the days following the death of Princess Diana, Blair successfully convinced Queen Elizabeth to express her compassion not only for Diana but for all citizens of the Commonwealth who revered the former princess. Blair was concerned about rising anger toward the monarchy because of an apparent lack of compassion. His objective was to defuse the fledgling crisis and preclude a greater one by having the monarch deliver a presentation reflecting her compassion.

On February 12, 2009, there was a tragic airline crash when Colgan Air's flight 3407 failed and forty-nine passengers perished outside of Buffalo, New York. Pinnacle Airlines Corporation is the parent company of Colgan Air. In addition to establishing a toll-free number for the families of those who perished, Pinnacle's CEO and president Philip H. Trenary traveled to nearby Amherst, New York, and issued the following statement.

> We are greatly saddened by this accident. Our prayers are extended to the family and loved ones of those aboard flight 3407 and those affected on the ground. Please know that we will commit all needed resources to assist the NTSB's [National Transportation Safety Board] investigation of this accident and work to ensure that a tragedy such as this does not occur again.[10]

Will Trenary's comment help to restore legitimacy?

With respect to the previous section on social networking, readers should be aware that "Buffalo Geek: A Blog for Smart People" also discussed issues germane to the Colgan accident.

COMPENSATION

A way to restore legitimacy is to compensate those who have been affected by the crisis.

Schwan did this when they offered to pay the medical costs not only for those who became ill from consuming its tainted food products but also for all of those consumers who needed to be examined to determine whether they would become ill because of what they had eaten.

Schwan was successful in part because their largesse was offered without an asterisk. When Intel was confronted with a problem related to flawed processors, the company offered to replace defective products with new ones. However, with Intel there was an asterisk that accompanied its offer of compensation. We will discuss the Intel crisis—and its asterisk—later in this chapter, in the section on "Minimization."

CORRECTIVE ACTION

Organizations take, or speak of taking, corrective action when they inform stakeholders about what they are doing to ensure that such a crisis never occurs again. This is a very common and, when genuine, effective form of image restoration.

When it was discovered that two Tufts University officials had embezzled thousands of dollars from the school, a Tufts spokesperson quickly outlined policies that would be enacted to preclude the possibility of such crises occurring in the future.

A famous crisis case in major league baseball also involved corrective action. Members of the Chicago White Sox were accused of taking money to intentionally lose to the Cincinnati Reds in the 1919 World Series. Eight White Sox players were indicted on October 22, 1920, and major league baseball lost a measure of legitimacy.

While other organizations during the early part of the twentieth century had been criticized by muckrakers for inappropriate corporate behaviors and consequently had lost legitimacy, baseball had "positioned itself as a public virtue" and had enjoyed strong perceptions of legitimacy. What became known as the "Black Sox scandal," however, highlighted that legitimacy could be an ephemeral phenomenon.

In order to restore its image, baseball team owners took unprecedented measures. They hired a disciplinarian, Justice Kennesaw Mountain Landis, to be the commissioner of baseball. Prior to hiring Landis, baseball was overseen by a group of three people. The hiring of the impartial and reputably tough Landis was an attempt to ensure that the game would be seen as impregnable, not a sport that would tolerate questionable behavior. Enforcing that perception, Landis banished the eight White Sox players from baseball despite the fact that they had been exonerated in court. While the players had not been found innocent of taking bribes and throwing the games, a jury had found them not guilty of defrauding baseball. Nevertheless, Landis banished the players stating that "Regardless of the verdict of juries no player who throws a ballgame . . . will ever play professional baseball."[11]

Another dimension of this case relates to the power of the media in crisis communication. Landis's hiring by the owners was an attempt to win over journalists who covered the game. Journalists had been critical of baseball for not policing itself in this scandal. Hiring Landis was intended to prove to reporters that to whatever extent baseball had been guilty of looking the other way, it was now committed to preserving the integrity of the game. The actions of the owners and Landis represent examples of corrective action. Sadly, as is documented in the 1988 film *Eight Men Out,* and books such as *Shoeless Joe,* not all of the banished players were guilty of the crime, yet all lost their honor and livelihood.[12] Also while Landis's actions have been lauded and he was enshrined in the hall of fame for his leadership, during his tenure he insisted that African-American players not be permitted to play major league baseball.

It makes sense for organizations to use corrective action as at least one dimension of their crisis activity. Many do. The question is to what extent these actions are genuine. As we saw above in the Superfund case, some people wondered whether the corrective action as a result of Love Canal was a genuine attempt to correct the policies that had created a crisis.

Is corrective action an essential component of all crisis communication efforts? In which situations, if any, would corrective action *not* be appropriate?

DEFEASIBILITY

Sometimes organizations argue that blame should not be attributed to them because it is not feasible for them to be held responsible for actions that have created a crisis. When Jack in the Box was affected by an outbreak of E. coli poisoning, one of the company's initial defense arguments was that new guidelines on cooking meat had not been distributed to the franchises. Hence, they claimed it was not feasible for them to be held accountable for the outbreak, since new information germane to food preparation had not been disseminated.

The *Harvard Business Review* compendium on crisis management includes an interesting case related to defeasibility.[13] The case involved a clothing retailer we will call X and its approach to making charitable contributions. X had many locations throughout the United States. In the past, all philanthropic decisions, that is, which charities would receive donations, were made by X's central office. In an attempt to give local retail managers autonomy, X allocated money to the various locations and allowed local managers to decide who should receive donations. One local branch decided to donate to an organization that, judging by its mission statement, had honorable objectives. The recipient's mission statement professed services to needy children. However, one splinter faction of this recipient included an aggressive antiabortion subgroup, to whom being of "service to children" meant that they should protest and even bomb abortion clinics. Subsequently, these people did indeed bomb a clinic.

X was mortified when it was revealed that they had, however indirectly, donated money to a virulent antiabortion group. The home office, aghast, expressed compassion for victims, but argued that it was not feasible to blame them for the event because not only had they not made the decision, the group that did so had no way of knowing the affiliations of the splinter group.

Would this claim by X reduce damage to its legitimacy?

DENIAL

An obvious but often shortsighted approach to crisis communication is to simply deny allegations that hold you responsible for the crisis.

During the 1972–74 Watergate crisis involving Republican president Richard Nixon, and during the 1992 primary campaign of Democratic senator Gary Hart, both politicians attempted to deal with crises by flatly denying their culpability. Denial might be an effective strategy if indeed the person or organization did not do what has been attributed. However, in the Watergate and Hart cases it was stunningly bad strategy as the denials soon proved to be spurious. President Nixon asserted that he had not obstructed justice. Senator Hart asserted he was not involved in an extramarital affair. In time, both denials were proved false. The politicians' images were tarnished not only because of their transgressions, but because of the denials they employed to avoid perceptions of culpability.

In the Dow Corning case, prior to attacking the FDA, the company flatly denied that its products were unsafe. The technical director of health care businesses, Robert LeVier, insisted that "the devices were safe and the data proved it."[14] Even after a change in leadership, representatives of Dow Corning commented "that they believed implants were safe and that any connection between the implants and health problems in women was coincidental."[15] Eventually, when evidence revealed that the accusations had been correct, the company accepted responsibility and took corrective action, but the denial approach was a staple of its initial image restoration strategies.[16] Instead of extricating the company from perceptions of irresponsibility, the denial made attempts at subsequent extrication much more difficult.

Can you identify any situation in which a denial is a good image restoration approach?

DIFFERENTIATION

Differentiation is a technique used to explain why what has occurred in your organization is different from an offense that has been committed by another organization.

When baseball pitcher Andy Pettitte was accused of having used illegal drugs, the athlete used differentiation as a complementary strategy to improve his image. Pettitte acknowledged his error, apologized to fans, and clearly expressed his embarrassment. However, in addition, he explained that he had taken the steroids because he hoped the drug would expedite the healing process for an injury he had sustained. By identifying the purpose for taking the drug, Pettitte intimated that what he was doing was different from the offenses of other baseball players who had used steroids to enhance performance.

Would differentiation in this instance affect perceptions of legitimacy? That is, would Pettitte's claim that he knew it was wrong, but did it to improve healing make him less illegitimate than someone who used drugs to enhance performance? When responding, remember that legitimacy is not defined in crisis communication in terms of legality—organizations must earn legitimacy.[17]

In what situations can differentiation be effective?

DISPLACEMENT

Displacement is a very common image restoration technique. The approach here is to displace blame onto another party.

When the *Exxon Valdez* ran aground, spilling oil in what had been relatively pristine harbors, Exxon claimed that the captain of the vessel had consumed alcohol and therefore he, independently, was to blame, not the company.

When the city of Boston could not contain the destructive exuberance of revelers after the New England Patriots defeated the Carolina Panthers in a February 2004 Super Bowl game, the mayor of Boston quickly blamed local universities for not policing the students more efficiently. The objective was to displace responsibility from the city for its poor preparation onto the universities in the vicinity.

After its 1996 crash, ValuJet blamed a contractor, Sabretech, for mislabeling products. Similarly, NASA blamed a supplier for photography problems with the Hubble Space Telescope. As we saw in the preceding chapter, Toshiba blamed its subsidiary the Toshiba Machine Company for the illicit sale of submarine technology to the Soviet Union.

It is a child's game to displace responsibility onto someone else—a child's game utilized by many adults when their backs are to the wall. The success of the approach is based on the integrity of the argument, the relationships established by the organization with its stakeholders, the reputation of the organization, and the regularity of crises besetting the organization.

For example, when NASA attempted to deflect blame to a contractor for the Hubble Telescope crisis it had to deal with NASA's legacy of attributing blame to Morton Thiokol, a contractor, for the O-ring that caused the Challenger explosion, and to North American Aviation for NASA's tragic Apollo fire. Organizations must be willing to accept responsibility. NASA, in many ways an outstanding organization, has been criticized because of displacement and other ineffective crisis communication efforts. James Kauffman reports that because of its poor communication policies, a joke circulated about NASA that the acronym was not shorthand for National Aeronautics and Space Administration, but rather for Never A Straight Answer.[18]

In what situations would displacement work as an image restoration approach?

INGRATIATION

Organizations may attempt to diffuse negative attitudes by ingratiating themselves with those who have lost respect for the company. In the language of scholars, "Ingratiation is intended to gain audience approval by conveying conformity to the normative institutional environment's rules."[19] In other words, ingratiation involves identifying values that the organization and stakeholder share, citing attributes of the company that are consistent with these values, and praising the stakeholder for believing and acting in accordance with these similar values.

For example, in the wake of 9/11, American citizens heard several speeches that involved ingratiation. This excerpt from President George Bush's speech to the nation on September 11th is an example.

> Good evening. Today, our fellow citizens, our way of life, our very freedom came under attack in a series of deliberate and deadly terrorist acts. The victims were in airplanes, or in their offices; secretaries, businessmen and women, military and federal workers; moms and dads, friends and neighbors. Thousands of lives were suddenly ended by evil, despicable acts of terror.
>
> The pictures of airplanes flying into buildings, fires burning, huge structures collapsing, have filled us with disbelief, terrible sadness, and a quiet, unyielding anger. These acts of mass murder were intended to frighten our nation into chaos and retreat. But they have failed; our country is strong.
>
> A great people has been moved to defend a great nation. Terrorist attacks can shake the foundations of our biggest buildings, but they cannot touch the foundation of America. These acts shattered steel, but they cannot dent the steel of American resolve.
>
> America was targeted for attack because we're the brightest beacon for freedom and opportunity in the world. And no one will keep that light from shining.[20]

These words may not have been strategically employed to restore legitimacy. In fact, this particular excerpt likely resonated positively with reasonable citizens of all nations and ethnicities. Nevertheless, this message is an example of ingratiation—the establishment of commonality in an audience in the interest of reducing or eliminating any fledgling notions of organizational irresponsibility.

Ingratiation is often used by political leaders in times of crisis. President Barack Obama's chief of staff Rahm Emanuel has said, "You never want a serious crisis to go to waste" in reference to the potential of crisis to be a catalyst for productive change.[21] Emanuel was alluding to the 2008–9 economic crisis in the United States when he made this remark. But can ingratiation serve as a springboard for either removing stigmas attached to a crisis or generating change? If an organization says, "Together we can arrest this demon," have they removed the demon from the organization's sphere of responsibility and helped restore its own legitimacy?

INTIMIDATION

Intimidation is often used in conjunction with attacks. During the Watergate crisis the conspirators suggested to *Washington Post* publisher Katharine Graham that continued newspaper coverage could make the renewal of her WJXT television license difficult. Unlike newspapers, radio stations must obtain and periodically renew their broadcast licenses. Since the Federal Communications Commission (FCC) is an arm of the government, the intimation was that persistent coverage might make the executive branch put pressure on the FCC to scrutinize Graham's request for renewal of her broadcast license.

Under what conditions might intimidation be an effective image restoration approach?

MINIMIZATION

Minimization is a technique used to downplay the significance and damage of a crisis. Intel used minimization when confronted with a crisis related to its Pentium processors.

In June 1994, Intel had discovered a flaw in their Pentium processor. The company considered the problem to be minor—because they felt that the flaw would almost never affect most consumers. The issue, they claimed, would affect the average person every 27,000 years. In their thinking, the only people affected by the problem would be those performing sophisticated mathematical computations. Intel corrected the flaw, but because it was so minor, they did not remove the flawed processors already in production. No new processor would have the flaw, but those already produced would be sold with the flaw since the problem would only surface every 27,000 years.

At the end of October 1994 a professor at Lynchburg College in Virginia noticed the error while he was performing computations. The professor sent some e-mails to colleagues identifying the issues with the processor. Some of the colleagues did computations to test the claim and confirmed there was indeed a problem. In early November, *Electrical Engineering Times* published an article describing the problem with the processor. By Thanksgiving, CNN, the *Boston Globe,* and *the New York Times* had run stories about problems with the chip.

Intel's response to the growing crisis was to minimize the problem, claiming, correctly, that it would rarely affect individuals who had purchased the product. The company also said they had already fixed the flaw in the production of new Pentium processors. Because a good deal of criticism had been communicated on a Web site, Intel posted an apology on the same Web site explaining how relatively inconsequential the error was. Even though the minimization was not an inaccurate claim, the public reacted negatively.

In addition to fixing the flaw, Intel took another corrective action. However, as discussed earlier in this chapter, it was corrective action with an asterisk. Reflecting its sense that the problem was minor and that it would affect only a few consumers, Intel said it would replace flawed machines only if a consumer could demonstrate that he or she conducted computations that would be affected by the problem. This idea proved to be less than effective. Customers were not pleased with this stipulation.

People who had purchased machines did not want a flawed computer regardless of the allegedly minimal effects of the problem. Customers also began to wonder about others who had purchased the product. For example, what if a medical researcher were doing computations with the product? What if the results of the research that could affect patients were tainted because of the "minor" technical error? In addition, consumers felt that if there was one identifiable flaw maybe there were others.

In mid-December the Intel crisis became more acute when IBM said it would no longer ship computers containing the Intel Pentium chip. IBM claimed that its calculations indicated that the problem would affect users every twenty-four days, not every 27,000 years. Faced with a tremendous loss of legitimacy, Intel then declared it would replace any Pentium processor with a pristine one.

The Intel case not only demonstrated an instance when minimization might not work but also explained how new technology affects crisis communication efforts. The Lynchburg professor ignited the dormant crisis by sending an e-mail. If not for disgruntled cyber conversation on comp.sys.intel, it is possible that the crisis would not have occurred. As word traveled through informal networks on the Web, Intel's legitimacy plummeted and the company was subjected to ridicule. Disparaging jokes appeared on the Web.

Q. How many Pentium designers does it take to screw in a lightbulb?
A. 1.99904274017—that's close enough for nontechnical people.
Q. Why didn't Intel call the Pentium the 586?
A. Because they added 486 and 100 and got 585.999983605.

The speed and effects of new media (facilitated by the very computers Intel produces) were made obvious in this case. The final analysis in the Intel case is that minimization was not the route to choose.[22] However, are there any situations when minimization might work as an image restoration strategy?

MORTIFICATION

When an organization humbly describes its embarrassment about what has occurred, it is, wittingly or otherwise, using the technique called mortification. This technique is often accompanied by an apology and, all too often, only after someone has been caught.

Elliot Spitzer expressed his embarrassment when he was identified as a frequent customer of a Washington, D.C., brothel. He was, no doubt, genuinely relaying how he felt.

Does mortification tend to increase your respect for someone? When Lee Iacocca was its CEO, Chrysler was attacked for selling used cars as new ones. The company used some cars as test vehicles, disconnecting the odometers while driving the cars during these tests. A test car might be driven up to 500 miles and still be sold as *new* with an odometer reading zeroes. Also in the course of the testing, some of the "new" vehicles were damaged. The damaged cars were then repaired and sold as new. Iacocca claimed to be unaware of the practice, but more than 60 percent of employees polled said that they had heard of it. The CEO expressed embarrassment, saying that disconnecting the odometers was "dumb." Selling damaged cars that had been repaired as new "went beyond dumb and reached all the way out to stupid."[23]

Would awareness of the act of disconnecting the odometers have affected your perception of Chrysler's legitimacy? If so, from your perspective would mortification have been an effective image restoration strategy? In the previous chapter we discussed the importance of communication infrastructure to preclude crises. If 60 percent of the employees knew about the practice, is the Chrysler case an example that supports Feynman's theory? Would navigable and credible communication networks have eliminated this crisis for Chrysler?

PENITENTIAL AND CAUSAL APOLOGIES

An apology in the vernacular of crisis communication means what it means in common usage. One party expresses remorse for what has occurred. Sen and Egelhoff claim that it is always important to show concern for the victim of a crisis.[24] That concern is often expressed as an apology. Benoit's comment on this matter is often cited in the crisis communication literature. "When a wrong is committed, one should admit it, apologize, and take corrective action."[25]

The default tendency of many organizations, however, is to consider apologies to be problematic because they leave an organization liable for lawsuits and financial damages. Companies simply do not like to apologize because they feel that an apology is a de facto admission of guilt. Because an admission of guilt might render the person issuing the apology vulnerable to a financial loss, "often offenders are explicitly instructed by their lawyers, or their insurance companies, *not* to apologize"[26] [emphasis in original].

In an exhaustive sixty-page article in the *Southern California Law Review,* law professor Jonathon Cohen challenges the advice that it is unwise to apologize. He argues that from ethical, cathartic, and pragmatic perspectives, apologies can be beneficial to organizations or individual clients. Cohen cites Massachusetts law specifically as prohibiting the equating of apologies with admissions of guilt. In addition, the author contends that apologies offer the advantage of repairing damaged relationships, facilitating negotiation between parties who might otherwise assume intransigent contentious postures, and therefore actually reducing chances that an injured party might sue.

> For a legal dispute to occur, injury alone is not sufficient. The injured party must also decide to bring a legal claim. Taking the step to make a legal claim is often triggered by the injured party's anger. An early apology can help defuse that anger and thereby prevent a legal dispute. The lesson here is an important one. While there are risks to making an apology there are also risks to not making an apology.[27]

Two types of apologies are described in the crisis communication literature. The first, a *penitential* apology, is recommended over the other, a *causal* apology. In a penitential apology, the organization expresses remorse and does not offer any explanation that describes why it is in a position to have to apologize. In a causal apology, the contrition is attenuated by a reason that accounts for why events evolved as they did.

A case that illustrates the distinction between the types of apologies took place in November 1998 in Lubbock, Texas. The case involved the wrongful arrest of three African-Americans.

In a Wal-Mart parking lot a white woman was duped in what is known as a pigeon scam. In a pigeon scam, the perpetrators approach a victim and say that they have found some money. The outlaws attempt to con the target by claiming that without a lawyer they—those who found the money—will not be able to retain the funds. The scammer then offers the target an opportunity to partner and receive some of the found money. If the target would be willing to front the money necessary for a lawyer, then the scammer would hire the lawyer. Then, according to the con, the scammer and the target would share the found money.

It is a bizarre con, and might lead readers to wonder who would be so foolish as to be victimized by it. Nevertheless, this scenario played out in the Wal-Mart parking lot. The woman in the car gave the scammers—who were black—money to obtain a lawyer. The target then went home and relayed the incident to her husband. The husband recognized the scam and contacted the police.

The police returned to the parking lot with the target. The police spotted two African-

Americans in a car. The police asked them if they had recently found some money. They said they had not. Eventually a third African-American came out of Wal-Mart and the three began driving away. The police followed the car.

The people in the car were the head coach of Hampton University's women's basketball team, the assistant coach, and the spouse of the head coach. Hampton University was in town to play Texas Tech the following evening. The lone characteristic that the scammers had in common with the coaches was that both the scammers and the coaches were black. Nevertheless, the police followed the coach's car back to the team's motel. The target rode with the police as they followed. When the police car arrived at the motel, the target was asked whether she could identify the scammers. The target did identify the coaches as the scammers. The coach, the assistant, and the spouse were arrested.

This arrest proved to be a nightmare not only for the city of Lubbock but also for Texas Tech University. The city especially was excoriated in the national media. The city police had arrested people who were shopping at Wal-Mart because of a positive identification that seemed to be based solely on skin color. Angry accusations were made that the city was racist. Subsequently, the target recanted her identification and the coaches were released. The image of the city, however, had taken a severe blow.

The mayor of the city traveled to Virginia to apologize for the incident. However, the police officials' implicit apology included an explanation. The police insisted that they had an excuse. The target had identified the perpetrators. The police claimed that since it was not until after the arrest that the target had recanted the incorrect identification, the officers' actions had some legitimacy. They expressed regret, but their apology was causal—there was a reason. There are many more issues related to this crisis, the city and the university's communication efforts, and legitimacy.[28] For the purposes of this section, however, consider the value of a penitential apology versus a causal one.

A penitential apology includes no causal explanation. It is simply a statement of remorse.

Would penitential apologies in the Lubbock case have been more effective? The duped woman had, in fact, identified the wrong persons.[29] The police did other highly questionable things in this case, but for a discussion point as it relates to apologies—if everything else the police had done was unimpeachable, should they have issued a penitential or a causal apology? Should causal apologies ever be used?

SUFFERING

Suffering refers to communications suggesting that, in addition to the victims, the company is also suffering.

This is a risky approach to image restoration and can exacerbate tensions. For example, a company that is laying off 2,000 workers may say that the layoff is hurting them as much as it is hurting the workers. This is hollow sounding as those declaring that they are suffering are still paid on a regular basis and do not have to look for work. Suffering can be a successful approach when the organization can indeed show it has been hurt. For example, "we too have suffered because of the action by our employees, our stock share has gone down, we have had to close two plants, our image in the business community has made it difficult for us to rebound."

In the air tragedy near Buffalo discussed earlier in the chapter, would the Pinnacle chairman's assertion that all at Colgen Air had suffered as well have been likely to reduce problems related to a loss of legitimacy?

TRANSCENDENCE

When an organization attempts to put a crisis in the perspective of something more significant, the communication strategy is referred to as transcendence. Essentially, other issues transcend the current one.

When baseball player Barry Bonds was accused of steroid use, he spoke about other matters, "This is just—this is old stuff. I mean, it's like watching *Sanford and Son,* you know, you just, rerun after rerun after rerun. You guys [reporters] it's like, what, I mean, you can't—it's almost comical, basically. I mean, we've got alcohol that's the number one killer in America and we legalize that to buy in the store. You've got, you know, you've got tobacco number two, three killer in America, we legalize that. There's other issues . . ."[30]

Apply the Principles

In the previous section we reviewed several image restoration approaches and discussed a number of crisis cases.

- Consider the cases in this chapter and in previous chapters.
  - 1919 White Sox
  - "A New Superstar"
  - American Peanut Corporation
  - Chrysler odometer
  - Colgan Air
  - Company X
  - Dow Chemical
  - Intel
  - Lubbock, Texas
  - Schwan Food Company
  - Superfund
  - "There Must Be Some Mistake"
- Review the image restoration strategies we have discussed.
- What combination of image restoration approaches would you employ for each of the crisis cases listed above?

TAXONOMIES

William Benoit has grouped image restoration approaches into five categories. Identifying these categories may be helpful to readers both as a review of the approaches and clarification of the nature of approaches taken. The categories Benoit uses are

- Denial
- Evasion of responsibility
- Reduction of offensiveness
- Corrective action
- Mortification

Denial strategies include
- Denial
- Attack
- Intimidation

Evasion of responsibility includes
- Defeasibility
- Displacement
- Reduction of offensiveness
- Minimization
- Transcendence
- Bolstering
- Differentiation

Corrective action includes
- Compensation
- Corrective action

Mortification includes
- Mortification
- Suffering
- Penitential apologies

Coombs has categorized response strategies by what he calls postures.
- Denial posture
  - Attack
  - Denial
  - Displacement
    - Diminishment posture
- Minimization
- Defeasibility
- Differentiation
  - Rebuilding posture
- Compensation
- Corrective action
- Penitential apology
  - Bolstering posture
- Bolstering
- Ingratiation
- Suffering[31]

Some scholars categorize crisis responses into more broad categories of accommodation and avoidance.

Accommodation includes
- Compensation
- Corrective action
- Mortification

- Penitential apologies
- Suffering

Avoidance includes
  - Attack
  - Bolstering
  - Defeasibility
  - Denial
  - Displacement
  - Intimidation
  - Minimization
  - Transcendence[32]

WHAT ARE THE BEST APPROACHES?

The best approach in a given situation will depend on that situation. The key factors that will determine the best response are the other three Rs in crisis communication: the relationships that the organizations have established with each stakeholder, the reputation that the company has earned in terms of stability, and the organization's responsibility for this particular crisis.

Coombs has developed what he has called "situational crisis communication theory" (SCCT). This is an attempt to identify the best approaches for certain categories of crisis. The idea, and it is a good one, is to help crisis communicators decide how to respond in a given crisis situation. By identifying features of a crisis and matching up these features with appropriate responses, SCCT aims to supply recommendations for making intelligent choices in the throes of crisis.

The problem with SCCT is that the permutations for crises are infinite. Consequently, the identification of the correct category for any one crisis is problematic if not impossible. For this reason, using SCCT recommendations could potentially be counterproductive. Since it is difficult to categorize a crisis that represents a unique set of delineating characteristics, it could be dangerous to select a response based on a categorization that might not be accurate. Users might attempt to place or force a unique crisis into a category and then select the response for the not-quite-right category. And that response might not be the best one or even a good one for the distinctive crisis faced. Nevertheless, it might be valuable to readers to review the SCCT chart on page 45 to see how it works and also to understand the complexities of applying it.

GENERAL RECOMMENDATIONS

Can any general recommendations be made?

Clearly, the answer is "yes." The recurring counsel from practitioners as well as scholars is that an organization is wise to adopt accommodation approaches as opposed to avoidance approaches. William Benoit's advice cited earlier is worth repeating. "When a wrong is committed, one should admit it, apologize, and take corrective action."[33] Business consultant Lauren Bloom's comments support Benoit's position. "We as a society [have] gotten sick of all the denials, all the stonewalls, all the legalese."[34]

Denial, concealment, deceit, and declining to accept responsibility are regularly cited as counterproductive.[35] David Henderson, a media consultant, emphasizes the point that we should follow the golden rule guideline. "Be open and timely and transparent. Admit the mistake, and admit you're human like everyone else."[36]

VALUE OF COMPASSION

A study conducted by Coombs is very revealing as it relates to avoidance versus accommodation strategies and the value of compassion. An understanding of the results of this research will be helpful in determining how to approach crisis situations.

The study tested the relative value of stakeholders' tendencies to (a) honor the account of the organization in explaining the crisis, (b) view the organization more positively in terms of reputation, and (c) potentially support the organization. The three types of crisis responses were compassion, instructing information, and compassion and instructing information. In other words would a response providing instructing information increase stakeholders' willingness to honor the account, support the organization, and view the organization more positively—or would a response expressing compassion be more likely to yield these results—or would a response including both instructing information and compassion be more likely to yield these results?

The results of the study are meaningful because they illustrate how powerful communications are when they recognize the emotional needs of stakeholders. Denial, intimidation, and attack are never as successful in terms of legitimacy as approaches recognizing that all stakeholders, as all of us, have human needs and are comforted by expressions that acknowledge these needs.

The results of Coombs's research showed that compassion tends to improve (a) account honoring, (b) legitimacy, and, to some extent, (c) the tendency to exhibit supporting information. However, instructing information alone does not have a positive effect on (a), (b), or (c); a combination of instructing information and compassion does not have an effect on (b) or (c); and there was only partial support for the hypothesis that this combination affects (a). In other words, compassion alone—of the three communication approaches—is the most powerful approach.[37]

Does this make sense to you? Does it make sense that accommodation approaches, those that reflect compassion, such as penitential apologies, mortification, and suffering, would be the most powerful—even when some others might logically seem to be the most applicable?

RECURRING COUNSEL FOR RESPONDING DURING CRISES

A review of the literature of researchers and practitioners reveals recurring counsel about how to respond to crises. Below is a list of these recommendations with a brief description of each.

BE VIGILANT ABOUT NOT HOPING THE PROBLEM WILL GO AWAY WITHOUT A RESPONSE

Crises rarely go away. In some instances, press coverage of events does not linger because other more important stories surface coincidentally. Yet even in these cases, the crises linger, stakeholders remember behaviors or the absence of action. The notion that a crisis will go away is wishfully myopic. Steven Fink comments, "The inability to communicate your message skillfully during a crisis can prove fatal. And it would be a totally needless demise, a wrongful death."[38]

KEEP IN MIND THAT STAKEHOLDERS REMEMBER HOW YOU COMMUNICATED DURING CRISES MORE THAN THEY REMEMBER THE CRISIS ITSELF

Communication in the aftermath of a crisis can either exacerbate a problem or reduce its effects. The communication effort can become part of the problem. We have previously discussed how errors made by Dow Chemical, Intel, politicians Nixon and Hart, and NASA in their communication responses exacerbated the crisis and remain central to what people tend to remember about the crisis.

In their article assessing the Union Carbide crisis, Sen and Egelhoff reinforce this point about the potential for communication to exacerbate a conflict:

> Carbide's inability or unwillingness to participate fully in the resolution of issues led to a further reinforcement of the views about Carbide. . . . It helped in the development and legitimacy of other constituencies who could now cast both Carbide and the Government of India as the villains. These were the voluntary agencies and a number of "grass roots" and other "mass" movements all over the world. As a matter of fact the Bhopal crisis, the unresolved issues, and Carbide's general handling [of the crisis] provided impetus to a number of environmental groups who organized on behalf of the victims.[39]

More about the Union Carbide case appears in Chapter 9.

AVOID STONEWALLING

Researchers and practitioners are nearly unanimous on this counsel.

> Remember the rule never to say "no comment." That phrase triggers two negative events. First 65 percent of the stakeholders who hear or see "no comment" equate it with an admission of guilt. . . . Second, "no comment" is a form of silence which is a very passive response. . . . In a crisis, being passive means that other actors in the crisis event get to speak and to interpret the crisis for your stakeholders.[40]

> Some of the major reasons incidents turn into crises include stonewalling—not being responsive to the media and the people who need to be informed, or responding with "no comment." . . . In a crisis, perception is stronger than reality and emotion stronger than fact.[41]

> They don't want you to hide behind a spokesman or written statement.[42]

STAY ON MESSAGE AND RESPOND AS QUICKLY AS POSSIBLE WITH THAT MESSAGE

> In crisis management, in an online world, timeliness is critical. If you wait, the world is going to define your image for you.[43]

In Chapter 2, we discussed the idea of nuggets as units of information that crisis communicators believe should be communicated to individual stakeholders. In Chapter 4, we discussed the importance of identifying nuggets during proactive planning.

When responding to crisis, it is important to remember to review these nuggets, revise the list for the unique conditions of the crisis, and then focus on them when communicating. A corporate communicator for Fidelity told me that she talks about a shark cage with her executives. She tells the executives that as long as they clearly identify the important nuggets and focus on them, they cannot get bitten by sharks, but if they stray into unknown waters or waters that have previously been determined to be inaccurate or misleading then they can be devoured by internal or external sharks.

BELIEVE IN YOUR MESSAGE AND DELIVER IT WITH CONVICTION

It is difficult to communicate a message if you do not believe in the message you are allegedly trying to communicate. Receivers tend to believe the nonverbal messages that accompany a message more than the words that are used. A message indicating remorse that sounds less than remorseful is likely to be perceived as indifferent. Sometimes spokespersons have every intention of being sincere but their delivery undermines them.

It is also important to designate a spokesperson for the crisis and urge employees not to act in that capacity. After a factory explosion a reporter collared an employee and asked about conditions. The uncoached employee said, "They got gas, they got blast furnace gas, they got everything there for an explosion. It's scary. It's nerve wracking. I've been here 23 years and I've seen seven people killed. So you know it's not like working at K-Mart."[44] This was not the best crisis communication message and was certainly not part of the communication package designed by the crisis communication team. It is important that the spokespersons be designated and available, in order to avoid the relaying of inaccurate or inappropriate messages.

REMEMBER YOUR INTERNAL STAKEHOLDERS

This was identified earlier as an often overlooked aspect of crisis communication. It is easy to think of the media and external stakeholders as primary. In fact, internal stakeholders need to know what has transpired and can also act as agents of the organization in the communication effort if they are informed. However, internal stakeholders are very important. It was remarkable that Union Carbide attempted to reduce anxiety by informing media that its plant in Bhopal was actually safe—as safe as their plant in West Virginia. This was certainly not comforting to the internal stakeholders in West Virginia who began to worry about their own safety given this claim.

ANTICIPATE POTENTIAL RESPONSES AND BE PREPARED TO RESPOND TO THESE REACTIONS

It is a standard recommendation that those making presentations consider questions that will be asked at the conclusion of a talk. Similarly, crisis communicators would be wise to anticipate responses and react to them.

SEE THE MEDIA AS POTENTIAL ALLIES

Organizations and individuals who believe they have been maligned by the media often lash out at the press as conveyors of innuendo and false accusations. The press can be seen as an ally and an agent that will help carry your message in time of crisis. During the first Gulf War, media priming and agenda setting actually worked to the benefit of the Bush administration. When media made the war the lead story, consumers identified the crisis as the most significant issue of the day and therefore evaluated the presidency on the basis of that issue as opposed to domestic matters. In this instance—and of course not in all—the president's approval ratings actually went up as media coverage of a successful enterprise primed the public to assess the performance of the president on this basis.

WHY DO CRISIS COMMUNICATION RESPONSES FAIL?

THE PLANS ARE INHERENTLY FLAWED

In order for a crisis communication plan to work, the plan itself must be intelligently conceived. Flaws in a plan include not identifying important stakeholders, not segmenting stakeholders into separate populations, and identifying nuggets that are beyond the understanding of audience members. Even if this flawed plan is enacted perfectly, it is doomed to fail.

POOR IMPLEMENTATION

A wise plan can prove ineffective because of sloppy communication. A poorly delivered presentation, an e-mail sent to the wrong e-mail addresses or an e-mail that excludes key persons, or a confrontational attitude taken in a press conference setting will doom a crisis plan despite the plan's inherent validity.

THERE IS A NONCREDIBLE DENIAL OF CRISIS OR CRISIS CULPABILITY

When as a child you were accused of wrongdoing, you might immediately have attempted to deny what had occurred. A few years ago I was sitting with a three-year-old niece. I saw a smashed piggy bank near where she was sitting. How did that happen? I asked. "It fell all by itself" was the toddler's response. I remember laughing aloud at the transparent fabrication.

And that is precisely what stakeholders do when they listen to noncredible denials of what cannot be denied. The organization becomes the subject of ridicule—for years. A three-year-old can be excused for claiming that the piggy bank smashed all by itself, but adults cannot. We can all remember the high school miscreant who might vandalize the school and then when confronted replies defiantly nevertheless. Even while holding the paint brush the fellow would stand tall near the graffiti and state, "It's my fault, right?"

Organizations that react childishly lose legitimacy, have difficulty regaining it, and earn a Velcro effect. Exxon's displacement in the *Valdez* spill has besmirched all the truly fine and high quality people who have worked at Exxon for two decades.

AN ORGANIZATION CLAIMS IT LACKS THE TIME TO DEAL WITH A CRISIS

This is a shortsighted approach since whatever is current can be affected by inactivity and the ignoring of a crisis.

Point/Counterpoint

In these exercises, two positions are presented. The first is consistent with a point made in the chapter. The second is a counterargument. Consider the counsel and counterargument. Then write a one-page position paper identifying your position on the issue.

- **Counsel**—Be honest when communicating to stakeholders.
- **Counterargument**—Those who understand linguistic relativity know why honesty will not work. The concepts of "honesty" and even "business" have been constructed such that honesty only means ersatz honesty and business refers to activity that is deceptive and condoned. We do not have the word honesty in our language system. The construct of honesty varies greatly and more often than not means something less than transparent and ethical behaviors. When we say "be honest" we cannot be honest, because the real concept does not live in our consciousness. Thus, the recommendation to be honest is valueless advice.
- **Counsel**—Act fast, identify nuggets, and stay on message.
- **Counterargument**—There is a tension between the necessity of acting fast during crises and identifying nuggets. As a practical matter, one cannot focus on the right nuggets if one is acting too quickly to identify what the right nuggets are. Acting fast trumps finding the right message.
- **Counsel**—The media are not the enemy. The media can be an agent that will help you with your crisis plan.
- **Counterargument**—Yeah, right. Tell me that's true when your assistant knocks on your door and tells you that a representative from *60 Minutes* is sitting in the lobby and has brought the cameras. The media are sharks out for a hot story. Crisis communicators have to keep the boat afloat at a time when scribes are hunting for some issue that will sell newspapers and torpedo the organizational enterprise. Broadcasters are interested in scooping their network rivals, and a good way to do that is to identify something sensational. Believing that the media are interested in just the facts, or concerned with organizational reputation, is like believing in the tooth fairy.

Summary: A Toolbox

Image restoration theory argues that perceptions of legitimacy can be improved by communicating effectively.

Several (nonmutually exclusive) image restoration techniques have been suggested including

- Apology
- Attack
  - Attacking those criticizing the company
- Bolstering
  - Identifying positive attributes about the company that are peripheral to the crisis
- Compensation
- Corrective action
  - Defeasibility
  - Arguing that circumstances make attributions of culpability illogical
- Differentiation
  - Claiming that there is a distinction between the organization's crisis and another crisis—typically one of greater magnitude
- Displacement
  - Blaming another party for the crisis
- Ingratiation
  - Identifying similarities between the organization and stakeholders in order to reduce deterioration of legitimacy and improve perceptions of legitimacy
- Intimidation

- Threats to critics
- Minimization
  - Arguing that the result of the crisis is relatively insignificant
- Mortification
- Suffering
  - Explaining that as well as stakeholders, the organization is also suffering
- Transcendence
  - There are grander issues to address.

Image restoration strategy is successful when the organization and its communicators

- Acknowledge that the crisis will not disappear without communication
- Recognize how communication can exacerbate crisis or aid in image restoration
- Avoid stonewalling
- Stay on message
- Deliver messages with conviction
- Apply stakeholder theory
- Are ready to respond to stakeholder feedback
- See the media as a potential ally

Exercises and Discussion Questions

1. Can you imagine any crisis situation for which attack and intimidation are the best image response?
2. Can you imagine a situation in which compensation and corrective action are not appropriate responses?
3. When you have heard displacement and bolstering used in crisis communication does it increase or decrease your sense of organizational legitimacy? Give examples.
4. Is there anything wrong with using differentiation, defeasibility, or minimization when (a) there really is a difference between your crisis and a competitor's, (b) it is not feasible to blame your organization for the crisis, or (c) when the problem really is not as major as detractors purport it to be?
5. Of the various items listed in this chapter describing "why crisis communication fails," which do you think is the biggest reason for failure? How can this problem be avoided?
6. Please read the following case and respond to points (a), (b), and (c):
   a. Evaluate US Air's crisis communication effort.
   b. What was positive about it?
   c. What would you have done differently?

Case for Analysis

A study by Benoit and Czerwinski analyzed the image restoration strategies of US Airways after a tragic crash that occurred in 1994. The article does not focus on the crash itself, but rather on the crisis that surfaced after the *New York Times* published an article suggesting that the crash occurred because the planes were unsafe, management had implemented policies that resulted in a likelihood that planes would be unsafe, and financial issues had trumped safety concerns at the airline.

The media analysis predictably was a concern for the airline, which thought this coverage would taint the company's image. To combat the damage, US Air used the media itself, taking out ads in forty-seven newspapers. The ads used bolstering, a denial of the *New York Times'* charges, and corrective action. The corrective action was to (a) hire an expert to oversee quality control, and (b) hire an independent auditor to examine quality.

On page 132 is the advertisement that appeared in the newspapers. Benoit and Scerwinski argued that the advertisements were ineffective because the bolstering was too vague and that the denial itself did not seem to be directed at the charges levied by the newspaper. Further, the authors claimed that the corrective action would not improve legitimacy, because for corrective action to be successful there would have to be an acknowledgment of error and US Air did not include such an acknowledgment.[45]

USAir

Dear Travelers:

On behalf of the 45,000 people of USAir, I would like to speak to you on a subject that is of vital importance to all of us – the safety of air travel in the United States.

We who are airline professionals know our system and our planes are safe. This is validated each and every day by federal regulators who fly with us, inspect our maintenance facilities and review our records.

To be certain that you share this conviction, I am announcing two important steps to assure you of the validity and integrity of our operating standards.

First, General Robert C. Oaks, a highly decorated command pilot and the former commander in chief of U.S. Air Forces in Europe, has agreed to oversee USAir's safety operations in the air and on the ground. He will report directly to me.

General Oaks is a proven dynamic leader of men and women who fly, maintain and support high-performance aircraft in a high-density, highly visible aviation environment. This is exactly the kind of environment in which we fly.

Second, I have asked one of the most respected groups of aviation experts in our country, PRC Aviation, to conduct a complete and independent audit of all our flight safety operations.

Under the leadership of R. Dixon Speas, whose industry background in airline safety operations is unsurpassed, an expert team will go anywhere, ask any questions, and look at any records, manuals, bulletins or messages they think are germane to safety at USAir. There will be no limits to their inquiry.

In closing, let me say that we will not rest until each and every member of the flying public shares in the certainty of our commitment to be the safest airlines.

Sincerely,

Seth E. Schofield

Seth E. Schofield
Chairman and
Chief Executive Officer

NOTES

1. The argument that language can be used to improve image is found in many places, including W. Timothy Coombs, "An Analytic Framework for Crisis Situations: Better Responses from a Better Understanding of the Situation," *Journal of Public Relations Research* 10, no. 3: 177–91. Some authors refer to image restoration theory as image repair discourse and the schemes/names for various strategies differ. An example of someone using image repair discourse is William Benoit, "Image Repair Discourse and Crisis Communication," *Public Relations Review* 23, no. 2 (Summer 1997): 177–86. In this article and in another he coauthored—William Benoit and Anne Czerwinski, "A Critical Analysis of US Air's Image Repair Discourse," *Business Communication Quarterly* 60, no. 3: 38–57—instead of using the term "defeasibility," for example, Benoit groups what he calls *provocation, accident, and good intentions,* with *defeasibility* and labels them all under the heading of *Evasion of Responsibility.* Many articles similar to Benoit's review the strategies in the introduction to their studies. Another example is Myria Watkins Allen and Rachel H. Caillouet, "Legitimation Endeavors: Impression Management Strategies Used by an Organization in Crisis," *Communication Monographs* 61, no. 1 (March 1994): 44–62. Those who study these articles will notice a slight variation in labeling, but the same essential types of responses.

2. Eric Dezenhall and John Weber, *Damage Control: Why Everything You Know about Crisis Management Is Wrong* (New York: Penguin, 2007), p. 9.

3. H. Burson, "Damage Control in a Crisis," *Management Review* 84 (December 1995): 42–45.

4. W. Small, "Exxon Valdez: How to Spend Billions and Still Get a Black Eye," *Public Relations Review* 17, no. 1 (1991): 9–26.

5. B. Lau, "Crisis Communication Planning for Organizations: Part II," *Management Quarterly* 28 (1987): 25–28.

6. Steven Fink, *Crisis Management: Planning for the Inevitable* (Cincinnati, OH: Authors Guild, 2002), p. 112.

7. W. Timothy Coombs, *Ongoing Crisis Communication,* 2d ed. (Thousand Oaks, CA: Sage, 2007), p. 133.

8. Susan L. Brinson, and William L. Benoit, "Attempting to Restore a Public Image: Dow Corning and the Breast Implant Crisis," *Communication Quarterly* 44, no. 1 (Winter 1996): 35.

9. Robert C. Rowland and Thea Rademacher, "The Passive Style of Rhetorical Crisis Management: A Case Study of the Superfund Controversy," *Communication Studies* 41, no. 4 (Winter 1990): 330.

10. http://memphis.bizjournals.com/memphis/stories/2009/02/09/daily40.html?surround=lfn.

11. Several books discuss this incident. Readers particularly interested in the Black Sox scandal from the perspective of crisis communication should see William B. Anderson "Saving the National Pastime's Image: Crisis Management During the 1919 Black Sox Scandal," *Journalism History* 27, no. 3 (Fall 2001): 105–11.

12. The film *Eight Men Out* was released in 1988 and written and directed by John Sayles.

13. Sandi Sonnenfeld, "Media Policy—What Media Policy?" in *Harvard Business Review on Crisis Management* (Boston: Harvard Business School Press, 2000), pp. 119–42. The editorial footnote at the conclusion of this Harvard Business Review (HBR) case in this compendium reads, "HBR's cases are derived from the experiences of real companies and real people. As written, they are hypothetical, and the names used are fictitious."

14. Brinson and Benoit, "Attempting to Restore a Public Image," p. 32.

15. Ibid., p. 37.

16. Ibid., p. 39.

17. Sellnow, Ulmer, and Snider, "The Compatibility of Corrective Action in Organizational Crisis Communication."

18. James Kauffman, "Adding Fuel to the Fire: NASA's Crisis Communications Regarding Apollo 1," *Public Relations Review* 25, no. 4 (Winter 1999): 427–28.

19. Watkins and Caillouet, "Legitimation Endeavors," p. 49.

20. http://georgewbush-whitehouse.archives.gov/infocus/nationalsecurity/archive.html Statement by the President in His Address to the Nation September 11, 2001, 8:30 pm eastern time.

21. http://www.youtube.com/watch?v=1yeA_kHHLow, accessed on July 22, 2009.

22. Keith Michael Hearit, "Newsgroups, Activist Publics, and Corporate Apologia: The Case of Intel and Its Pentium Chip," *Public Relations Review* 25, no. 3 (Fall 1999): 291–309.

23. John Holusha, "Chrysler Enters No Contest Plea Over Odometers," http://query.nytimes.com/gst/fullpage.html?res=9B0DE5DD163AF936A25751C1A961948260, accessed on June 22, 2009.

24. Falguni Sen and William G. Egelhoff, "Six Years and Counting: Learning from Crisis Management at Bhopal," *Public Relations Review* 17, no. 1 (Spring 1991): 81.

25. W. Benoit, "Sears' Repair of Its Auto Service Image: Image Restoration Discourse in the Corporate Sector," *Communication Studies* (Spring/Summer 1995): 46.

26. J.R. Cohen, "Advising Clients to Apologize," *Southern California Law Review* 72 (1999): 1012.

27. Ibid., p. 1022. The points made in the preceding paragraph are from pp. 1019–22. Cohen includes other benefits of apologizing in these pages.

28. David E. Williams and Bolanle A. Olaniran, "Crisis Communication in Racial Issues," *Journal of Applied Communication Research* 30, no. 4 (November 2002): 293–313.

29. Quoted in Peter Schworm, "Apologies Become 'Tenor of the Times,'" *Boston Globe,* February 16, 2009, Metro, p. B 4.

30. http://www.barrybonds.mlb.com/players/bonds_barry/news/pressconf0222.html, accessed on July 22, 2009.

30. Many sources address this, for example, P. Lagadec, "Communication Strategies in Crisis," *Industrial Crisis Quarterly* 2, no. 1: 19–26.

31. Coombs uses terms other than those used in this list. For example, he uses "scapegoating" for "displacement," and "excuses and justification" for "defeasiblilty and minimization." Coombs, *Ongoing Crisis Communication,* p. 140.

32. For a continuum from defensive to accommodative strategies with a less inclusive list, see Coombs, "An Analytic Framework for Crisis Situations," p. 189.

33. Benoit, "Sears' Repair of Its Auto Service Image."

34. Schworm, "Apologies Become 'Tenor of the Times.'"

35. Coombs, *Ongoing Crisis Communication,* pp. 83–84.

36. Rene Henry, *You'd Better Have a Hose If You Want to Put Out a Fire* (Windsor, CA: Gollywobbler Productions, 2000), pp. 4–5.

37. W. Timothy Coombs, "Information and Compassion in Crisis Responses: A Test of Their Effects," *Journal of Public Relations Research* 11, no. 2 (1999): 125–42.

38. Fink, *Crisis Management,* p. 92.

39. Sen and Egelhoff, "Six Years and Counting: Learning from Crisis Management at Bhopal."

40. Schworm, "Apologies Become 'Tenor of the Times.'"

41. Ibid.

42. Ibid.

43. Ibid.

44. Steve Wilson, *Real People, Real Crises: An Inside Look at Corporate Crisis Communications* (Winchester, VA: Oak Hill Press, 2002), p. 73.

45. Benoit and Czerwinski, "A Critical Analysis of US Air's Image Repair Discourse," pp. 38–57.

6 Ethical Issues in Crisis Communication

Chapter in a Nutshell

Ethics is a pervasive factor that affects organizations and crisis communication decisions. If lying to the media will affect company stock prices, is lying justifiable? Do crisis communicators have an obligation to tell the truth to internal and external stakeholders or do they have an obligation to be deceptive for the sake of the company that signs the paycheck? This chapter discusses ethical issues as they apply to crisis communication.

Specifically, at the end of this chapter, students will be able to

- Explain why ethics is a factor in crisis communication.
- Define lying.
- Discuss issues related to ambiguity, significant choice, and deception.
- Discuss what is meant by ethical scientific argument.
- Describe the tension that exists between ethical behavior and legal decision making.
- Identify and describe types of fallacious arguments.

CASE 6.1: JELLY BEANS

In the mid-1990s Texaco's corporate literature included sections asserting that the organization was "committed to diversity" and sought to hire "minority employees." Texaco, at least officially, believed that "each person deserves to be treated with respect and dignity . . . without regard to race, religion, sex, age, national origin, disability or position in the company." Certainly, many people who worked at Texaco believed genuinely in these sentiments. However, these people and the company as a whole were nevertheless tarnished by a crisis that had national and even international repercussions.

In 1994 Texaco employees filed a lawsuit against the company arguing that Texaco was a racist organization. The plaintiffs claimed that their ability to progress at Texaco was limited and the general comfort level for African-Americans at the company was very bad. As discourse regarding the suit intensified, many anecdotal references were supplied indicating that there was at least a sentiment among people at Texaco that the company did not treat minorities equitably. The lawsuit and larger conversations about the lawsuit threatened to damage Texaco's legitimacy with its stakeholders. What ignited the situation, however, was a revelation germane to the crisis that surfaced two years later.

In 1996 white Texaco executives were caught on tape discussing the lawsuit. In the recording the executives used racial epithets and what were disparaging references to African-Americans at Texaco and African-Americans in general. In the taped conversation, the executives refer to the employees as "black jelly beans."

> —You can't just have we and them. You can't just have black jelly beans and other jelly beans. It doesn't work.
> —Yeah, but they're perpetuating the black jelly beans.

The jelly bean allusion was apparently a reference to a diversity workshop held at Texaco in which a trainer used jelly beans to indicate different races and to illustrate how all "jelly beans" regardless of color needed to work as one. Apparently, the trainer's lessons did not stick. One of the executives was heard saying:

> I'm still getting used to Hanukkah. Now, we have Kwanzaa . . . [expletive] n*ggers, they have s**tted all over us with this.

The taped conversation also included references to how evidence pertaining to the lawsuit would be destroyed.

> We're gonna purge the s**t out of these books, though. We're not gonna have any damn thing that . . . we don't need to be in them.

When these tapes were revealed, Texaco had a major crisis. The company's crisis response involved a number of techniques discussed in the previous chapter.

1. Bolstering—discussed Texaco's official policies against discrimination.
2. Corrective action—announced there would be an investigation into the incident designed to prevent a recurrence of the event.
3. Displacement—identified those on the recording as anomalies at Texaco who behaved reprehensibly. They were "bad apples" who did not represent the workforce as a whole.
4. Mortification/apology—expressed humiliation for this horrendous behavior and apologized for Texaco's behavior.

In addition to these four approaches, Texaco hired an audio expert. The expert enhanced the tape recording and analyzed it. He concluded that the executive did not use the N word on the tape. The executive, according to the analyst did not say, "I'm still getting used to Hanukkah. Now, we have Kwanzaa . . . [expletive] n*ggers, they have s**tted all over us with this." According to the expert, the executive actually said, "I'm still struggling with Hanukkah, and now we have Kwanzaa—I mean, I lost Christmas, poor St. Nicholas—they [expletive] all over his beard."

QUESTIONS FOR ANALYSIS

- What determines whether Texaco's image restoration approach will be successful?
- How could organizational culture have created the evolution of this crisis?
- Does any organization have the ethical responsibility to purge racists from its workforce regardless of how capable they might be at their jobs?
- Assume for the sake of this exercise that these people were representative of the norm at Texaco. Did Texaco do anything unethical by claiming that the people on tape were "bad apples?"
- Assume for the sake of the exercise that Texaco had not been "committed to diversity." Was it unethical to include this reference in its literature?
- Assume for the sake of the exercise that the person on the tape had used the racial epithet. Did the company do anything unethical by trying to make it seem as if he had said, "St. Nicholas?" Did they do anything foolish by trying to make it seem as if he had said, "St. Nicholas"?

WHY DO ETHICAL DECISIONS AFFECT CRISIS COMMUNICATION?

> People that [sic] behave best during a crisis are not those with the best plan but those that are value driven. . . . While tactical notions are very important in dealing with a crisis, values provide a kind of enduring logic that lends coherence to an organization's actions.[1]
>
> —Public relations executive, John Scanlon

> In many ways this story is about human nature, about people and choices. It shows how power and money can change people and how easy it is to rationalize, give in to fear, and cave under pressure and intimidation. It speaks of the importance of living a life of integrity and making decisions we can look back on without regret. It illuminates the value of developing strong boundaries, keeping our paths straight, and guarding against the temptations, and trappings of material success.[2]
>
> —Former WorldCom employee and whistleblower Cynthia Cooper

> People say we must have had a plan because we came out so well. But there was no canned plan, only a value system based on our corporate credo, and we tried to conduct business in accordance with our credo.[3]
>
> —Tylenol general counsel Roger S. Fine

These quotes—from a public relations executive, a corporate whistleblower, and an attorney—all address the question that heads this section. Ethical decisions do, in fact, affect crisis and crisis communication. Very much. Ethics affects proactive crisis communication behavior as well as postcrisis behavior. A management consultant colleague describes the reason for this very clearly: "A company that is not focused on real value creation, or lacks a set of internal values, is operating without a reliable compass. During crisis, management is very likely to drive the company into a wall or over a cliff."[4]

Ethics is a factor in crisis communication for practical and moral reasons. The practical reasons are likely self-evident. Ethical corporate behavior can preclude some crises from surfacing. And ethical behavior during a crisis may reduce the damage to an organization's legitimacy. The moral reasons are also self-evident to any person who values truth or who has been insulted by deception. We are taught as children that being truthful is what is right. We are offended when we have been victims of duplicity.

As Cooper suggests, unethical behavior can become embedded in the character of an organization and can flourish when even decent people become seduced by their own capacities to rationalize. Cultural theorists argue that routine communications can seed a culture that breeds crisis conditions. Formal and informal interactions that reflect reverence for the bottom line and the relative marginalization of other concerns such as safety, transparency, human needs, and fairness can create fertile corporate soil for developing crises.

Before we proceed in this chapter, take a moment to consider some ethical situations you may confront as a member of an organization. It will probably be no surprise as you read through these that each instance represents an actual situation that some person has faced in an organization.

1. You become aware of a cheating scandal in your class. A work-study student who had the responsibility of duplicating the professor's exam made extra copies and distributed them. If you tell student affairs officers there will be a scandal. You are going to ace the exam anyway as you have prepared thoroughly for the test. Nevertheless, you know that what these others are doing is wrong. Do you report the work-study student's behavior?

2. You become aware that a colleague at work is sexually harassing a coworker. You are not friendly with the coworker, but this behavior is wholly inappropriate. Your company seems to be aware of the miscreant's actions but is nevertheless ignoring them. Do you contact the local newspapers with this information? To complicate matters your company purports to be concerned with sexual harassment and has an item to this effect in its mission statement.

3. Part of the sales plan for products in your organization involves rebates to customers who mail documentation confirming that they have purchased the product. Your company is notoriously slow about paying the rebates and it is prescribed policy to be so slow even though this policy does not appear in any written documentation. If contacted by customers, representatives say that they are processing the rebates. If contacted again, the policy is to apologize to the customer. Only if the company is contacted a third time does it submit payment. Do you report this to the Federal Trade Commission and create a problem for the company that pays your salary?

4. The treasurer for your club is a friend. One day he takes you out for a drink and after consuming one becomes talkative. He says that the drinks are "on the house." You ask what that means. He says that he believes that his work for the club deserves some compensation so he takes 1 percent of all dues and treats himself to drinks and a dinner every month. He feels that people do

not appreciate his efforts, so he appreciates himself. That is why your drink is "on the house." You know this is absolutely illegal and the university would put your club on probation if you were to report this. Do you report this to anyone?

5. You are part of a search committee for a new sales director. Your colleague on the committee has a friend who is an applicant. You discover that the colleague is contacting his friend and telling him what questions will be asked, who the competition is, and characteristics of committee members so he will be prepared for the interview. This is beyond unfair since the competitors do not have this advantage. Do you report the behavior?

6. As you work in the kitchen of a fancy restaurant you notice some things that would startle you if you did not observe them so often. The hygiene of food handlers is such that you yourself will not eat any meal there unless a certain clean cook has prepared it. The kitchen itself does not meet health regulations and is paying off the city inspector who periodically is required to assert that the kitchen meets these standards. You need this job and, besides, it is temporary. In three months you will graduate and get a real job. Now you are just making tips as a waitperson. Do you contact the board of health?

7. You have lunch with someone who is considering giving you a promotion. In the course of the discussion he makes disparaging comments about ethnic groups. At one point he swivels his head left and right and then says that "between you and me there are too many [x, y, z] in this company and it is about time we kept a promotion in the family, if you know what I mean." You feel uncomfortable even to be in the same ethnic group as this person, but you really could use the promotion. On the other hand, this racist could do damage to the company with the way he thinks and speaks, let alone to the people who are denied opportunities. Do you take any action on the basis of your conversation at lunch?

8. A skilled basketball teammate seems to be spending time with characters who do not look or act like Rhodes Scholars. In fact, if you had to guess by appearances, they look like gamblers. As you watch him play you see uncharacteristic errors. You begin to suspect that your teammate has conspired with the gamblers to reduce the deficit of your team's victories. This would be a huge scandal for your university and it would end your teammate's professional aspirations. When you talk with him, first he denies his involvement. When you tell him what you have observed he offers to give you money if you too will conspire with the gamblers to shave points. You refuse to have any part of the illicit activities on the court, but wonder if you should speak to your coach about this. Do you?

9. Your company is not going to make its estimates this quarter. If you report the actual bottom line, the disparity between the estimates and the figures will cause your stock share value to plummet. This would be disastrous for several reasons, not the least of which is that you yourself have stock options that you were hoping to cash in the near future. One possibility is to cook

the books so the health of the company will look better than it is. Your boss asks you to do this. He says that everyone does it. All indications are that the next quarter will be better. Should you cook the books? Should you contact anyone about the request made by your supervisor?

10. You work for a state representative. Your boss has been trying to get support for a new tax bill for years without success. The state needs the money for good reasons, but those reasons do not seem to be swaying the citizens. You read a report generated by your representative and others indicating that a huge deficit in the treasury needs to be addressed or the state prison system will be underfunded and marginal criminals will be allowed to go on work release. You know this is completely untrue. That is, you know whatever treasury deficit there is has been exaggerated. Also, you know from conversations you are privy to, that there is no way the prison system will be affected by whatever deficit might exist. Your supervisor is actually creating the illusion of a crisis to get the taxpayers to agree to his request for more funds that will be used for other reasons. Do you contact media officials with this information?

The above are all whistleblower-type questions. They relate to decisions organizations and people in them have made that can create crises. When companies or individuals make these unethical decisions they may be doing so because they are sloppy or because they are driven by their sense of what is appropriate behavior in a capitalist system. They are applying what is called "instrumental rationality." Their reasoning is driven by the business objectives of the organizations. Organizations can also be driven by what is called "value rationality." That is, they can be driven by underlying beliefs and ethical values. For example, an organization can have and express its value for the satisfaction of consumers. Another value might be a respect for truth and transparency. Another could be concern for the safety of the company's employees.

There may be tension between instrumental rationality and value rationality—that is, between the criteria that should fuel decision making in a company. When confronted with a choice between doing something that is in the financial health of a company and the safety of your employees, which rationality, what set of foundational guidelines steers decision making and decision makers?

Experts in crisis communication and people such as Cynthia Cooper who have been through the tribulations that accompany corporate misdeeds argue that instrumental rationality at the expense of ethical corporate values can breed crises. WorldCom, Enron, Arthur Andersen, are all companies whose image and fortunes came crashing down because of unethical practices.

Practitioners should also be concerned about the residual effects of ethical decisions for reasons that go beyond one's own organization. Unethical behavior can breed unethical behavior in other organizations. Sellnow and Brand discuss this in their article about the Nike Corporation, arguing that unethical behavior can become normalized. "In organizations these resemblances can take the form of standard industry practices. In other words, an entire industry could regularly engage in profitable practices that key publics see as socially irresponsible."[5]

STAKEHOLDER EXPECTATIONS AND TRUTH

O'Hair, Stewart, and Rubenstein comment that, "One of the most consistent expectations that we as listeners bring to any speech situation is that the speakers will be honest with us."[6] In addition, Kraut has argued that people are not particularly adept at detecting lies.[7] Ford makes corroborating comments in *Lies! Lies!! Lies!!! The Psychology of Deceit.* Not only are most people able to identify lies at a rate only "slightly greater than chance," but even those people who are *coached* to detect signs of deceit are unlikely to become more efficient at identifying lies and liars.[8]

Stakeholders are vulnerable. Stakeholders are not necessarily fools because they can be deceived. In her book, *Lying,* Sisela Bok argues that those who are deceived become "resentful, disappointed and suspicious. . . . They see that they have been manipulated, that the deceit made them unable to make choices for themselves according to the most adequate information available."[9] She comments that even those who are inclined to deceive others desire to be treated without deceit.[10] Further, she argues that the damage of deceit transcends the effects on the deceived and includes the erosion of societal trust.[11]

The Greek scholar Isocrates claimed that above all else a speaker must be "a good person."[12] The great Roman rhetorician Quintilian defined the ideal speaker as "a good person speaking well."[13] Crisis communicators must consider ethics because an organization, like any individual, is not only good because of the quality of its message, but because of the quality of its character. The repercussions of unethical behavior can be significant. Unethical communication behavior can dramatically affect consumers, organizations, nations, and even the careers of the unethical speakers themselves.

WHAT IS A LIE?

> And, after all, what is a lie? 'Tis but the truth in masquerade.
>
> —Lord Byron

If you say that all the researchers at your company have PhDs in chemistry from Harvard University and the fact is that they do not, then that is clearly a lie.

However, what if people who conduct the research in your organization are not actually called *researchers,* but are called *aides*? What if only two people have the title *researcher* in your organization? These two do hold a PhD in chemistry from Harvard, and these two supervise all research activities, but the truth is that they do not do the research. It is really the ten aides who actually conduct the research, draw all conclusions, and write the findings. The ten aides are recent graduates with BSs from various institutions. In this scenario, have you lied? You did, after all, say that your researchers, not your research aides, have the degrees. Certainly your objective was to mislead the receivers into thinking that those who conduct the research have advanced degrees from Harvard University. But did you lie, since what you said was, literally, the truth?

Ekman has defined a lie as "a deliberate attempt to mislead without the prior consent of the target."[14] Many people discuss the importance of transparent communication in crisis, but what constitutes honesty is sometimes—conveniently—ambiguously conceived and defined. It is important to be clear with yourself and others concerning what is meant by transparent communication in any discussion of its importance. Ekman's definition is the standard one used by deception scholars. Let us review the key elements. Lying is a *conscious* attempt to *mislead without the consent* of the person you are misleading. If this definition is used, then all of the following behaviors are lies:

- Making a statement that is not true;
- Omitting something from a message that will or could mislead the receiver;
- Using ambiguous language to create an illusion;
- Using statistics to confuse stakeholders.

Consider the following statements from companies in crisis:

> 1. We are devastated by the actions of this apparently deranged employee. We had no idea of his instability. Our organization thoroughly scrutinizes all applicants before hiring to make sure there is no history of mental disorder. Our review of Charlie was like all other reviews.

If employees had complained about Charlie's erratic behavior then this statement is certainly untrue. However, the statement is also a lie if nobody had complained about Charlie, but the extent of your scrutiny of potential employees is no more or less than what is the industry standard, and that standard hardly provides for thorough scrutiny. It may be true that you do what all others do and meet that standard, but you do not thoroughly scrutinize. Therefore, this statement is a deliberate attempt to make the receiver think you do something other than what you do. It is not true and your organization could not be considered transparent if a spokesperson said this after a workplace tragedy.

> 2. Our chief safety officer has impeccable credentials having worked at Merck and Coors previously.

If your chief safety officer did work at Merck and Coors, but neither job had to do with corporate safety and both were part-time temporary positions, then this statement is probably a lie. It would be a lie if it were a deliberate attempt to suggest to the stakeholders that the person responsible for safety had experience in this area at other major corporations.

> 3. The charges that our food products have little nutritional value are false. Few people are aware that our products contain more food energy than competitive brands.

Most people are unaware that *food energy* means *calories.* It is unlikely that the company would have attempted to defuse allegations of limited nutritional value by saying that their product had more calories than the competing product. This would be a deliberate attempt to mislead the target: a lie. Beyond this, it is shortsighted to think that such deliberate ambiguity will go completely undetected. Most people may not get it, but someone will, and then any crisis would be compounded.

> 4. In the past year we have increased our hazardous waste training by 100 percent and there has been a 50 percent decrease in injuries due to accidents.

An organization may have had one obligatory training session and has now added a second. This would represent a 100 percent increase. The company may have had an outrageous twenty incidents of injury due to hazardous waste accidents and now has a still outrageous ten incidents. The claims made are true, the facts are misleading. According to the Ekman definition, this statement is a lie.

Apply the Principles

- Assume that you were hired by an organization that polluted the air. You were told by your employer to make presentations throughout the country describing the charitable and humanitarian activities of the company. The goal of these presentations was to deflect attention from the company's polluting behavior. Is it ethical to deflect attention from the pollution issue by bolstering the company with the other messages?
- Assume you are a famous nutritionist and a consultant for the food industry. There is some question as to whether consumption of a particular product has caused the death of a customer. Because of your fame you are invited to appear on the *Today Show* to debate the controversy with a consumer group's representative. Must you disclose that in addition to being an expert you are also a paid consultant?

THE NORMALIZATION OF DEVIANCE

> My business life had fostered the conviction in me that, outside of the family, the human world was as brutally selfish as the jungle, and that it was worm-eaten with hypocrisy into the bargain. From time to time the newspapers published sensational revelations concerning some pillar of society who had turned out to be a common thief on an uncommon scale. I saw that political speeches, sermons, and editorials had, with very few exceptions, no more sincerity in them than the rhetoric of an advertisement. . . . I saw that civilization was honeycombed with . . . conventional lies, with sham ecstasy, sham sympathy, sham smiles, sham laughter. . . . I imagined mountains of powder and paint, a deafening chorus of affected laughter, a huge heart, as large as a city, full of falsehood and mischief.[15]
> —David Levinsky in the novel *The Rise of David Levinsky* first published in 1917

The phrase "normalization of deviance" has been attributed to sociologist Diane Vaughan. In her book about the Challenger explosion she writes, "repetition, seemingly small choices, and the banality of daily decisions in organizational life,—indeed in most social life—can camouflage from the participants a cumulative directionality that too often is discernible only in hindsight."[16]

The normalization of deviance means what you might think. Doing the wrong thing can become normalized. Deviant behavior can become common because a "cumulative directionality" may be camouflaged by repetitive steps in the wrong direction.

Let us assume you hear someone talk about how they are going to take a sick day for a personal day. If after a time it becomes common in your organization to use a sick day for a personal day, this deviant behavior will become normalized. You yourself might want to take the kids to Washington and use a sick day simply because this is done in your organization.

Now, consider something less benign. Assume you work as a flight attendant for an airline. One night you noticed that a pilot consumed three drinks before takeoff. After the plane took off, flew, and landed you might have felt relieved. Now assume that the next time you flew with this pilot he again consumed three drinks before takeoff. And again the plane took off, flew, and landed. Again you would feel relieved. Still you might be concerned, so you mention your observation to a veteran colleague who said "Don't worry." Apparently, several pilots drink before takeoff. This startles you, but after reviewing the flights piloted by these drinkers you found that nothing problematic had occurred on these trips. You might not only be relieved after this review, but perhaps now might consider preflight consumption the norm and inconsequential. What you know in your head and heart is wrong no longer seems unconscionable to you. The deviance has become normalized. Maybe now you too will have a few drinks before takeoff.

Consider another example. If everyone at your clothing store shoplifts items, and you do it too because it is done, the deviance of stealing has become normalized. You know that should this stealing "get out," you will be in a good deal of trouble, but the deviance has been normalized. You do it. You rationalize it.

Consider this final example. Someone in your class asks you to help him cheat on an exam. Cheating is pervasive in school. You have witnessed it for as long as you can remember. This person wants you not only to help him cheat but also to help his pals on the swim team cheat. The class is a large lecture class. The teacher never takes attendance and has no idea who is in the class and who is not. What you have to do is sit in a row beneath the row in the lecture hall where all the swimmers are perched during the test. You have to leave your answer sheet exposed so that a glance from the row above will provide correct answers to the swimmers. It would be a passive act. Has this deviant behavior become normalized so that there is nothing wrong with it?

It is likely not difficult at all for you to consider organizational situations that could instantly become crises if they were exposed, in which the offenders had rationalized the behavior as normative and therefore benign. Our political history provides numerous examples. As recently as November 2008 a Massachusetts state senator was caught accepting bribes. To some, her reaction seemed to be, "What is all the fuss? This is done." In the infamous ABSCAM scandals in the 1970s, senators were overheard saying, "This is the way of the world."

Let us assume that what has become normalized is not drinking or stealing or cheating or accepting bribes. Assume that what has become normalized is lying: Lying about company achievements, company policies during crises, company policies about transparency. What has become normative is the deception, the deviance of lying.

IS HONESTY OVERRATED?

For several years I conducted a survey and held discussions with graduate and undergraduate students on the subject of deceptive communication. In the course of one such conversation, an MBA student made the following comment:

What is so wrong about lying in certain situations? Isn't honesty overrated?

At another time when discussing the same survey with an undergraduate class, a student commented that if she did not preface her remarks with the words, "this is the truth," then she was not obliged to be honest in her subsequent message.

The comments met with some eyeball rolling, but these students were not anomalies. Over the years I have conducted dozens of similar exercises related to ethics with undergrads, graduate students, and executives in MBA programs. The results are nearly always the same. Many argue that deception is not inherently inappropriate, particularly in business contexts. A reason often used to support deceit is that it is common and therefore to be expected—essentially, deception can be condoned because it is done. A corollary to this reasoning is often used as a complementary argument. A discussant will say that a type of deception is fine because "I do it myself." Other rationalizations are used to condone deception: "I work for this company. I am paid by this company. If I have to lie for the best interests of my company, I will do it because this is my job."

A problem in many organizations is that unethical and deceptive communication has become normalized, thus disorienting organizational cultures. This normalization and the concomitant disorientation is particularly insidious because the disoriented organizations operate under a dangerous illusion rationalizing decisions with skewed reasoning that to them, "logically," justify dangerous actions. Deceptive communication can confuse even those who are being duplicitous. In other words, you may begin to believe in your own nonsense. If you add two plus two and get five, and believe that the arithmetic is correct, then all of your future computations are off. In Vaughan's classic analysis of the Challenger case and in Tompkins's books on this subject, this phenomenon is apparent. Very bright individuals were swayed by their own acceptance of deviance. Can indeed, "repetition, seemingly small choices, and the banality of daily decisions in organizational life . . . camouflage from the participants a cumulative directionality that too often is discernible only in hindsight?"

TRANSPARENCY, AMBIGUITY, AND CRISIS COMMUNICATION

THE CASE OF JACK IN THE BOX

In their article, "Ambiguous Argument as Advocacy in Organizational Crisis Communication," Sellnow and Ulmer describe the crisis faced by the Jack in the Box chain when a large number of customers became ill after consuming hamburgers in their Seattle-area restaurants. Jack in the Box employed several image restoration techniques in attempting to address the crisis. They used bolstering, displacement, defeasibility, minimization, and compensation. They also deliberately used ambiguous argument in an attempt to restore legitimacy. As you read through the description of the case consider whether Jack in the Box acted ethically in its responses to this crisis.

Four hundred Seattle-area residents became ill and three children died as a result of the spread of E. coli bacteria in January 1993. State health officials traced the problem back to hamburgers served at Jack in the Box restaurants and notified executives at the company. Jack in the Box immediately sent a research team to Seattle to investigate the problem. In the three-week period between the outbreak on January 13 and February 6, when the *New York Times* printed a story about the crisis, the share value of Jack in the Box's parent company plummeted.

Initially, Jack in the Box denied responsibility for the outbreak. They contended that the problem was not theirs, but related to the meat inspection system, which they deemed inadequate. Because of these inadequacies Jack in the Box's meat supplier, Von's, had provided the restaurant with tainted meat. Since Von's, not Jack in the Box, was responsible for the meat, and the meat had been inadequately assessed, Jack in the Box contended that it could not be held accountable for the crisis. The CEO of Jack in the Box, Robert Nugent, testified before Congress urging legislation for improved meat inspection guidelines. Jack in the Box also filed suit against the meat supplier Von's.

Jack in the Box argued that it was not feasible for it to be blamed for another reason. The company claimed that certain information pertaining to meat cooking temperatures had not been communicated to them. The Washington State Board of Health had issued a directive regarding the correct temperatures for cooking meat to ensure the destruction of any potential bacteria in a meat product. Jack in the Box claimed that it had adhered to federal guidelines requiring a lower cooking temperature, because the new state guidelines mandating the higher temperature had never been received at the corporate headquarters. The company stated, "While the Washington Health Department recently, and we think appropriately, upgraded their temperature regulations of hamburger, it is clear that Jack in the Box was not properly informed of the change."[17]

Subsequently, however, Jack in the Box was forced to acknowledge that it had indeed received notifications. It seemed they said that "these items were not previously brought to the attention of appropriate management."[18] In other words, the problem was related to *internal* communication. Jack in the Box had not distributed the information to its managers. Still Jack in the Box did not acknowledge responsibility. It intimated that it had not done consciously anything wrong. Internal communication procedures had failed and therefore managers at restaurants had not been properly informed. The company also claimed that there were hundreds of cases of E. coli poisoning reported in the state of Washington every year.

Jack in the Box was vague at best with its communications pertaining to its responsibility. It claimed that its supplier was at fault; the information about cooking had not reached it; there were hundreds of cases of E. coli bacteria each year. It did replace its meat, but was vague about accepting blame. Was this wise? Was this morally correct? By suggesting that it was possible that the company was not responsible for the illness, was it lying?

Sellnow and Ulmer "contend that ambiguity, when viewed in the context of a crisis situation, enables organizations to strategically communicate seemingly contradictory messages to distinct audiences."[19] Goss and Williams claim that if a message is vague people will attach a meaning to the message which is consistent with their previously held attitudes.[20] Advocates of ambiguity argue that this is advantageous since attribution of meaning can reduce perceptions of illegitimacy that would not occur if messages were stated clearly.

STRATEGIC AMBIGUITY

A group of scholars has endorsed an approach to organizational communication called "strategic ambiguity." Strategic ambiguity, as the label suggests, refers to purposefully being vague in order to derive some personal or organizational benefit. Proponents explain that "strategic ambiguity complicates the task of interpretation for the receiver,"[21] and that "at all levels, members of an organization stand to gain by the strategic use of ambiguity."[22]

This perspective endorsing "strategic ambiguity" was first developed in a 1984 article published in *Communication Monographs*. It has continued to be discussed in academic publications as a valuable approach to organizational communication. Contemporary textbook anthologies contain articles endorsing strategic ambiguity, and current textbooks describe the advantages of being strategically ambiguous.[23]

Tension exists between endorsing an ethical framework for crisis communication and simultaneously advocating strategic ambiguity. Let us consider this theory of strategic ambiguity in terms of its purported benefits and problems.

PLAUSIBLE DENIABILITY

In their textbook, *Organizational Communication: Balancing Creativity and Constraint,* Eric Eisenberg and H.L. Goodall Jr. describe the advantages of strategic ambiguity. Among other advantages, Eisenberg and Goodall argue that strategic ambiguity preserves privileged positions and allows for deniability. Eric Eisenberg and Marsha Witten, in "Reconsidering Openness in Organizational Communication," comment that by using strategic ambiguity "organizational participants can express their feelings and can deny specific interpretations, should they arise."[24] In essence, supporters of strategic ambiguity argue that those in authority can use ambiguity to "plausibly deny" blame and maintain their privileged positions. Jack in the Box can be ambiguous about when it received information from the state health department in an attempt to plausibly deny responsibility for the E. coli outbreak.

The following are comments from textbooks supporting the advantages of plausible deniability.

1. "Students and employers often are told that clarity is a virtue. But in organizational situations ambiguity can be strategic. It allows someone to speak without being accountable for what she or he says."[25]
2. "Strategic Ambiguity also allows one to deny a stand if it becomes unpopular. 'That's not what I meant at all' gives a person a way to back down gracefully."[26]

PROBLEMS WITH STRATEGIC AMBIGUITY

The identification of "strategic ambiguity" as an academic theory is discomforting. Journal article titles such as "Reconsidering Openness" or "Flirting with Meaning" create a membrane of legitimacy for behavior that is morally indefensible. Statements made in support of strategic ambiguity seem to be contrary to ethical principles. Here are a number of examples.

- "The use of strategic ambiguity complicates the task of interpretation for the receiver. . . . By complicating the sense-making responsibilities of the receiver, strategically ambiguous communication allows the source to both reveal and conceal, expressing and protecting, should it be necessary to save face."[27]
- "Ambiguity can be used to allow specific interpretations of policy which do more harm than good, to be denied, should they arise."[28]
- "Strategic ambiguity preserves privileged positions by shielding persons with power from close scrutiny by others."[29]
- "[S]trategic ambiguity is said to be deniable; that is the words seem to mean one thing, but under pressure they can seem to mean something else."[30]
- "Strategic ambiguity . . . may be used to allow certain people to have access to the 'correct' interpretation, while purposefully mystifying or alienating others."[31]
- "In organizations, strategic ambiguity is one way in which supervisors can take out 'character insurance' in order to maintain their formal or informal standing in the company."[32]
- [Others have claimed] " 'There is much to be gained in venturing nothing,' there is even more to be gained by giving the appearance of venturing something which, on closer inspection, may be made to seem like nothing."[33]
- "As an alternative to unrestricted candor, secrecy, or lying, information control is often accomplished through the strategic use of ambiguity."[34]

ETHICS AND STRATEGIC AMBIGUITY

Tompkins refers to the dangers of strategic ambiguity in *Organizational Communication Imperatives.* Writing about the space shuttle Challenger disaster he remarks:

> Those who find the concept of "strategic ambiguity" appealing should read the addendum to Chapter V of the Roger's Commission Report. They will be sobered by the possible consequences of ambiguity, strategic or not. Ambiguity was a factor in the Challenger accident.[35]

The problem with promoting the idea of strategic ambiguity is that it provides a license for people to be misleading. Strategic ambiguity promotes the notion that deception is defensible and can be advantageous. Deception is dangerous.

SIGNIFICANT CHOICE

Ulmer and Sellnow published another article related to crisis communication and ambiguity, in which they argue that something they refer to as "significant choice" is an imperative for those engaging in crisis communication.

"Significant choice" is a phrase derived from the writings of Thomas Nilsen. "Significant choice" essentially means that receivers who consume messages have to be able to make an intelligent decision (a significant choice) based on the data they receive. If information is vague or misleading, receivers will not be able to make a "significant choice." Nilsen contended that persons in "positions of influence" were obliged to provide receivers with "the best information available when the decision must be made." In the course of communicating, "there should be no less information provided, no less rigor of reasoning communicated, and no less democratic spirit fostered than circumstances make feasible."[36]

Crisis communicators as much, if not more, than others are obliged to meet this litmus test. Ulmer and Sellnow argue that the tobacco industry's crisis communication responses during its 1994 crisis included several arguments that might seem spurious and others that did not meet the criterion of significant choice.

In April 1994, Dr. David Kessler presented a report to a congressional committee arguing that cigarette products were addictive and that there was an awareness in the tobacco industry of the addiction. Among other criticisms, Kessler argued that the industry had not provided customers with complete information about the hazards of smoking. Most damaging were his assertions suggesting that the industry, aware of the addictive power of cigarettes, attempted to hook consumers with the addiction so that they would continue to purchase the products. In response to Kessler's charges, leaders of the seven major tobacco companies asserted before the committee that there was uncertainty regarding the addictive qualities of cigarettes. Each leader contended that he did not believe the product was in fact addictive.

The executives used several arguments in their presentation that Ulmer and Sellnow considered misleading.

1. Cigarettes are not intoxicating. Would you prefer to fly a plane with a pilot who had just had a cigarette or with a pilot who had "snorted cocaine or shot heroin or popped some pills?"
2. People do quit smoking. If people do quit smoking then cigarettes cannot be truly addictive. To whatever extent it is addictive it must be a relatively insignificant addiction.
3. The surgeon general has referred to overeating, television, and video games as addictions. Do we want to call food, television, and video games a drug?[37]

Ulmer and Sellnow contend that these arguments did not meet the ethical criterion of significant choice because the industry did not provide complete information to consumers so that they could make a reasoned judgment on the basis of the absent comprehensive research. They further claim that the arguments are misleading and deliberately ambiguous. The result of this ambiguity "may contribute to a further decline in the public's ability to make informed choices regarding the complex issues in its environment." The authors conclude that the "tobacco industry's concerns for profitability over social responsibility is identified as a downfall in their crisis communication . . . the role of social responsibility and ethical communication . . . [are] essential variables in a crisis response."[38]

- Do you agree? Is significant choice a factor that trumps any advantages of deception?
- Do executives have a moral obligation to stakeholders or stockholders?

ETHICS OF SCIENTIFIC ARGUMENT

Scientific arguments are often used by organizations when they face crises. When confronted with charges of irresponsibility, organizations, naturally, desire to exonerate themselves by citing scientific "proof" that repudiates any claims of impropriety. It was the intention of the cigarette manufacturers to do just this in their refutation of Kessler's testimony. Dow Corning would have liked to cite scientific proof to refute claims that its breast implants created physical problems for women. When charges were made that Procter & Gamble's Rely tampons created toxic shock syndrome, the company hired scientists in an attempt to refute the charges.[39]

A company may be enticed to conduct a study that does not meet the norms of scientific research. In other words, while science ostensibly provides dispassionate results, a company seeking redemption would like to find scientific evidence to support the repudiation of charges and could conduct studies that do not meet the norms for scientific research. The phrase "scientific ethos" has been used to describe the extent to which science and scientists abide by ethical criteria for research.

Sellnow discuss four criteria that affect scientific ethos.[40] Readers will see that these categories are not discrete and the areas overlap.

UNIVERSALISM VERSUS PARTICULARISM

Ethical research should meet the criterion of universalism. This means that an evaluation of events should be based on a universal established criteria. Let us assume that Exxon wished to claim that what it did in response to the Velez crisis was appropriate. Studying Exxon's actions against an established protocol for behavior in such situations would result in conclusions that meet the criterion of universalism. It is possible, however, that a checklist developed by a company could be designed in such a way as to permit a subsequent claim that "studying the situation reveals that Exxon met all criteria that are appropriate in such disasters." If you were to make a list of all things that you did well, and then evaluated your behavior on the basis of this "protocol," then you could determine that you met all criteria. You would not, however, have met the research criterion of universalism.

COMMONALITY VERSUS SOLITARINESS

Ethical research should meet the standard of commonality as opposed to solitariness. In other words, the goal of the research and the end result of the study are to obtain results that are intended to be shared with all who might be interested in the findings. If the objective of the research is to horde the data within an organization, then the standard of commonality is not met. The latter does not raise the level of scientific ethos since the organization is conducting the research for its own interests and not to share results with a broader audience. The results will be promulgated only if findings support its needs. If findings are inconsistent with its needs the research will be suppressed.

DISINTERESTEDNESS VERSUS INTERESTEDNESS

Disinterested researchers have one self-interest objective and that is to complete the research as dispassionately as possible to discover the truths about whatever it is they are exploring. Interestedness means that a researcher is working toward the interests of a group or organization. Conducting research on a presidential aspirant who may be an opponent would fall into the category of disinterestedness if the researcher simply wants the facts. It would be in the category of interestedness if the researchers are seeking facts consistent with the needs of the party to which they are affiliated. In the latter case, the researcher may seek out only facts that may embarrass the opponent.

ORGANIZED SKEPTICISM VERSUS ORGANIZED DOGMATISM

A disinterested researcher approaches scientific investigation with no biases and with the desire to discover what there is to discover. Similarly organized skepticism suggests that scrutiny of any data is based on objectivity. Organized dogmatism does not involve an objective analysis. The dogmatic researcher approaches the data with a desire to prove a point.

Consider the Texaco case as an example to illustrate the meaning of these four criteria of scientific ethos.

- Organized Skepticism versus Organized Dogmatism
  - An organized skeptic in the Texaco case looks at the tapes and attempts to understand what they mean.
  - A dogmatic researcher examines the tapes in order to find evidence to prove that Texaco was racist.
- Disinterestedness versus Interestedness
  - A disinterested researcher attempts to explore all evidence in the Texaco case to find out what has taken place.
  - Interested researchers are interested in unearthing only information that supports their cause.
- Commonality versus Solitariness
  - Researchers who meet the goal of commonality in the Texaco case will share information with all.
  - Researchers who fit into the area of solitariness will reveal the data only if it serves their point.
- Universalism versus Particularism
  - Meeting the criterion of universalism in the Texaco case means applying established criteria for racist behavior to the case.
  - Particularism involves identifying a protocol for racism that is in the best interests of proving the point of the partisan. For example, Texaco cites a list of what is or is not racist behavior that excludes the actions of their executives.

Do organizations in the throes of crisis have an obligation to conduct research to maintain high ethos or because of their organizational responsibilities are they entitled to conduct research for their partisan interests? One author writes, "The competitive nature of profit seeking organizations makes the presence of counter norms in their scientific argument both likely and to a certain extent, culturally acceptable."[41]

Do you agree? Is this an example of the normalization of deviance?

The asbestos industry has been described as having what was called "myopia" in failing to acknowledge that its product was deleterious to health even after research suggested that it indeed was.[42] Is myopia an accurate word for this? Cheney comments that such myopia can stem from the "propensity of organizational members to preserve, protect and defend the organization even against the best interests of the publics it is supposed to serve."[43] Is this behavior condonable or do individuals have an obligation to force their way through this propensity, deconstruct their rationalizations, and reveal findings as they really are as opposed to how they would like them to be?

Apply the Principles

Your organization makes tires for automobiles. A car manufacturer buys your tires for its products. There are a series of accidents involving tire malfunctions. You believe that the tires have malfunctioned because of problems with the construction and operation of the vehicle. To exonerate yourself you intend to do some studies.

- How would you apply the principle of
  - Universalism?
  - Commonality?
  - Skepticism?
  - Disinterestedness?

Would it be your ethical responsibility to apply these principles?

ETHICAL BEHAVIOR AND LEGAL DECISION MAKING

One issue that surfaces in discussions of ethics and crisis communication relates to a company's legal liabilities. Specifically, if an organization is honest and identifies its transgressions, is it not likely to be subjected to costly litigation? In Chapter 5, when discussing penitential apologies as an image restoration approach, we reviewed law professor Jonathan Cohen's perspective on this issue of apologies and legal ramifications. Cohen contends that there are practical reasons for apologizing. He also argues that apologizing is ethically correct. In essence he suggests that there does not need to be tension between ethical behavior and legal decision making.

Kathy Fitzpatrick, an attorney and professor of public relations, makes a case similar to Cohen's. She suggests that the key to effective crisis management is to balance both appropriate crisis communication behavior and legal concerns. She suggests that crisis communication professionals should see lawyers as a resource, establish positive relationships with the legal team ahead of time, and understand the perspective that a legal team has. She emphasizes that hiring ethical spokespersons, having a meaningful and enforced code of ethics, and being value driven are factors that contribute to reducing legal risks.[44]

Despite these recommendations, data suggest that companies tend to default to what Fitzpatrick calls a legal versus a public relations approach when communicating during a crisis. She characterizes a legal approach as one in which the spokesperson says nothing, says as little as possible—citing privacy laws, company policy, or sensitivity—denies guilt, and displaces guilt. She calls a public relations policy one whereby the company investigates allegations, is candid, voluntarily admits that a problem exists if it does exist, then announces and implements corrective action quickly. In a study she conducted involving thirty-nine cases of company communications involving charges of sexual harassment, she reported that companies, three to one, tended to the legal versus the more ethical public relations approach.[45]

Rehm and Beatty suggest, like Cohen, that despite legal concerns, the consequences of apologizing are not as dire as one might suspect. The authors argue that an apology does not mean guilt. Their article provides another platform to reject the notion that apologies mean one is guilty and a plea of guilt will inevitably lead to liability. As mentioned previously, in Massachusetts, in particular, state law specifies that apologies do not in and of themselves constitute guilt. The authors suggest that attorneys who claim that apologies are grounds for lawsuits may be overly cautious or defaulting to that conclusion believing it is logical in the absence of evidence to support the assumption. The authors write that judges and juries seem to like apologies and treat them favorably. In some proceedings, an apology can be a mitigating factor and the lack of an apology an exacerbating factor.[46]

In one case, while performing a therapeutic abortion, a doctor perforated a woman's uterus. There was a lawsuit. The doctor apologized and said that "she made a mistake and that she was sorry and this had never happened before." The doctor was found not guilty since the defense had proven that she had performed a regular procedure. The court concluded that her apology did not mean she had done anything wrong, just that something anomalous had occurred. The plaintiff appealed, saying that on the basis of the defendant's own statement the physician had obviously been negligent. The appellate court found that while it is true that a defendant's statement could mean something negligent was done, the description of what the doctor had done in this case—despite her statement that she had made a mistake—revealed no negligence—even though the result of the procedure was a perforation. Therefore, the court concluded that the act of apologizing was not equivalent to a negligent error.

This case suggests that plaintiffs armed with an apology as a peremptory argument in support of their claim must prove their cases just as if the apology did not exist. It appears safe to offer an apology as long as it does not contain an admission of negligence. "Statements, writings or benevolent gestures expressing sympathy or a general sense of benevolence relating to the pain, suffering or death of a person involved in an accident and made to such person or to the family of such person shall be inadmissible as evidence of an admission of liability in a civil action."[47] Rhem and Beatty also cite cases in which apologizing was not an aggravating factor and in fact was a mitigating factor.

This counsel is not supported by all. In *Management Communication Quarterly,* Tyler writes:

> Management has a legal and moral obligation to consider a variety of stakeholders in making its decision including stockholders and creditors. . . . The threat of legal liability and consequent threat of corporate extinction make an admission of guilt unwise and perhaps even immoral, even when some audiences (such as victims of the crisis or members of the general public who are not shareholders in the company implicated in the crisis) might find such an admission of guilt highly desirable. Corporate executives are thus trapped, because much as they may like to apologize, they cannot do so without violating their fiduciary responsibility to stockholders.[48]

Tyler's argument assumes that Cohen's and Fitzpatrick's contention is not correct. There is debate in the literature regarding these antithetical sides. The fine line appears to be that while an apology does not necessarily mean an acknowledgment of guilt, some apologies are implicit acknowledgments of guilt. "I am sorry my patient was injured" does not imply guilt, but "I am sorry our consumers were taken ill because of the product we manufactured" does.

Nevertheless, a key ethical question remains. Does management have a legal and moral obligation to consider stockholders and creditors that trumps any moral obligation to apologize?

There is no categorically correct answer to this question. It should be emphasized that most writers argue that in the long run, even for stockholders and creditors, a golden-rule approach to crisis communication is wise. It is also important to remember Cohen's article in the *California Law Review* discussed in Chapter 5.[49] Apologies can have mitigating effects.

IDENTIFYING FALLACIES

Sometimes unethical communicators attempt to persuade stakeholders by using fallacious arguments. Even those who wish to be ethical often employ fallacious arguments and are unaware that they are doing so.

A fallacious argument is one that contains a fallacy—some flaw of reasoning that undermines and corrupts a claim. The words "specious," "spurious," and "bogus" all have similar meanings. They are all adjectives describing something that is counterfeit. A specious gem may look real, but under scrutiny is a cheap imitation. A spurious argument is one that contains faulty reasoning. Something bogus is simply not true. Perhaps the reason there are so many variations of words meaning phony is that so much is phony.

Crisis communicators who are concerned about ethics must be careful not to employ fallacious arguments when speaking for their organizations. Similarly all of us who listen and read statements from government, business, and nonprofits during times of crisis should be able to examine the claims and detect which ones are accurate and which are not. The following section describes several common types of fallacious arguments. An awareness of these will help ethical individuals behave ethically when communicating during crisis situations.

HASTY GENERALIZATION

> When the vegans tested our product they found it to be toxic. When the Green party tested our product they found it to be toxic. No surprise. Apparently all liberal organiza-

tions are against us and it is they who are discrediting us. It is time that objective people stopped listening to this cacophony from radicals so that we can all hear the truth about our product.

The so-called hasty generalization fallacy occurs when conclusions are drawn on the basis of a number of incidents that do not sufficiently support the conclusion. In this case, an organization attempting to portray itself as victimized by the liberal left has identified organizations that have criticized them, and hastily concluded that any attributions of guilt have been contrived by groups with an antithetical political agenda. The facts may be that other groups have criticized the product or that, regardless of political orientation, the groups identified have been objective in their analysis.

POST HOC ERGO PROPTER HOC

As soon as we decided to decrease our entrance standards we saw increased violence on campus. Therefore, we must acknowledge that the source of the present crisis on campus is not poor security, but an influx of nonacademically oriented students.

Post hoc ergo propter hoc literally means "after the fact, therefore because of the fact." In other words, this type of argument suggests that because something occurred after another occurrence, the second phenomenon was caused by the first.

The argument in the example is fallacious because (1) there may be no evidence that the admissions' change created the effect; (2) there may be other causes for the effect, such as the university's reduction of its campus police force; or (3) there may be evidence that this alleged relationship is an aberration. For example, perhaps if the study were conducted four more times with admission standards remaining constant, the increase in violence this year may be the only year when there was a problem in comparison with years when the admission standards were higher. Therefore, the alleged correlation is nothing more than a coincidence.

RED HERRING

It is absurd to think that our company should be punished for these alleged polluting offenses. After all, we have more researchers with advanced degrees, give the most to charities, and have employed more local women and men than all other companies in this area combined.

The red herring argument gets its name from a practice used by farmers to distract hunters. They would drag a red herring through their property hoping that the smell would discourage fox hunters since the hunters' dogs would be thrown off by the scent of the herring.[50] When people employ a red herring argument consciously, they attempt to persuade by including an unrelated argument that they hope will distract the listeners from examining the central issues of their case. Bolstering, when it is intended to distract stakeholders, is an example of a red herring argument.

AD HOMINEM

> It is no secret that Elliot Johnson is an enemy of big business. His entire career has been based on trying to stymie industry. Therefore, his claim that we are pollutants should be rejected in light of his agenda. Can you really take seriously anything that Elliot Johnson might say?

An ad hominem argument is one which is not based on the integrity of the argument, but rather is founded on the characteristics of the person or group supporting the argument. It is irrelevant that Elliot Johnson is making the claim if in fact the company is a polluter.

MISPLACED AUTHORITY

An individual who is an authority in one area is not necessarily an expert in many others. Speakers sometimes invoke the name of an authority to support a position when the authority is misplaced, that is, not a genuine expert in this area. For example,

> Currently our nation is in financial crisis. The Dow is plummeting, people are losing their jobs. We must address this crisis by infusing money into the system and that is why I am proposing this bill to stimulate the economy. The need to use federal money to stimulate the economy has been endorsed by Toni Morrison, Meryl Streep, and several renowned physicians.

Toni Morrison is a Pulitzer Prize winning novelist. Meryl Streep is revered as one of the best movie actors of all time. An epidemiologist may have saved countless lives. However, neither, Morrison, Streep, or a physician becomes an expert in the area of finance because of their skill in other areas.

APPEAL TO TRADITION

> For 100 years our community has always permitted the sale of guns to law-abiding citizens. We should not stop now just because a deranged student behaved unconscionably.

The fact that something has always been the case does not mean that it was ever legitimate or that its historic existence was based on intelligent choices. In the example, the argument is fallacious since no evidence has been provided to suggest that traditionally it was good or wise to sell guns to law-abiding citizens.

AD POPULUM

> CBS has endorsed our findings. So has NBC. So has the Fox network, which typically has nothing good to say about us. All reasonable media people seem to be supporting this report, so we know it is of unimpeachable quality.

The ad populum argument is also called the "bandwagon fallacy." Speakers occasionally attempt to make a case for a proposal because others have endorsed the proposal. In the example, the ad populum argument is fallacious because it offers no proof other than its popularity.

SLIPPERY SLOPE

The slippery slope argument is based on the assumption that the domino effect is inevitable. Speakers who employ this argument suggest that while one step is innocuous it will inevitably lead to something corrosive. For example,

> Once we begin to penalize companies for polluting lakes, where will it end? Will we penalize workers who drive to work in cars that do not meet gas mileage criteria established by government? Will we penalize employees who smoke outside of the building because somehow they are polluting the air? Will we penalize citizens who absent-mindedly toss a gum wrapper away? Once government starts to penalize companies, they will become big brother for all of us.

The slippery slope assumes that the effects of one action will inevitably result in an avalanche. It is fallacious unless supporting evidence can be provided, justifying the notion that the alleged consequences are likely to occur.

FALSE DICHOTOMY (SOMETIMES CALLED "FALSE DILEMMA")

In this argument speakers present their solution as the better of two choices. It is a false dichotomy if more than only two choices are involved. For example,

> We have two choices here. We can pay for the damage we did in this instance and go out of business, leaving close to half the people in this community without work, or we can suggest that the cleanup effort in this matter be a community initiative that is paid for cooperatively, and thus continue to help put food on the table for 48 percent of this town's citizens.

This argument is fallacious since there are likely to be more than the two choices presented by the speaker. The creation of the dichotomy is employed to contrast an absurd and unattractive alternative—going out of business and costing the community's residents their jobs—with the alternative desired by the speaker. This can be a convincing argument unless one realizes the multiple options that may exist but have not been identified.

Apply the Principles

A student group has taken funds allocated by the university and employed them to fund activities that are inconsistent with the purposes of these funds. Instead of using the moneys for a charitable enterprise, they have spent the money to finance spring-break vacations.

- What fallacious arguments might you hear from this club that are based on
  - False dichotomy?
  - Hasty generalization?
  - Ad populum?
  - *Post hoc ergo propter hoc?*
  - Slippery slope?
  - Appeal to tradition?
  - Misplaced authority?
  - Red herring?
  - Ad hominem?
- If you were a member of this club would you employ any of these arguments?

Point/Counterpoint

In these exercises, two positions are presented. The first is consistent with a point made in the chapter. The second is a counterargument. Consider the counsel and counterargument. Then write a one-page position paper identifying your position on the issue.

- Counsel—Ethical behavior is expected by stakeholders. We are all stakeholders at one time or another. We have the obligation to be ethical to our organization and our society at large when we communicate during crises. This means we speak the truth, the whole truth, and nothing but the truth. There is a reason why we pledge to do this in a court of law.
- Counterargument—Few issues are black and white. Most crises involve gray. Crisis communicators are not being unethical because they are ambiguous, they are simply expecting the stakeholders to make reasoned decisions and analyze the gray. There is no such thing as the "whole truth."

Summary: A Toolbox

- Ethical decision making has a practical effect on crisis communication efforts.
- The guiding definition of lying is
  - A deliberate attempt to mislead without the consent of the target
- Crisis communicators are wise not to lie and to be transparent.
  - Allow stakeholders significant choice and avoid what has been referred to as "strategic ambiguity"
  - When using evidence apply the principles of scientific argument
    - Universalism versus particularism
    - Commonality versus solitariness
    - Disinterestedness versus interestedness
    - Organized skepticism versus organized dogmatism
- Avoid fallacious arguments
  - Slippery slope
    - Hasty generalizations
    - *Post hoc ergo propter hoc*
    - Misplaced authority
    - Red herring
    - Ad hominem
    - False dichotomy
- There is evidence to suggest that apologizing does not necessarily increase liability and may reduce liability.

Exercises and Discussion Questions

1. Assume you have a friend who works as a researcher for an automobile manufacturer. How would you define the following in words she or he could understand?

- Universalism
- Commonality
- Skepticism
- Disinterestedness

2. In crisis communication is lying ever justified?
3. How did Ekman define lying? How would you define lying?
4. If you present a false dichotomy to stakeholders, are you lying according to your own definition? Ekman's?
5. What is more important, the ethical considerations of lying during crisis or the practical ramifications of lying during crisis?
6. Should legal counsel trump the counsel of crisis communicators?

Practitioner Perspective: Sue Phillips

Sue Phillips is a lawyer and has served as vice president and senior in-house counsel for several companies headquartered in St. Louis, Missouri.

It is important to think about the long-term ramifications of what you say when communicating with stakeholders during crises. It is also important to be truthful and to respect an audience's need to receive relevant information. When an organization gets into cocoon mode it is acting counterproductively. Not commenting—or saying "no comment" when you do communicate—is likely to be a mistake.

Apologizing in the aftermath of a crisis might be in the best interest of the organization, but it often takes a long time to discover who is responsible for the crisis and consequently, to know if an apology is called for. That said, if faced with a crisis, I would approach the management team and ask what their concerns are. If the biggest concern is litigation, I would recommend avoiding saying anything that could be used to establish liability. But if the biggest concern is that the customer base will be alienated without an apology, then apologizing might be appropriate despite the liability consequences. It is a matter of trying to figure out what approach would end up serving the company's best interests. In the McDonald's case, for example—the case that involved the hot coffee allegedly scalding a customer—the cost of apologizing for what happened to the customer might be preferable to losing business from other customers who feel that an apology is due. Of course, sometimes it is possible to find something to say that can both avoid admitting liability, but at the same time appease those who would be inclined to want an apology.

Organizations can do several things to prepare for crises. They can establish the principles that will guide the organization in determining what they will communicate during crises. The company can agree on a team that will assemble to map out a communication plan if there is a crisis. Finally, the organization can attempt to simulate crisis situations and have the team practice working out a communication plan applying the company's principles. This way the company will have had some experience practicing prior to being confronted with an actual crisis. A public relations firm can be engaged to guide the company through each of these preparation steps, as well as to be on call when a crisis occurs.

The benefits of working in teams can be significant. Different perspectives will be brought to the table. The team can examine a case from the human resources perspective, the investor perspective, the government relations perspective, the legal perspective, and the like. This will improve the eventual plan. A team does not eliminate the need for quality leadership, but allows the leadership to have the input it needs to make the best decisions.

NOTES

1. Quoted in Lynn Sharp Paine, "Managing for Organizational Integrity," *Harvard Business Review* (March/April 1994): 111.

2. Cynthia Cooper, *Extraordinary Circumstances: The Journey of a Corporate Whistleblower* (New York: Wiley), p. 362.

3. Quoted in Kathy Fitzpatrick, "Ten Guidelines for Reducing Legal Risks in Crisis," *Management Public Relations Quarterly* (Summer 1995): 33–38.

4. Interview with Boston-based consultant Paul O'Malley, November 2008.

5. Timothy Sellnow and Jeffrey Brand, "Model and Anti-Model Arguments," *Journal of Applied Communication Research,* no. 3 (August 2001): 285.

6. Dan O'Hair, Rob Stewart, and Hannah Rubenstein, *A Speaker's Handbook* (Boston: Bedford/ St. Martin), p. 38.

7. Robert Kraut, "Humans as Lie Detectors: Some Second Thoughts," *Journal of Communication* 30, no. 4: 209.

8. Charles Ford, *Lies! Lies!! Lies!!! The Psychology of Deceit* (Washington, DC: American Psychiatric Press, 1996), pp. 211–14. The "slightly better than chance" characterization is used by Kraut in "Humans as Lie Detectors" as well as Ford.

9. Sissela Bok, *Lying* (New York: Vintage Books, 1999), p. 20.

10. Ibid., p. 23.

11. Ibid.

12. Isocrates was born in 436 B.C. and lived to age ninety-seven. He was a prolific author of works related to rhetoric. Ironically, despite his knowledge of oratory, he was a nervous and shy individual and rarely spoke. See John Frederic Dobson, *The Greek Orators* (New York: Books for Libraries Press, 1967; originally published in 1919), p. 128. Dobson conjectures that Isocrates, a brilliant rhetorician, may "never have delivered a public speech" (p. 130).

13. Marcus Fabius Quintilianus, known as Quintilian, lived in the first century A.D. He is famous for his *De Institutione Oratoria* [On the Education of the Orator]. Sometimes this comprehensive treatise on oratory is simply referred to as the *Institutio.* The discussion relevant to the quote appears in book XII, Chapter I, section 1 of the *Institutio.*

14. Quoted in Mary Frank and Thomas Feeley, "To Catch a Liar: Challenges for Research in Lie Detection Training," *Journal of Applied Communication Research* 31, no. 1 (February 2003): 60.

15. Abraham Cahan, *The Rise of David Levinsky* (New York: Harper Torchbooks, 1960; originally published in 1917), p. 380.

16. Diane Vaughan, *The Challenger Launch Decision* (Chicago: University of Chicago Press, 1996), p. 119.

17. Timothy L. Sellnow and Robert R. Ulmer, "Ambiguous Argument as Advocacy in Organizational Crisis Communication," *Argumentation and Advocacy* 31, no. 3 (Winter 1995): 138–50.

18. Ibid.

19. Ibid.

20. Ibid.

21. Eric Eisenberg, "Ambiguity as Strategy in Organizational Communication," *Communication Monographs,* 51, 1984, page 236.

22. Eric Eisenberg and Marsha Witten, "Reconsidering Openness in Organizational Communication," in *Readings in Organizational Communication,* ed. Kevin Hutchinson and Wm C. Brown (Dubuque, IA: Wm C. Brown 1992), p. 127. Originally published in *Academy of Management Review* 12, no. 3: 418–26, 198. Eisenberg and Witten reference the 1984 Eisenberg article (see footnote 1) as support for the claim.

23. Steven Corman, Stephen Banks, Charles Bantz, and Michael Mayer include the seminal article in their reader *Foundations of Organizational Communication* (White Plains, NY: Longman, 1995), p. 246; a similar article by Eric Eisenberg and Marsha Witten, "Reconsidering Openness in Organizational

Communication" is included in *Readings in Organizational Communication,* ed. Kevin Hutchinson (Dubuque, IA: Brown), p. 122. Two texts refer to the benefits of strategic ambiguity: Eric Eisenberg and H.L. Goodall Jr., *Organizational Communication, Balancing Creativity and Constraint,* 3d. ed. (Boston: Bedford/St. Martins, 2001), p. 24; and Sarah Trenholm, *Thinking Through Communication* 3d edition (Boston: Allyn & Bacon, 2001), p. 95. The original article, "Ambiguity as Strategy in Organizational Communication," appeared in a 1984 issue of *Communication Monographs*, 51, pp. 227–242.

24 Eisenberg and Witten, "Reconsidering Openness in Organizational Communication," p. 127.

25. Charles Conrad and Marshall Scott Poole, *Strategic Organizational Communication,* 5th ed. (Fort Worth, TX: Harcourt College Publishers, 2002), pp. 238–39.

26. Trenholm, *Thinking Through Communication,* p. 95.

27. Eisenberg, "Ambiguity as Strategy," p. 236.

28. Ibid., p. 235.

29. Eisenberg and Goodall, *Organizational Communication, Balancing Creativity and Constraint,* p. 25.

30. Ibid.

31. Eisenberg, "Ambiguity as Strategy," p. 234.

32. Ibid., p. 235.

33. Ibid., p. 236.

34. Ibid., p. 234.

35. Tompkins, Phillip Organizational Communication Imperatives, (Roxbury Press, CA 1993). p. 137.

36. Robert R. Ulmer and Timothy L. Sellnow, "Strategic Ambiguity and the Ethic of Significant Choice in the Tobacco Industry's Crisis Communication," *Communication Studies* 48, no. 3 (Fall 1997): 215–33.

37. Ibid., p. 224.

38. Ibid., p. 231.

39. Timothy L. Sellnow, "Scientific Argument in Organizational Crisis Communication: The Case of Exxon," *Argumentation and Advocacy* 30, no. 1 (Summer1993): 28–42.

40. Ibid.

41. Ibid.

42. R. Heath, "Effects of internal rhetoric on management response to external issues: how corporate culture failed the asbestos industry." *Journal of Applied Communication Research* 18 (1990): 153–167 cited in op cit Sellnow.

43. Cheney quoted in op cit Sellnow.

44. K.R. Fitzpatrick, "Ten Guidelines for Reducing Legal Risks in Crisis Management," *Public Relations Quarterly* 40, no. 2 (1995): 33–38.

45. Kathy R. Fitzpatrick and Maureen Shubow Rubin, "Public Relations vs. Legal Strategies in Organizational Crisis Decisions," *Public Relations Review* 21, no. 1 (Spring 1995): 21–33.

46. P.H. Rehm and D.R. Beatty, "The Legal Consequences of Apologizing," *Journal of Dispute Resolution* (1996): 115–30.

47. Ibid.

48. L. Tyler, "Liability means never being able to say you're sorry: Corporate guilt, legal constraints, and defensiveness in corporate communication." *Management Communication Quarterly* 11 (1997): 51–73.

49. J.R. Cohen, "Advising Clients to Apologize," *Southern California Law Review* 72 (1999): 1012.

50. Interested students might enjoy reading a detailed description of the etymology of the phrase "red herring" at www.word-detective.com/042601.html.

7 | Crisis Communication Teams

Chapter in a Nutshell

Crisis communication planning is done in teams. These teams are active during crises as well, generating messages to stakeholders, assessing reactions, and responding to feedback from stakeholders. Communication in teams can be problematic for various reasons. There may be personality issues, discordant or hidden agendas, or leadership problems. An ability to effectively interact in crisis teams can reduce or eliminate impediments that would otherwise increase the challenges to communicating effectively during crisis. This chapter discusses issues pertaining to team interaction with specific applications to crisis situations.

Specifically, at the end of this chapter, readers will be able to

- Resolve primary and secondary conflict.
- Understand the principles of nonsummativity and multiple causation.
- Recognize common variables affecting group success.
- Implement methods for improving team success.
- Detail elements of effective crisis communication teams.

CASE 7.1: FEELINGS OF BETRAYAL AND ANGER

Many people feel very strongly about their faith. Whether one is a believer or a nonbeliever, it is undeniable that for millions of citizens worldwide religion provides a meaningful and valuable foundation for life. Places of worship are sanctuaries and the ability to find refuge and comfort in the walls of churches and synagogues should be a birthright for all people. Many of us belong to a church or synagogue and speak with pride of our particular place of worship and those who lead our congregations. We have seen people point to a building and heard them say with a sense of belonging, "That is my father's church," or "This is my synagogue," or "We are very fortunate to have Pastor Paul for our congregation." It is important for all believers to trust that the place they go to seek spiritual comfort is indeed inviolable and sacrosanct.

It was, therefore, a blow to the parishioners at St. Vincent Ferrer Catholic Church in Delray Beach, Florida, when two priests, the reverends John Skehan and Francis Guinan, were charged with stealing over $100,000 of church money and using it for their personal enjoyment, including cruises, trips to Las Vegas, and time spent with mistresses. On September 27, 2006, Father Skehan was arrested at Palm Beach International Airport as he returned from Ireland. On October 23, 2006, Father Guinan was arrested after he returned from a cruise to Australia. The parishioners' reactions ranged from incredulity, to dismay, to a tendency to defend the religious leaders. In January 2009, Father Skehan pleaded guilty to the charges. Father Guinan maintained his innocence. On February 17, 2009, Father Guinan's criminal trial began.

On September 28, 2006, one day after Father Skehan's arrest, Bishop Gerald Barbarito of the Diocese of Palm Beach issued the following statement.

> We have been informed by the State Attorney's office that arrest warrants for grand theft were issued for Father Frank Guinan and Father John Skehan and that Father Skehan has been arrested.
>
> When diocesan officials received credible evidence against Father Guinan regarding financial impropriety at St. Vincent Ferrer Parish, which pointed to using parish monies not in keeping with his priestly ministry, I immediately withdrew his ability to administer financially the parish of St. Vincent Ferrer and approved an internal diocesan investigation, which included an independent audit. The information gathered in the investigation was turned over to the Delray Beach Police Department who had simultaneously received an anonymous complaint about Father Guinan. The Delray police and the Florida Department of Law Enforcement launched a separate lengthy investigation with which we fully cooperated at all times. Because of evidence uncovered at St. Vincent Ferrer, I also authorized a forensic investigation at St. Patrick Parish, where Father Guinan had previously served as pastor.
>
> Credible evidence also prompted me to initiate a canonical process for Father Guinan's removal as pastor. During this process he volunteered to resign and retire. I accepted his resignation. In the course of the investigation evidence was then uncovered against Father Skehan, Father Guinan's retired predecessor at St. Vincent Ferrer. Because of the ongoing nature of the criminal investigation I will not elaborate further on the specifics of the case, except to say that we intend to continue to cooperate fully and to fulfill the requirements of justice.
>
> I wish to assure all that, independent of this matter, a policy of regular biennial audits of every diocesan entity and a system for the handling of parish funds were established during the past three years. Parishes are required to follow these polices. While no policies can totally prevent financial improprieties, especially in cases of collusion, the current policies and procedures are intended to prevent future improprieties such as those that have been alleged.
>
> Until such time as this matter is concluded in the criminal court, Fathers Guinan and Skehan are being placed on administrative leave and will not have permission to exercise publicly their priestly ministry. Upon the conclusion of the criminal process, their canonical status will be reviewed.
>
> As these allegations give rise to grave concern and possible feelings of betrayal and anger, let us remain steadfast in faith and in the sacramental life of the Church knowing that the power of grace is operative at this time.
>
> I ask for your prayers for the parish communities of St. Vincent Ferrer and St. Patrick's, for our diocese, as well as for Fathers Guinan and Skehan.
>
> May God bless you.

QUESTIONS FOR ANALYSIS

- Evaluate the quality of Bishop Barbarito's message.
  - What, if anything, would you have added or eliminated?
  - What crisis communication strategies did he employ?

- Assume it is October 2006 and you are a member of a crisis communication team hired to work with the diocese of Palm Beach.
    - Who would you consider to be the primary internal stakeholders?
        - What would the message be to these people?
    - Who would you consider to be the primary external stakeholders?
        - What would the message be to these people?
    - What difficulties might your team have in coming to consensus regarding any recommendations you might make to the bishop?
    - How might you attempt to address these tensions?
    - If you were to break up your class into teams acting as crisis communication experts making recommendations to the bishop in October 2006 in attempting to come to consensus, would your class group experience tension different from those of any group actually hired by the diocese?
        - What would be the source of your group's tension?
        - How might you overcome the tension?
- Assume you are working for the archdiocese as the trial began in February 2009. What recommendations would you make to the bishop in terms of crisis communication pertaining to this event?

INTRODUCTION

Crisis communication planning is done in teams. As we discussed in Chapter 4, planning involves identifying potential crises, considering stakeholders, generating nuggets to be disseminated to these stakeholders, determining the best methods for distributing these messages, anticipating the appropriate sequencing for disseminating the messages, and simulating crisis efforts.

In addition to the precrisis work, crisis teams are also active during crises. In what is sometimes (unfortunately) referred to as "war rooms," team members meet and adjust their plans to the unique circumstances defining a given crisis. Then team members must collectively make decisions under intense internal and external pressures regarding what and how to communicate to the varied stakeholders.

Meetings are often identified as stressful communication contexts in the best of times. While your experience with meetings may be more positive, it is likely that you have experienced tensions when working on team projects either in school or at work. Sometimes the sources of these tensions are innocent, that is, people are not delinquent or deliberately trying to derail the process, but the meetings are problematic regardless. Sometimes the sources of tension are less benign; someone may not be working as diligently as necessary, or may have an objective that differs from that stated by the group. Sometimes groups are rudderless and there is at best a vague sense of leadership, understanding of process, or clear identification of purpose—even in crisis.

Problems identified by participants in meeting sessions often reflect what might be considered minor issues—certainly when juxtaposed with major issues that loom during crisis—but these minor issues can accrue and create tensions. These tensions can be an additional force that increases the challenges during crisis and actually derails the making of intelligent choices. In other words, problems related to communicating in teams—instead of facilitating stronger solutions because of input from many people—can result in choices made during crisis that are counterintuitive and destructive. Students may be familiar with the classic Bay of Pigs case when the United States decided to take a covert action in Cuba that was, at least in retrospect, very foolish. The attribution of responsibility for this crisis is often placed not at the foot of any single fool who participated in the decision, but at the feet of a committee that reached a stunningly illogical conclusion—because of poor team interaction.

Teams that are proactively examining crises will encounter types of problems that differ from the problems encountered by teams in the throes of crisis decision making. In the proactive stage, the imminent dangers of the crisis are not apparent and some issues related to responsibility and apathy may surface that are unlikely to evolve during crisis. However, the reactive stage also has its share of issues that can develop because of the intensity of the moment. Not listening to others, allowing one's ego to dominate, not using what we will discuss later as "risk technique"— these are all insidious tendencies that can undermine team decision making when examining crises.

Let us consider some common remarks about problems that people make during meetings.

1. There is always an elephant in the room. We are talking about an issue, but we all know that someone or a few people in the room are responsible for the issue, so we all dance around the fact that negligence in the first place caused us to have to meet. If the negligent person misses the meeting and there is no elephant, we talk about what is really going on. Otherwise, there are elephants in the room and we do not talk frankly. The result is an incomplete solution because we did not address a central part of the problem.

2. We have one guy on our team who is overly concerned with policy and precedent. He always wants to know where something is "written." Can he see the policy? I think he is afraid of getting in trouble. Sometimes you have to act, damn it, and you can't just make sure you are not violating some arcane company policy. This drives me crazy when time is valuable.

3. The problem is that all our meetings are crisis meetings or become crisis meetings. We never meet unless something is presented as absolutely urgent to be addressed. So all decisions seem to be made with a gun to our heads and that scenario does not create a solid foundation for logical decision making.

4. I really don't know why we meet. It is actually a ruse. The head makes the calls and it is less about discussing and more about presenting. I think the idea is to create an illusion that there is collaborative input, but in reality if we have a voice at all it is to mutter "Yes, sir" periodically.

5. The issue we have is regular attendance and psychological attendance even when all are present. Often one or two people in our group call in their regrets, so the next meeting really does not start anew as it should. It is difficult to

have an ongoing planning session when we must "fill someone in" on what
we did in the preceding session. We have minutes, and they are pretty good,
but I do not get the sense that people read them prior to the session. Also,
it is bothersome to be in a session and have someone step outside for a cell
phone call and then have to repeat what was said. Worse yet is discussing an
item and knowing that a key decision maker is looking at his BlackBerry,
so you waste time going over the same ground. There have been instances
when someone who was immersed in a BlackBerry pretended to know what
was going on and weighed in on a decision that swayed the vote and sent us
reeling in the wrong direction.

6. The problem we have is too many chiefs and not enough Indians, and the
   reason we have this problem is that the designated chief is not taking an active
   role. So, we have these meetings supposedly called and led by one person, but
   in the absence of anything more than nominal leadership it becomes chaotic
   with everyone shouting out their ideas at once. At the last minute apropos
   of nothing that has preceded it we make a rash decision because a decision
   needs to be made before we all have to leave.

   • Do you think these voices are atypical?
   • Have you experienced any similar problems when working on committees?
   • What are the ramifications of the problems suggested by these complaints
     for crisis communication decision making?

VALUES OF MEETINGS

Despite the common tensions, there are reasons for crisis communication to be done
in teams. Several of these advantages are listed here.

• A stage in crisis communication planning involves predicting crises. Individuals in a parochial area may not be able to comprehensively predict what can go
  wrong. Therefore, a team comprised of people from various groups will allow
  for a more comprehensive list of potential crises.
• Members of the team have expertise in specific areas. The safety officer is aware
  of safety issues, and the CFO knows about financial issues. Crisis communication is multifaceted and crisis communicators require informed input in order to
  make quality decisions.
• Even very intelligent people can be assisted by listening to the perspectives of
  others. A team allows for the presentation of diverse viewpoints that increase if
  participants represent different parts of an organization.
• Team interaction allows for "buy in" or acceptance of a decision through participation.
• Team members can play "devil's advocate" to identify flaws in any potential
  solution.

Because of these advantages, crisis planning should be done in teams. However, because of the problems inherent in team interaction, crisis communicators should examine common problems in team contexts and employ intervention techniques to preempt the corrosive effects of these tensions.

PRIMARY AND SECONDARY CONFLICT

Almost any group you have ever belonged to and worked within has experienced primary and secondary conflicts that have negatively affected the quality of team interaction.

WHAT IS PRIMARY CONFLICT?

Primary conflict refers to anxiety that surfaces *before* any crisis team meeting occurs. It can occur before an initial planning meeting and/or prior to any subsequent session, even after a group has met dozens of times in the past. Team members may experience primary conflict for many of the following reasons.

Anticipated inequity and irresponsibility

Responsible individuals may fear that others on the team will be less diligent. The head of human resources may have some negative experience with the legal team and assume that prior work that was done superficially will be characteristic of work done in this meeting.

Preexisting personality tensions

In organizations people become aware of colleagues who are easy to work with and others who are contentious. After an initial group project in a class, you know with whom you want to work on the second project. Primary tension can surface when team members know the other participants on the team and expect that some will be obnoxious, tyrannical, or verbose.

Past experience

Since groups are often problematic it is likely that team members have had previous bad experiences in meeting with other groups. These tense memories may be recalled prior to the beginning of a session and create anxiety. If a crisis team has met in the past and these past meetings were disorganized then any subsequent session may make participants feel tense as if this session will also be difficult.

Poor communication skills

Some people experience primary tension because they do not speak well or become anxious in speaking situations. This creates anxiety because other members expect communication and thus, tense shy individuals know they will be put on the spot and unable to hide. Even someone who is extraordinarily knowledgeable and bright may feel as if he speaks poorly, or will be ridiculed because of the way he talks. This anxiety can create primary conflict.

Other organizational projects

In organizational and university life we multitask. It is rare for someone to have only one responsibility—to work on committees. If other business and school matters are on your agenda and you fear that the team meetings will usurp precious time, you will experience primary tension. This is unlikely to surface during actual crises because of their urgency: the crisis has priority. However, in proactive planning this can surface often. A participant may not have bought into the notion that planning for crisis is wise or helpful. Therefore a planning meeting may seem to be a waste of time and make the participant nervous.

Personal matters

We multitask at work, but we are essentially always multitasking since our personal lives are also important. If parents are ill, roommate is ornery, romantic partner is aloof, or children are having issues at school, even work on a crisis matter may be relatively meaningless. Team members may become anxious before a meeting when they have more significant personal items on their schedules.

Sense of marginalization

Critical theorists talk about individuals sometimes being invited to the table, but not given any silverware. A person on a crisis team may feel as if his presence is window dressing and that he will not have meaningful input in the decisions of the group.

Significance and pressure related to assignment

In crisis situations, primary tension can surface because a great deal may depend on the quality of the team interaction and decisions. If the team is meeting to respond to a financial crisis that could, if poorly managed, result in loss of jobs, then the pressure can create preliminary anxiety. In crisis situations then, the enormity of the problem can increase the primary tensions related to other problems. For example, if participants are concerned that Joe from information technology will be part of the committee because Joe tends to be condescending and dismissive, the primary tension associated with Joe's presence is exacerbated because the group outcome has great significance.

Workload

A participant may experience primary conflict because while the issue is significant, the amount of work on the project will similarly be significant and this assignment may make it impossible to complete other projects in a timely way.

Preparation

Participants may have assignments from a previous meeting and be unprepared to present what they were supposed to prepare for the meeting. This can create primary tension. Because individuals do not want to be embarrassed in front of peers, attending a meeting unprepared will create preliminary anxiety.

Any one of these or any combination could result in primary tension and make it difficult for work in groups to be successful from the beginning.

How many of these have affected your attitude prior to attending a meeting?

SECONDARY TENSION

Once the meeting begins secondary tensions or conflicts are likely to surface. These can be categorized into four areas: *procedural; equity; affective; and substantive tensions.*

Procedural

These tensions stem from feelings that the process of interacting in the group is unproductive. A member or members of the group may feel that the agenda is weak or feel dispirited because the leader is not adhering to the agenda. There may be no agenda at all, which could cause procedural anxiety. In a proactive crisis meeting this can create tension because time is being wasted. In a reactive crisis meeting, the lack of process not only wastes time but also reduces the already limited time available to the extent that intelligent choices are not made because there have been inadequate deliberations. Individuals who experience this type of conflict feel that if the session were to be conducted differently it would be more effective and productive.

Equity

Equity tensions occur when there is a perception of inequality. Participants in the group feel that something is not fair. Typically, equity tensions fall into two sub-categories.

The first occurs when members feel that they are assuming a disproportionate share of the responsibilities. The HR representatives may feel that it would be nice if legal did some more of the legwork on a document. HR may resent always being saddled with the time-intensive proactive responsibilities. It may sometimes seem as if other participants are slackers or "social loafers"—a phrase used in the literature of group interaction to describe those who are derelict and allow, if not compel, other group members to do their work.[1] If participants sense that they must carry the weight of noncontributing members, tension may surface because of the inequity.

A second type of equity tension occurs when participants want to be involved in the group but are ignored by more powerful or controlling members. In this situation a potential contributor feels bruised because what he says is not taken seriously. Members begin to wonder, "Why am I here?" They offer a suggestion about a stakeholder population and it seems to them that after they offer their opinion it evaporates from the consciousness of all members who, except for claiming subsequently that they "heard" all voices, disregard the input. Women and minorities often feel such equity conflict.

Affective

Affective tension surfaces when people in the group begin to dislike one another. This may be the result of residual procedural, equity, or even primary tensions, but when it surfaces, group interaction becomes very difficult. Participants find it difficult to "hear" what adversaries are saying, let alone to consider the wisdom of any suggestions. The personality tensions may make individuals contrary and the discussions gratuitously argumentative. A perceived foe may suggest a plan that is well-grounded in logic, but the rival is unable to see through the personal tension to legitimately evaluate the proposal.

Substantive

A positive type of tension is called substantive conflict. This refers to conflict that surfaces because of legitimate disagreements regarding the subject being discussed. Typically, most people think of conflict as something negative, but it is not necessarily the case. Kreps identifies three beneficial aspects of conflict. It can:

- promote creativity and therefore facilitate problem solving
- promote the sharing of different ideas and therefore increase the amount of relevant information available
- serve to test the strength of opposing ideas.[2]

For example, let us assume your organization produces office equipment. You work on a committee that has been formed to address a crisis that surfaced because a particular product—a printer—regularly malfunctions. The blogs, Web sites, and assorted social networks are ridiculing your company. Your committee is meeting to discuss, among other things, what to offer in terms of compensation to disgruntled customers. If one member of the committee suggests compensation in the form of a replacement, another member suggests compensation in terms of a credit for future products, a third suggests writing a check to consumers, and a fourth suggests no compensation at all, there is conflict between these four positions. And the conflict may well yield a better solution for the organization.

In short, substantive conflict is something you desire when you meet as a group. Leaders and all participants should actively try to create disagreement even when there seems to be total agreement on a particular subject. In the section of this chapter that deals with interventions we discuss methods of generating substantive conflict.

NONSUMMATIVITY AND MULTIPLE CAUSATION

Two terms used in the literature of team interaction are nonsummativity and multiple causation.

WHAT IS NONSUMMATIVITY?

We have heard the expression "the whole is greater than the sum of its parts." While this expression is very relevant to team interaction, it is not completely accurate. In group situations, the whole *could* be greater than the sum of its parts. However, the whole—or result of group interaction—could in fact be less than the sum of its parts. Because of primary and secondary tensions it is not impossible for the result to be *negatively* nonsummative. Nonsummativity means that the result of group interaction is not the additive sum of each person's potential contributions. Because of collective wisdom and the ideas that such collectivity can spawn, the whole can be positively nonsummative, that is, the whole can be greater than the sum of its parts. If, however, there is a good deal of tension the result can be negatively nonsummative.

Let us assume a crisis committee is meeting to decide what image restoration strategy to use in an embezzling crisis. Someone at the company has stolen funds from the employees' retirement accounts. This committee includes a representative from the ranks of employees, the chief financial officer, a human resources representative, the chief executive officer, and the chief information officer. Each of these five people could work collectively to consider alternatives. However, if there is procedural conflict, equity conflict, or affective conflict, it is possible that some of the five members will choose not to participate in the discussion. Therefore, any decision to use denial and intimidation, for example, would not reflect that the whole is greater than the sum of its parts but that the whole is less than the sum of its parts. The principle of nonsummativity argues that it is extraordinarily unlikely that the result will be summative, and very likely that it will either be positively or negatively nonsummative. The reason for the nonsummativity is referred to as multiple causation.

WHAT IS MULTIPLE CAUSATION?

Multiple causation means what you would think it means if you tried to deconstruct the phrase. Essentially, multiple factors or causes can create the phenomenon of nonsummativity.

Poor organization of meetings, inadequate leaders, poor communication skill sets, lack of quality space, financial pressures of crisis, inadequate representation, highly ego-involved members, and great amounts of affective conflict are all causes that can create a negative nonsummative result. Conversely, large measures of substantive conflict, effective leadership, solicitation of comments from all members, and the use of meeting interventions are multiple causes that can result in a whole that is greater than the sum of its parts. Therefore, multiple causes create a nonsummative result.

COUNTERPRODUCTIVE TENDENCIES

Groups often default to counterproductive behaviors. That is, the natural tendency is for group members to behave in ways that are likely to create a negative nonsummative result. The following are several of these counterproductive tendencies.

Conformity

Groupthink, the Asch effect, and goal lining all refer to threats to group success based on group tendencies to conform. An assumption when convening in groups is that "two heads are better than one." However, if two or more "heads" *actually act as one* then the value of collective communication is diminished. When this occurs, crisis meeting sessions will *not* do what they purport to do, which is to provide an arena for sharing multiple perspectives on an issue. For illustration, the decision to use a press conference to disseminate information determined by a committee may have been the product of a single person's idea cloaked in the spurious claim that it was a group decision.

What is groupthink?

As is the case with many neologisms, "groupthink" is a term that has morphed from its original conception and taken on some ambiguous dimensions. Understanding the precise meaning of groupthink is important for crisis communicators lest they fall victims to it. Irving Janis popularized the word in a book about political decision making and an article in *Psychology Today*.[3]

Groupthink refers to the tendency for groups to make decisions without considering alternatives. Janis described it as

> a mode of thinking that people engage in when they are deeply involved in a cohesive in-group, when members' striving for unanimity override their motivation to realistically appraise alternative courses of action.[4]

Essentially, when groupthink occurs, there is no group debate after an individual presents an option. An alternative to a crisis is offered and the team adopts the alternative without anything other than superficial discussion. This may occur because of power issues in a group, a desire to conform, or apathy. The aforementioned 1961 decision of the Kennedy administration to invade the Bay of Pigs is typically cited as an example of groupthink.[5] Without groupthink it is difficult to imagine how the team could have reached a decision that had such a high probability of failure. Because of groupthink, meetings sometimes result in stunningly shortsighted solutions to organizational crises.

Is it possible that a group of executives really thought, after weighing all issues, that denying the proven debilitating effects of the breast implants made sense for Dow Corning?

Could a committee really have thought that releasing the audio expert's "conclusion" in the Texaco case would be met by anything other than ridicule?

What is the Asch effect?

The Asch effect is a frightening example of how crisis decisions can be easily affected by desires to conform. In the early 1950s, Solomon Asch conducted an experiment to gauge how willing individuals would be to conform to clearly incorrect conclusions. Since then his study has been replicated and his conclusions confirmed by these subsequent experiments. The Asch effect is the derivative of the experiment and it explains a good deal about conformity and how conformity can affect groups. The potential impact of the Asch effect on crisis communication decisions is enormous, as will soon be obvious.

Asch's experiment involved graduate students who were asked to compare twelve pairs of cards. Each pair consisted of what was called a "standard line" card and a "comparison line" card. On the standard line card was a single line. On the comparison line card were three lines of varying lengths.

The procedure for each study was the same.

1. The students are brought into a room.
2. Each student views the first of the twelve pairs of standard line cards and comparison line cards.
3. The first student then announces which line on the "comparison line card" is the same length as the line on the "standard line card."
4. Then the remaining students, one by one, announce which line from the comparison line card is the same length as the standard line card.
5. When all students have announced the selection for the first pair, the students view the second pair and follow the same procedure.
6. The study continues until each of the twelve pairs has been viewed, and each of the subjects has orally declared his/her vote.

The correct answer in each case was obvious. For each of the twelve pairs of cards, only one line on the comparison card could possibly be construed as the correct match. However, among the students involved in the experiment *all but one was working with the researcher.* There was only one true subject assessing the lines.

For each of the twelve comparisons, the conspirators were told to declare aloud and unequivocally that *another* line—clearly the incorrect one—was the line matching the one on the standard line card. After each of the conspirators stated that the *incorrect* line was the match, the lone actual subject was put in the position of conforming to the clearly incorrect conclusion or disagreeing with the unanimous majority and identifying the clearly incorrect answer.

It was as if one were in a long line of individuals who were asked to compute the sum of two plus two. And each person in the line ahead of you announced boldly that the answer was five. Then you, the last in line, were asked to declare the result of adding two to two. And then the process continued with a researcher asking all to add four plus three and you were at the end of a line and had to respond after hearing everyone of the others say that four plus three equals nine.

What would you do?

Incredibly, in the Asch experiment, approximately 80 percent of the (real) subjects yielded to the pressures at least one time out of the twelve. Nearly 60 percent of the (real) subjects yielded to the pressure at least two times out of twelve. In

Figrue 7.1 **The Asch Effect**

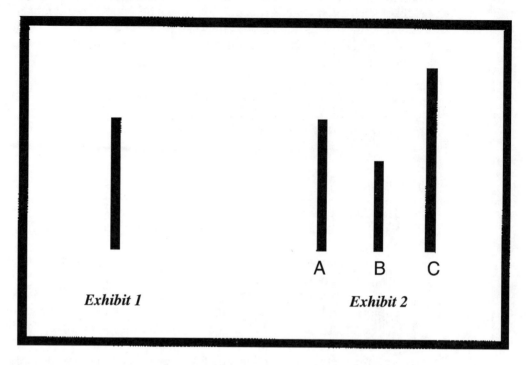

Exhibit 1   *Exhibit 2*

other words, nearly three out of every five participants were willing to say four plus three equals nine or some such nonsense at least one time out of six. As Goldhaber points out, what may be the most stunning feature of this study is that these groups were neither cohesive groups nor any kind of standing committee.[6] These were collections of strangers. No person owed anybody in the group a favor to go along with her or him. No person feared that a nonconforming answer might result in some organizational penalty. What might have been the tendency to conform had these people been part of a cohesive group? There is some evidence to suggest that cultural issues such as power distance and uncertainty avoidance (discussed in Chapter 4), do not influence the Asch effect results. Bond and Smith report Asch studies with similar results conducted in Portugal, Kuwait, Brazil, France, Zimbabwe, Fiji, and Ghana.[7]

If people are willing to succumb to peer pressure in crisis decision making when to do so is to agree to an absurd conclusion, how likely are people to succumb to such pressure when the idea, however inappropriate, is not entirely beyond reason?

If a company is accused of inadvertently placing toxins in foodstuffs, and there is no denying that this offense, however inadvertent, is real, how difficult is it to imagine a crisis team agreeing to deny the charge in the face of a powerful, if frightened, CEO who suggests denial is the way to go and then "polls" the team ostensibly to solicit different opinions?

Is it really possible that a team at Jack in the Box thought it was wise strategy to claim that the reason there were toxins in its hamburgers was because the company had not received the new cooking temperature guidelines that had been distributed by the state? Is it not reasonable to think that some person on a team might have opined that given the nature of the fast food hamburger business, stakeholders might not consider this a credible response and therefore the claim will not improve the company's image? Is it not reasonable to predict that some team member might wonder about how such a claim could damage relationships with customers in the future?

What Is Goal Lining?

Goal lining is a conforming tendency that results in an absence of valuable substantive conflict. When goal lining occurs, participants see reaching the goal as the lone criterion determining quality meeting interaction. If a group is meeting to determine how to respond to accusations that the organization did not vet its employees sufficiently to avoid hiring an embezzler, then the objective of the meeting is seen by goal liners as that and that alone.

At first, one might wonder what is wrong with this. Why should the group be concerned with anything other than the goal? The problem with goal lining is that it tends to encourage participants to seek a conclusion without necessarily seeking a *group* conclusion. In the rush to cross the goal line, the group loses the potential value of discussion, creativity, and interaction. A member might consider bolstering in the embezzling example and this could seem a great way to cross the goal, so the group accepts the solution because it meets the objective without vetting that solution—in perhaps the same way it did not vet the embezzler before the hiring.

AGENDAS AND PROCESS

Mosvick and Nelson asked 1,600 managers what went wrong with meetings. Of the top six items cited as obstacles, five related to either a poor agenda, no agenda, or not following an agenda.[8] An agenda is a list of topics to be addressed at a meeting session. Problems relating to agendas occur if (a) agendas are created to provide an illusion of structure and order as opposed to being designed to actually facilitate structure and order, or (b) they are ignored. Most readers have attended meetings where either (a) or (b) is the case.

Think of an agenda as a road map. If groups want to get from a starting point to the correct destination they need to follow the directions. Crisis meetings, particularly reactive ones, typically arrive at a destination because the urgency of the situation compels the group to reach a decision. However, the decision might be a bad one because no intelligent process was followed to allow for a meaningful journey and result. If you hastily get into your car and drive three hours you will get someplace, but if it is not where you should be you will have created another problem. In addition to still needing to get to the right place, you have now delayed your arrival because of an ill-advised method or process. An agenda is a roadmap that needs to be followed to allow groups to reach their meeting objectives.

WHAT IS A HIDDEN AGENDA?

A hidden agenda refers to personal and/or political meeting objectives that are "hidden" from the group. Let us assume that a group meets to discuss what to do in the aftermath of the revelation regarding the Reebok crisis with the Incubus shoe. The alleged goal of the department is to determine what image restoration strategy to select. The hidden agenda, however, for an individual member may be different from the alleged goal.

Some members who tacitly or otherwise approved the name might seek to communicate a message that does not besmirch their own reputations despite their complicity. Another member might worry that an expensive approach will inevitably sabotage a project for which she just received funding approval. Someone else might be delighted to topple a company adversary and select an approach that will torpedo that person's promotions even at the expense of making the wisest organizational decisions.

As is obvious, these hidden agendas can undermine the success of any discussion. They can also create *affective* conflict that may carry over to subsequent discussions on entirely other matters.

INTERNAL COMPETITION

A spirit of cooperation, as opposed to a spirit of competition, facilitates effective communication in teams. What often happens, however, is that participants tend to become ego-involved and competitive. Differences of opinion are good for groups, but fighting for your opinion *simply because it is yours* can create affective conflict.

What is ego involvement?

As discussions develop in meetings, individuals may become more and more attached to their stated perspectives on an issue and be reluctant to consider opposing points of view. A discussant's position on an issue may become intertwined with that person's ego.

Julie's *position* on the Reebok matter may become *Julie's* position. If you disagree with the position it may seem to Julie to be a personal attack. What can occur is that participants cease discussing the merits of an issue and simply want to win. Very highly ego-involved individuals are a bane in groups because the meeting may not develop beyond these individuals' need to be victorious. Cooperation versus competition is a key to success in groups, yet cooperation should not be construed as bogus team playing. Cooperative participants seek substantive conflict. They do not, however, consider the meeting a battleground where the successful members are the ones whose ideas are adopted by the group.

Apply the Principles

Assume you are on a crisis communication team addressing the St. Vincent Ferrer case. The members of the group include other parishioners, community members, priests from other churches in the diocese, diocese administrators, and two external consultants. There are ten members of the team. It is February 2009 and the court trial has just begun. Assume that you do not know the verdict.

- Assume you are one of the two external consultants. Which of the following would you fear would derail the crisis communication efforts?
  - Ego involvement
  - Hidden agendas
  - Affective conflict
  - Equity conflict
  - Procedural conflict
  - Lack of substantive conflict
  - Asch effect conformity
- Assume you are one of the parishioners. Which of the following would you fear would derail the crisis communication efforts?
  - Ego involvement
  - Hidden agendas
  - Affective conflict
  - Equity conflict
  - Procedural conflict
  - Lack of substantive conflict
  - Asch effect conformity
- Of the various constituents on this committee
  - Which do you believe will have the greatest influence on crisis decisions?
  - Which do you believe will have the least influence on crisis communication decisions?

INTERVENTIONS

WHAT IS AN INTERVENTION?

In the previous section we discussed what can and often does go wrong in meetings. The underlying assumption that crises should be analyzed in teams is correct. However, it is undeniable that meetings are inherently difficult contexts for effective communication. Interventions are techniques that can be used to address tensions in teams. If used properly, interventions can help teams interact efficiently so that substantive conflict will prevail and the maxim, "two heads are better than one" will apply.

In general, an intervention is a tool or technique used to alter behavior that would likely not be altered without intervention. You may have heard the term "intervention" used to describe a procedure for stopping the counterproductive behavior of a family member. For example, if someone in a family is addicted to drugs and denies the dependency, an intervention takes place in which attempts are made to confront the family member, and, subsequently, alter the debilitating behavior. Interventions as applied to the team context are also procedures. Without interventions in teams—and without interventions in some family situations—counterproductive behaviors are likely to continue to encumber individuals and relationships.

TYPES OF TEAM INTERVENTIONS

Buzz groups

Assume that you are working in a large group discussing the Vincent Ferrer case. Despite the dozen participants representing the diocese, other clergy, local government, consultants, and church membership, only some people are participating in the discussion. You might want to employ the intervention technique called "buzz groups" to increase participation and decrease the potential for problems related to *equity* conflict. Buzz groups can also reduce issues related to conformity and apathy.

With buzz groups, larger groups are divided into smaller ones. A group of twelve individuals discussing the merits of how to communicate regarding the alleged theft would be broken into six groups of two each. Each group of two would discuss the same issue. After a period of time, the six buzz groups of two each would reconvene as a group of twelve. Each buzz group would express to the group of the whole what they had discussed within their particular dyad.

The main value associated with buzz groups is that they require the participation of all and therefore tend to reduce equity tensions. A shy participant is likely to feel more comfortable speaking to just one other than speaking to a larger group. Since everyone participates it is unlikely that conformity will reign since all members are compelled to discuss the issue as part of the intervention.

Brainstorming

Brainstorming is a commonly used term and technique that is applied incorrectly. Brainstorming has a precise meaning and if employed properly, consistently with its actual meaning, can be a very effective intervention technique that can generate desirable substantive conflict.

The following is *not* an example of brainstorming.

> A group meets to discuss the February 14, 2008, JetBlue incident and how to respond to a stakeholder group identified as the TrueBlue customers. TrueBlue is JetBlue's frequent flier program. TrueBlue members are regular fliers and, in this example, we assume that JetBlue needs to get a message to these stakeholders. The team leader suggests that they "brainstorm" on the issue. One participant offers that it is probably a good idea to offer a free flight to TrueBlue members so that people will be willing to fly them again in case they had reservations. Another member responds and comments that the previous speaker is incorrect because people will not be more or less motivated because of compensation. A third person remarks that compensation will be good, but only if it is given to those TrueBlue members who have flown six times in the prior three months.

While this type of conversation might result in a valuable discussion, it is not an illustration of brainstorming, even though many people tend to think of brainstorming this way. Brainstorming is not an "advantages and disadvantages" discussion.

Brainstorming is an idea-generating intervention that involves the identification and recording of any and all ideas germane to the topic being discussed. A key and essential feature of brainstorming is that at no point during the intervention is anyone permitted to criticize a "brainstormed" idea that another has offered. Indeed, some have argued that even outlandish ideas are welcome, because these ideas might be springboards for perhaps less bizarre but more creative ideas than others would consider and offer.[9] The following is the way a brainstorming session might work using the illustration of the JetBlue case.

The leader of the group asks to hear suggestions for how to respond to TrueBlue stakeholders. Group members then identify, even shout out, any advantages they consider appropriate. A member of the group records, perhaps on a chalkboard or on a flipchart, any comments made.

- Give a free one-way ticket to all TrueBlue customers.
- Apologize in a personal letter sent to the e-mail addresses of these stakeholders.
- Bolster the image of JetBlue by identifying its impeccable safety record.
- Differentiate between this problem and other, more serious, safety problems, that have occurred on other airlines.
- Give a free trip to Disneyworld.
- Minimize problems related to delay.
- Post a note on a Web site indicating how embarrassed the company is.

Even outrageously poor ideas such as "Minimize problems related to the delay" or peculiar suggestions such as a trip to Disneyworld are not derided during brainstorming. They are simply recorded. True brainstorming encourages any and all notions. Subsequently, the ideas are discussed and evaluated. Brilhart and Galanes suggest that the group take a break after creating the brainstormed list and before evaluating it. Further, the authors comment that it might be wise to wait for a separate session for the evaluative discussion or have another group examine the brainstormed ideas.[10] Regardless of when it is done, the next step in brainstorming, the discussion phase, is one when you analyze the ideas. While going to Disneyworld is not the best solution, maybe thinking about Disneyworld can create some compensation idea that would work—apply double the dollar value of a flight for use at a partnering hotel, for example.

A variation of traditional brainstorming is polling brainstorming, in which the leader "polls" group members. Using the JetBlue example, each participant in turn would be asked to identify an image restoration plan. When their turn came, members would offer an advantage until such time as all individuals had exhausted all ideas.

The advantage of polling brainstorming is that it encourages the participation of shy group members who may have valuable suggestions but are unwilling to speak in a brainstorming session unless compelled to do so. A related advantage is that polling brainstorming makes it difficult for a dominating personality to overwhelm the session.

The polling approach can result, however, in a loss of spontaneity. Participants may focus on having something to say only when their turn comes and the session may not intensify in the way it otherwise could. A way to deal with this disadvantage is to use the alternative of *brainwriting*. With brainwriting all individuals write down ideas and then subsequently draw from their individual list during a brainstorming session. Brainwriting does not fully address the concerns of not being able to piggy back off of others' ideas. However, with brainwriting a participant is not restricted to the prewritten list so she or he can react to another's idea.

Nominal group techniques

Nominal group technique (NGT) developed by Delbecq and Van de Ven attempts to avoid affective and procedural tensions.[11] This technique involves very little group interaction. The word nominal means "in name only," and this technique limits the group interaction. In effect, the group becomes a group in name only. NGT participants are asked to write down their solutions to a particular problem as they would in brainwriting. In a polling format, they then express their ideas for solving the problem. Subsequently, all of these ideas are written on a board or flipchart. The leader proceeds to review each item so that the authors can clarify what is meant by each suggestion. At this point in the process there is no defense or criticism of any of the presented ideas.

After the clarifications are made, each participant votes on the most preferred ideas and ranks the top five solutions that have been advanced. The leader collects the written rankings and tallies the votes. The ideas that receive the most votes are then discussed and evaluated. Since discussion is reduced, this is considered a "nominal group technique"; a group in name only. NGT is designed to decrease the negative effects of affective conflict.

An intervention that involves division of labor is a more common type of nominal group technique. This approach is used so frequently in task-related groups that it is likely you have employed this technique when working on group projects at your college. When given a task, some teams divide the task into subsections equal to the number of people in the group. A group of five assigned to address the JetBlue case may break up the work by assigning one person to identify stakeholders, another messages, a third methods, a fourth other similar situations, and a fifth the design of a survey to be used to poll TrueBlue members.

The alleged advantages of this approach are it

- Saves time
- Allows individuals to go into greater depth on their individual subjects
- Avoids affective tensions that might surface otherwise
- Avoids equity conflict if the separation of responsibilities is indeed equitable

The disadvantages of this approach for crisis communication are major and overwhelm the advantages. Dividing responsibilities

- Reduces positive substantive conflict
- Can create affective and equity conflicts if individuals do not (legitimately or otherwise) or cannot do their work comprehensively
- Can result in a disjointed product as different sections may not seamlessly fit together. In the scenario above, for example, identifying nuggets without knowing the stakeholders is nearly impossible to do completely.

This approach of dividing tasks in problem-solving groups is very risky. It can be used to avoid affective and equity tensions, but if participants are not responsibly willing to complete their share *and* to work toward the seamless joining of individual sections, the solution to the problem may be incomplete, disjointed, and inadequate. The technique also circumvents and subverts the ostensible goal of collaborative meetings, which is to gain collective insights that would be lost if work was done individually.

If parishioners, other clergy, community members, and members of the diocese have been asked to participate in a discussion of crisis communication approaches in the St. Vincent Ferrer case, they have been so invited, allegedly, to gain multiple perspectives. Teams in general—but particularly in crisis—should be wary of using NGT in group problem solving.

PROBLEM CENSUS

What is problem census?

Let us assume you are on the committee to discuss how to proceed in the St. Vincent Ferrer case. You begin discussing the matter and find that the comments from members are all good but the conversation is disjointed.

Someone says, "Well, we have to address the media. There is no doubt about that. The media will overwhelm us. What should we do about the newspapers and radio?" A discussion begins on this stream, but before it is completed another comment takes the discussion in another direction. "What about donations and our programs? No one is going to want to give money now and we need the funds to run our church programs. These programs are valuable. Remember our mission is not only to make the church good for us, but to serve our community." Some react to this remark before another committee member inadvertently steers the discussion another way, "We ought to have our new priest do some sort of community tour for his sake and also the image of the church."

All of these are good points, but in order to focus and avoid procedural conflicts, the group might want to conduct a problem census. In this technique, initially members are polled regarding their perceptions of the problem. Before discussion takes place the group has identified all aspects that need to be addressed, in other words, a census has been taken on the breadth of the problem before beginning to identify each problem individually.

By using problem census you may, before you actually begin, derive a better sense of the task at hand and a clearer method of how your group intends to proceed to meet the group goals.

RISK TECHNIQUE

What is risk technique?

To avoid issues that surface relating to the Asch effect or groupthink, meeting members might consider using risk technique. This approach requires each participant to play the role of "devil's advocate."

"Devil's advocacy" is a phrase used to mean arguing for a perspective that is contrary to whatever position has been advanced. For example, a team may meet in the wake of the Howard Dean Iowa speech. The team may propose that supporters for Dean take out an advertisement in *USA Today* apologizing for the Dean scream. If so, before you place the advertisement, you will want the committee members to play devil's advocate to that proposition.

To play "devil's advocate," regardless of their actual perspective on the matter, members would take the stance that the advertisement is not a good idea. The value of devil's advocacy is that it forces groups to examine a proposal in depth by exploring opposite perspectives. Risk technique works as a polling technique. After a group has decided on a solution, each member of the group plays the devil's advocate and identifies a risk associated with implementing that solution. These lists of risks are recorded. Subsequently, the group reviews the list of risks and reevaluates the proposal. Most of the time the reevaluation does not result in the elimination of the proposal, but with the fine-tuning of the resolution so that it addresses the concerns suggested by the risks.

For example, assume that in the wake of Dean's rant, your group has decided to implement a new slogan to be used in all advertisements in the campaign. When using risk technique you would ask each group member *who had already decided to employ this new slogan* to play devil's advocate and identify problems with the slogan. For example, Donna might say that changing the slogan would be too confusing to voters. Jermaine might suggest that it will be costly to implement. Rita may argue that the new slogan will be seen as a desperation move.

On the basis of these risks your group may fine-tune your proposal, adopting a revised version that accommodates these risks. It is possible that you might decide to retain what your group had originally identified, despite the risks, because the value of that proposal exceeds the problems that were identified by the risks. In either case the risk technique has strengthened the quality of your group activity and solution.

It can be difficult for people to assume the role of devil's advocate, particularly, if moments earlier they presented the logic behind, and supported, the plan that is being considered. Yet, in order for risk technique to work, each person regardless of how involved she or he may have been in the composition of the plan, must play the devil's advocate and assume the posture of someone who identifies proposed flaws. This reduces the potential for groupthink, Asch effect conformity, and ego involvement. One must criticize one's own ideas with this intervention.

GENERAL PROCEDURAL MODEL

An intervention that combines many of the techniques described previously is called the "general procedural model" (GPM).[12] GPM is an effective approach for problem-solving meetings and an excellent technique for groups that are experiencing procedural conflict and perhaps affective and equity conflict as a result.

It is a five-stage model. In Chapter 4, we outlined a multistep process for creating a crisis communication plan. Let us assume that you are at the stage where you are identifying units of messages that you desire to relay to individual stakeholders.

1. Identify the problem. The group clarifies the objective for the meeting or the particular topic being discussed within the meeting. It is a good idea in this stage to use problem census. For example,
   - We need to identify units of information/nuggets that we wish to relay to
     a. Parishioners
     b. Members of the Delray community
     c. Other churches in the diocese

2. Brainstorm. The group uses brainstorming as it was designed to be used, that is, without any evaluative component. Individuals identify solutions—which may be wild—to the problem or the dimensions of the problem. A group representative records the brainstormed ideas. The more ideas the group generates the better for the solution.
   - These are the nuggets offered as potential units of information to communicate to
     a. Parishioners
     b. Members of the Delray community
     c. Other churches in the diocese

3. Evaluation. In this stage of the GPM, group members assess the merit of the brainstormed ideas. With large groups it is a good idea to consider buzz groups for step (3) of the GPM. This reduces equity conflict and increases substantive conflict.
   - Buzz groups meet to evaluate the brainstormed ideas.

4. Selection of the best idea. At this point, the group attempts to come up with a consensus on the best solution, or more likely, the best combination of solutions to the group issue. At the conclusion of this stage you should consider using risk technique to evaluate the merit of the proposal. After using risk technique, fine-tune your solution so that it reflects the concerns identified during the risk technique intervention.
   - These are the nuggets we will relay to the three groups
   - Risk technique
     a. These are the reasons why some of these nuggets are inappropriate
   - This is a revised list of nuggets

5. Put the solution into effect
   - Create messages composed of the nuggets
   - Determine the best methods for disseminating the messages
     a. Use the GPM to determine these best methods

Apply the Principles

Crisis communication teams should meet prior to crises to plan, and must meet during crisis.

- Indicate which of the following techniques would work in
  - Proactive planning
  - Reactive planning meetings (during a crisis)
  - Both proactive and reactive
  - Neither proactive nor reactive
    - Risk technique
    - Buzz groups
    - Problem census
    - General procedural model
    - Brainstorming
    - Nominal group technique
- Describe the rationale for your opinions

MAKING INTERVENTIONS WORK

GROUP MEMBERS AS PARTICIPANT-OBSERVERS

In order for interventions to work, members need to become "participant-observers." A participant-observer is someone in a group who concurrently participates and observes the process of participation.[13] For example, a participant-observer comments on the agenda items and also ensures that the agenda is followed.

This is work. Most people are not accustomed to being participant-observers. Some individuals may be conscientiously active contributors, but few typically will concurrently evaluate the interaction process. However, in order for groups to function effectively, members have to be vigilant. Interventions can work, but participants need to be committed to working at the interventions for them to be successful. *Intelligence, knowledge, even communication skill* does not guarantee effective group interaction. Members have to be both responsible participants and responsible observers of the process.

EXAMINING LEADERSHIP STYLES

There are three basic leadership styles.

- *Authoritarian* or *Autocratic* leaders are, as the label suggests, dictatorial and nondemocratic.
- *Laissez-faire* leaders are the opposite of authoritarians. They believe that the best way to lead a group is by keeping your "hands off." A laissez-faire leader believes that a group can run itself and, therefore, to guide it is to wield power that is not only unnecessary but counterproductive.
- A *democratic* leader is different from both a laissez faire and an authoritarian. The democratic leader seeks input and advice from group members. She or he may make the eventual decisions regarding directions for the group, but those

decisions are not made without considering the concerns of other members of the group.

For example, an authoritarian leader would determine the agenda for a session. A laissez-faire leader would assume that if those meeting needed an agenda the group would decide to create one. A democratic leader would solicit input for the agenda and use that input to create a process that has been developed with the input of all members of the committee.

DE FACTO LEADERSHIP

Sometimes a group has no designated leader. Other times the leader is not doing an effective job. A *de facto* leader is someone who, essentially, becomes the leader despite the fact that someone else is a *designated* or *nominal* leader. This is a very natural process and you have likely observed it when working in groups. A department has a chair, but the meetings seem to be run by Sharon because the chair is shy, inept, a lame duck, or for whatever reason does not lead. Someone emerges as the leader and assumes the responsibilities. Occasionally an autocratic leader may incur the wrath of a group such that another member becomes the de facto leader. In these instances the de facto leader emerges because the other group members are not attending to the directives of the designated autocratic leader.

Leadership is important for most crisis groups. If it were not, then there would be no such phenomenon as a de facto leader. The democratic leadership style is likely to be most effective. In some low performance groups an authoritarian leader might be necessary, and in some highly responsible groups anything other than a laissez-faire leader is inappropriate. However, your team requires someone who is willing to assume the responsibility of leader. Leaders should:

- *Plan for the meeting.* Define the meeting objectives. Solicit agenda topics, prepare, and distribute an agenda.
- *Get the meeting started.* Sometimes meetings can start slowly. This is more likely to happen in proactive crisis sessions, but can also occur in postcrisis meetings. For example, discussants will engage in chatting until some member calls the session to order. The duration of the preliminary conversation sometimes exceeds the appropriate few minutes for such orientation. A leader has the responsibility to ensure that not too much time is wasted at the beginning of a session.
- *Keep the discussion on track.* Meetings are notorious for lengthy digressions. Crises create urgency, but the urgency does not obviate digressions.

    Discussions that begin with an analysis of how to respond to the Dean scream can turn into commiserating about Jay's mortgage, which will not be met if Dean quits the campaign, which can further digress to discussions about whether it is ethical to join another campaign, which can further digress to what the word "loyalty" means exactly.

    A leader is responsible for keeping the discussion on topic. Because meetings typically have time limits, lengthy digressions cause the last few items on the agenda to be jammed into an inappropriate time space.

- *Summarize periodically.* Because of different inputs and tangential comments, it is wise to periodically summarize what has been brought out. After discussing one area on an agenda, a summary statement by the leader can provide closure for that area and allow the group to seamlessly segue to the next topic of the session.
- *Solicit comments from taciturn members.* Effective meetings require input from all participants. Quiet members often need prodding to voice their opinions. Quiet, here, is not synonymous with irresponsible. Quiet members may simply be shy and require encouragement. Leaders, to the extent that they can, should ensure that reserved participants do contribute to the discussion.
- *Curtail verbose members.* The other side of the problem is related to someone who dominates. Some people do not realize that they are monopolizing conversation. Others are aware and have no qualms about such inconsiderate behavior. When a group member is hogging time, a leader has the uncomfortable task of intervening to allow for others' comments and to facilitate progress toward the completion of the meeting's agenda. It does no good to invite parishioners if discussion time is dominated by administrators from the diocese.
- *Employ interventions.* A leader should consider and utilize approaches that can reduce negative group tensions.
- *Conclude the meeting.* The leader is responsible for starting as well as ending the meeting. At the conclusion, the leader should summarize the progress of the session, indicate what remains to be done, and, if the information is available, announce when the next meeting will take place.
- *Plan for the next session.* Between meetings the leader has the job of planning for the next session. This includes sending out the minutes of the preceding session to committee members; taking care of the logistics for the next meeting (e.g., reserving meeting rooms; ensuring that the meeting time is appropriate for all parties and any guests who are to be invited to the next meeting); and soliciting additional agenda topics for the next session.

Point/Counterpoint

In this exercise, two positions are presented. The first is consistent with a point made in the chapter. The second is a counterargument. Consider the counsel and counterargument. Then write a one-page position paper identifying your position on the issue.

- **Counsel**—Intervention techniques in meetings can be used to create substantive conflict, which will yield better solutions to crisis communication problems.
- **Counterpoint**—This is highly unlikely. Even in the relatively calm atmosphere of precrisis planning meetings, the power of conformity and default tendencies will overwhelm the most intelligent and theoretically sound intervention techniques. Human tendencies to maintain power, compete, avoid ruffling the wrong powerful figure, and "goal line," can and will trump even the desire for organizational survival. The value of group collaboration is undermined by ego. Communication techniques are as likely to be followed as high school manuals describing how to abstain from intimate relations. Human urges make it impossible to follow the steps.

Summary: A Toolbox

- Crisis communication planning involves working in teams.
- Teams should be comprised of individuals representing diverse sections of the organization.
- It is natural that conflicts will surface in teams regardless of a common sense of urgency.
  - Some conflicts exist prior to the first or any subsequent team meeting sessions.
  - Secondary conflicts surface during team meetings based on
    - Equity
    - Procedure
    - Personality tensions.
- Conformity is a common problem that is particularly insidious during crisis work.
- Inadequate procedure and weak leaders also create problems for crisis teams.
- The residual effects of these conflicts and problems can include
  - Ignoring important stakeholders.
  - Having incomplete or offensive communications during crisis.
  - Selecting an ineffective medium for communication.
- Crisis teams can employ interventions to overcome common conflicts, including
  - Smaller (buzz) groups to avoid equity conflicts.
  - Risk technique to engineer substantive conflict.
  - General procedural model to avoid procedural conflict.
- Leaders have specific responsibilities and must be more than just nominal heads of the crisis team.
- Crisis teams work best when all members view themselves concurrently as participants and observers.

PRACTITIONER PERSPECTIVE: JOE LUKAS

Joe Lukas is the Vice President of PMCenters USA, a national project management consulting company. With over 30 years of experience working in a range of industries including manufacturing, information technology, and construction, Mr. Lukas has expertise in many areas including risk management. He has a degree in chemical engineering, holds a professional engineer license, and is a certified Project Management Professional (PMP).

There are several keys to effective crisis communication and management. An organization must be quick to respond to a crisis and not hold back information from the media and other stakeholders. The organization must also be honest and open with their communications. This does not mean relaying information that is confidential. There was a situation when a worker was fatally injured in an industrial explosion. While the company had the name of the deceased, we had not yet notified family members, so we retained that information in the communications. However, unless you are faced with a similar situation, being honest with your publics is an important criterion for success. It is also important to provide updates when new information becomes available.

Some companies make the mistake of not communicating internally to employees. Employees must know the protocol for communicating during a crisis. They must know, for example, who the company spokespersons are and to whom to direct inquiries. Organizations can prepare for crises by clearly describing these procedures and also by simulating actual crisis conditions. At some companies, such simulations were regularly conducted. At one company, it was assumed that an industrial accident had occurred, and they went through their procedures for communicating to various publics attempting to simulate time pressures, concerned audiences, and the overall stressful conditions. This preparation and these simulations are important for all. Spokespersons in particular need to have practice and experience in their roles. You want your spokesperson during a crisis to reflect a confident "we are in control" attitude. It is important that the company representative do an effective job of communicating messages confidently.

There is a real value in working with teams in crisis situations. The only downside surfaces when team members may become defensive during discussions. This can be overcome with strong team leadership that emphasizes the objectives of the team and the values of the organization. In these team contexts people present different ideas that individuals might not have considered if they had been working independently. Team members play devil's advocate when considering crisis responses and these contrary points can help a company refine important messages that might otherwise be misconstrued.

Leadership, organizational culture, and ethics are factors that can facilitate the effective execution of a crisis plan. As is obvious, a company with weak leadership and a culture of distrust will be hobbled by these realities when they face organizational crises.

Exercises and Discussion Questions

1. Assume you are the head of crisis communication for your college or university. Who would you want to sit on your crisis communication team?
2. Does the potential for positive in-team interaction overwhelm the potential for negative conflict in teams?
3. Would the identification of stakeholders and nuggets inevitably vary depending on who sat on the crisis team? Explain.
4. If the answer to question (3) is yes, would this phenomenon render teams counterproductive? If the answer to question (3) is no, are you suggesting that all teams will always come up with the same solutions?
5. In your experience, does the nature of crisis trump tendencies to conform or does it increase the tendency to conform?

NOTES

1. The term "social loafing" was first used in an article by B.K. Latane and S. Harkins, "Many Hands Make Light the Work: The Causes and Consequences of Social Loafing," *Journal of Personality and Social Psychology* 37 (1979): 822–32. See also Beatrice Schultz, "Improving Group Communication Performance: An Overview of Diagnosis and Intervention," in *The Handbook of Group Communication Theory and Research,* ed. Lawrence R. Frey (Thousand Oaks, CA: Sage, 1999), pp. 388–89.

2. Gary Kreps, *Organizational Communication,* 2d. ed. (New York: Longman, 1990), pp. 191–92.

3. Irving L. Janis, *Groupthink: Psychological Studies of Policy Decisions and Fiascoes* (Boston: Houghton Mifflin, 1982); and Janis, "Groupthink," *Psychology Today,* 5, no. 6 (November 1971): 43–36, 74–76.

4. Janis, *Groupthink,* p. 9.

5. For example, Irving Janis, *Crucial Decisions: Leadership in Policymaking and Crisis Management* (New York: Free Press, 1989), p. 57.

6. Gerald Goldhaber, *Organizational Communication,* 6th ed. (Madison, WI: Brown and Bench-mark, 1993), p. 249.

7. Rod Bond and Peter Smith, "Culture and Conformity: A Meta Analysis of Studies Using Asch's (1952b, 1956) Line Judgment Task," *Psychological Bulletin* (January 1996): 112.

8. Roger Mosvick and Robert Nelson, *We've Got to Start Meeting Like This* (Indianapolis: Park Avenue, 1996), p. 31. The sixth item, ranked number two on the list was "Inconclusive: No results, decisions, assignments or follow up."

9. Sunwolf, and David Seibold, "The Impact of Formal Procedures on Group Processes Members and Task Outcomes," in Frey, *The Handbook of Group Communication Theory and Research,* p. 400.

10. John Brilhart and Gloria Galanes, *Effective Group Discussion,* 9th ed. (New York: McGraw–Hill), p. 302.

11. Andre Delbecq, Andrew H. Van de Ven, and David H. Gustafson, *Group Techniques for Program Planning: A Guide to Nominal Group and Delphi Processes* (Glenview, IL: Scott, Foresman, 1975), pp. 7–10.

12. John Brilhart and Gloria Galanes *Effective Group Discussion,* 7th ed. (Dubuque, IA: Wm. C. Brown, 1992), p. 238.

13. Brilhart and Galanes, *Effective Group Discussion,* 9th ed., p. 16.

8 | Training the Spokesperson

Chapter in a Nutshell

Knowing what to do in crisis situations does not guarantee being able to do it. Even when a committee or individual accurately identifies stakeholders, intelligently selects nuggets, and creates a wise statement to make to the media and other stakeholders, someone has to deliver that message effectively. Crises can increase the pressure on spokespersons and make delivering these messages difficult even for the most eloquent speaker. Company executives, who often serve as spokespersons, may not necessarily be skilled speakers. However, all people can be trained to be effective even during times of pressure. This chapter identifies several factors that affect presentations especially during times of crisis.

Specifically, at the end of this chapter, students will be able to

- Explain the importance of speaking skill for crisis spokespersons
- Identify ways to deal with anxiety
- Identify advantages and disadvantages of delivery styles
- Describe key components of statement content
- Explain how to deal with questions in question and answer sessions
- List factors that affect the use of visual support
- Describe verbal and nonverbal considerations that affect delivery

---

CASE 8.1: MEETING THE PRESS

A private boarding school in New England prided itself on a disciplined approach to education for young women. Located in an affluent suburb, the school's rules were strict, protocol clearly articulated, and proscriptions numerous. Many parents sought out the school for their daughters precisely because of the regimen. The headmaster's approach to education would be considered unenlightened by many contemporary educators. Nevertheless parents enjoyed listening to his statements at the beginning of each school year assuring students and parents—explicitly with unambiguous word choice and implicitly with imperious intonation—that this was a school where young women adhered to rules and became educated ladies.

One Sunday morning a young woman failed to appear for the weekly Sunday brunch meal. Several of her friends looked anxious and bleary-eyed as they attempted, without success, to convince supervisors that they had no idea where the missing student might be. An investigation revealed that a group had broken school rules and left the dormitory the prior evening to attend an unsupervised party in a neighboring development. The party was attended mostly by students from a nearby public high school and hosted by a student whose parents were away for a weekend.

The party lasted into the early hours of Sunday and there had been no shortage of alcoholic beverages available to the revelers. When it was time for the boarding school women to return they realized that one of their number was missing. She apparently had wandered off outside the house by herself. The students were worried but gave up looking, accepted a ride back, and hoped the missing student would somehow find her way back to the dormitories.

She was not back in the dormitories. Late Sunday afternoon, the student was found dead, having drowned in a pond near the place of the party. Evidently she had taken a walk while inebriated, stepped out on what appeared to be solid ice, fell through the ice, and was unable to escape. In a hastily called assembly, the schoolmaster informed all students of the tragedy, reprimanded the miscreants for leaving the school on Saturday night, and assured all that severe penalties would be doled out to the offenders and any persons who took similar excursions in the future. In the talk the headmaster forbade any student and all teachers to speak to the media. He informed those assembled that a "press conference" had been scheduled for Monday morning, at which time he would make a presentation to parents, community members, and reporters. After his talk he would take questions.

QUESTIONS FOR ANALYSIS

- What should the headmaster's message be at the press conference?
  - What are the nuggets?
  - Should anything written be distributed to those assembled?
  - What recommendations would you make to him in terms of appropriate message delivery?
  - What questions should the headmaster anticipate?
  - How should he respond to these questions?
- How would the following factors affect what crisis communicators refer to as "honoring the account" and "supporting behavior?"
  - Paralingual and rhetorical sensitivity
  - Speech accommodation theory
- Assume the private school has a school board that oversees the program, hires the faculty and administrators, and essentially determines policy at the school.
  - What primary and secondary tensions might exist if that group met to discuss what should be communicated regarding this crisis?
- Evaluate the message the headmaster delivered to the students on Sunday night.
  - What other messages might you have suggested he communicate?
  - Will the "no communication to the media" edict be effective?
  - Will there be gender-related problems because all the students are women and he is male?

- Who are the other external stakeholders in this crisis?
  - What are the nuggets for these groups?
- Who are the other internal stakeholders in this crisis?
  - What are the nuggets for these groups?
- Will an imperious schoolmaster be able to deliver a compassionate message to the stakeholders at the press conference?
- Does the neighboring public school system have a crisis that requires communication?

INTRODUCTION

When faced with a crisis, an organization often releases a written statement and then complements that statement with an oral presentation at some form of press conference. As illustrated in the case of the boarding school (a real case with some changes to disguise the actual people involved), the headmaster made two presentations: one to the students and another to external stakeholders, including the media.

Over a century ago, the eloquent American statesman Daniel Webster said, "If all my possessions and powers were to be taken from me with one exception I would choose to keep the power of speech, for by it I could soon recover all the rest."[1] This may be an exaggerated claim for crisis communicators, but knowing how to speak effectively immediately after a crisis can facilitate image restoration. The opposite is also true.

Persons who are chosen to lead organizations are selected for many reasons. Frequently, job postings list "excellent communicator" as one of the desired attributes of a successful candidate. Despite this criterion, there is no guarantee that the chosen leader—often the spokesperson in crisis situations—will be able to speak effectively during crises. In Chapter 4 we discussed preparation for crises. One aspect of preparation involves training spokespersons and simulating speaking in crisis situations.

This chapter identifies several factors that affect presentations especially during times of crisis.

MISCONCEPTIONS REGARDING SPEAKING SKILL

SOME PEOPLE HAVE THE GIFT OF GAB. OTHERS ARE NOT AS FORTUNATE

The ability to speak well is not a gift any more than the ability to divide by four is "a gift." Those of us who can divide numbers by four learned how to do so and then were compelled to do many exercises to reinforce what we had learned. We were not born with the gift of arithmetic. Similarly, presentation skills can be, and are, learned. Some people may be more naturally adept at speaking than others, but learning how to speak effectively requires understanding the principles, and then practicing. Sellnow makes this point emphatically when she writes that effective speakers "are those who choose to work at developing their skills and ineffective speakers are those who choose not to do so."[2]

EFFECTIVE SPOKESPERSONS ARE NOT APPREHENSIVE

Most, if not all, people are apprehensive in speaking situations. It may even be somewhat abnormal not to feel any anxiety prior to speaking to the media after a crisis. Edward R. Murrow, the famous broadcaster, remarked that "the best speakers know enough to be scared. . . . The only difference between the pros and the novices is the pros have trained the butterflies to fly in formation."[3]

EDUCATED PERSONS CAN AND SHOULD BE ABLE TO SPEAK EFFECTIVELY

Depth of knowledge does not necessarily translate into speaking prowess. Advanced degrees certainly do not, even when the advanced degree may be in a communication-related field.

CREATING A QUALITY POWERPOINT® PRESENTATION IS THE KEY TO EFFECTIVE SPEAKING

PowerPoint presentations may help a speaker, but they are not the cure for speaking ills. Often presentations seem to be nothing more than a collection of PowerPoint slides. The misapprehension that effective graphics—even those that are esthetically engaging—will make a crisis presentation a good one, almost guarantees that a spokesperson will be unsuccessful.

COMMUNICATION NOISE

WHAT IS COMMUNICATION NOISE?

Communication noise refers to impediments that affect the receivers' ability to get a message in any communication context. Noise can literally be external noise such as rail traffic outside an open window or distracting side conversations during a press conference. Noise can also refer to psychological interference. In the boarding school case, media members who never liked the imperious manner of the headmaster may bring an attitude about the speaker that interferes with listening dispassionately to his message.

Communication noise is omnipresent. Some writers define noise as that which creates message distortion.[4] A better way to think of noise is as a factor that reduces the chances of successful communication but does not guarantee failure. If a train rushes by while you are speaking, you might have to increase your volume, or receivers might have to work harder to hear your message, but it is still possible to understand what you are saying.

In short, noise should be viewed as an impediment, but like most impediments noise can be overcome. Spokespersons in crisis situations must identify potential sources of noise and overcome the obstacles. It is wise, for example, for the headmaster to know about attitudes media members may have toward him as he prepares his message.

A GAME CONCEPTUALIZATION

Crisis spokespersons might find it valuable to think of three games when considering their messages: catch, pool, and chess.

When engaged in a game of catch your objective is to throw an object so that your partner can catch it. In catch, throwing the ball esthetically is not as crucial as throwing it so your friend can receive it. Similarly, when speaking to stakeholders, your objective is to ensure their receipt of the message, not to compose a rhetorical gem that may be admired by unrelated audiences.

Pool players are aware that they have two objectives when it is their turn to strike the ball. They must attempt to sink the shot and also set themselves up for the next attempt. Crisis spokespersons send a series of messages in their oral statement and, subsequently, will likely relay other messages to these stakeholders. Spokespersons must "sink" each of their messages, and also put themselves in a position to increase chances for a subsequent message to be received as intended. The headmaster may say, "This is the way we do things here. We are proud of it. And we will continue to follow the strict regimen that has brought us success for twenty years." That message will be sunk. However, the headmaster's imperious manner may tinge the meaning of subsequently communicated messages.

Rules govern the game of chess. Rooks cannot move diagonally. A king cannot move more than one space at a time. If you move your rook diagonally, an opponent might first explain the rules patiently, but if you continue to break the rules, your opponent might simply quit. Similarly, stakeholders come to press conferences with expectations about what should be addressed and how it should be addressed. Should a spokesperson break these rules—avoid a sensitive subject, issue a noncredible claim, appear disorganized— either reflecting ineptitude or disregard—then stakeholders are likely to disengage, or in the parlance of a game, stop participating, "quit" at least mentally. Instead of restoring the company image the spokesperson may have accelerated its erosion.

REDUCING ANXIETY

Some studies suggest that the greatest fear of more than 40 percent of the population is public speaking—even greater than the fear of death. This is likely an exaggeration, but it is indisputable that many people become anxious when they are forced to speak. In crisis situations, the anxiety level is likely to spike even higher. Below is a list of recommendations for reducing anxiety.

- Recognize that anxiety is normal
- Realize that anxiety often goes undetected
- Prepare thoroughly
- Visualize success

- Address physical manifestations of apprehension
- Use nervous energy
- Make the presentation context less uncommon

RECOGNIZE THAT ANXIETY IS NORMAL

You are not an underachiever because you feel tense. If you do not experience tension before you deliver a crisis presentation, the absence of anxiety might reflect a deficiency. Mark Sanborn is a professional speaker who has spoken to organizations throughout the world. His comment about the natural presence of anxiety is unequivocal. "Successful speaking doesn't mean eliminating anxiety; it means controlling it."[5]

REALIZE THAT ANXIETY OFTEN GOES UNDETECTED

A second step toward reducing anxiety involves accepting a simple proven fact. Audience members typically do not see a spokesperson's apprehension.[6] You may have witnessed this phenomenon yourself if you have ever had a presentation videotaped. While viewing tapes of their presentations, students and professional clients often comment that it was "better than I thought" and that the apprehension they felt was not apparent through the lens of the camera.

PREPARE THOROUGHLY

Thorough preparation is consistently identified as a significant factor that reduces anxiety. Preparation involves studying the subject, analyzing the audience, crafting and practicing the delivery of the message, and examining the speaking location. In crisis situations, of course, one does not always have the luxury of preparation time. However, if an organization takes the proactive steps identified in Chapter 4, crisis teams can simulate scenarios and prepare. The nuances of unique crises cannot, of course, be predicted, but teams can identify likely stakeholders, craft messages, and practice delivery in simulated scenarios. These simulations will not eliminate anxiety but can reduce it when spokespersons are confronted with actual crises.

VISUALIZE SUCCESS

Visualization is not for everyone, but this technique—employed by athletes and stage performers—is an approach to consider before categorical rejection. Proponents argue that creating a mental picture of achievement facilitates performance that is consistent with the visualization.

ADDRESS PHYSIOLOGICAL MANIFESTATIONS OF APPREHENSION

A high level of communication apprehension can have physiological effects. Recommendations for reducing physical tension include running or exercising prior to the presentation,[7] breathing exercises,[8] stretching, and pre-speech silent concentration.[9] In the song, "I Whistle a Happy Tune" from *The King and I,* the character Anna suggests that others follow her advice when they become apprehensive. She comments that when she is fearful she is able to overcome the anxiety by "whistling a happy tune" and acting as if she is unafraid.

Rodgers and Hammerstein were not communication scholars, but several researchers who are offer the same basic advice. Zarefsky as well as Brydon and Scott comment that during a presentation spokespersons act confidently even when they feel apprehensive.[10]

USE NERVOUS ENERGY

Your nervous energy can be channeled into something positive. Tension can be used to invigorate your voice, emphasize key words, and reflect enthusiasm for the subject.

AUDIENCE ANALYSIS

In Barron's *Dictionary of Business Terms* an effective presentation is described as one that is "usually *planned, organized and tailored to a specific audience* to help facilitate the behavior change desired by the presenter"[11] [emphasis added].

While audience analysis may seem to be a very natural preliminary behavior for those preparing to address the media or other stakeholders, many presentations do not reflect such preparation. Some spokespersons actually attempt to analyze their receivers *while* they are speaking. This is foolish. When spokespersons have the opportunity to study their audiences ahead of time, they should use this to their advantage.

RAMIFICATIONS OF POOR AUDIENCE ANALYSIS

There are several potential repercussions of not taking the time to analyze your audience.

You may anger the audience

In almost all contexts, but particularly in crisis contexts, listeners do not want to have their time wasted. If they are called to listen to a presentation that is irrelevant to them they may become angry that their time has been stolen. Even if time is not an issue, stakeholders may feel anger at being disrespected. They may feel as if the spokesperson was not concerned enough to determine who the audience was prior to delivery and what information was needed.

You may reduce your chances of success in future speaking situations

After misreading stakeholders on an initial occasion, it may be difficult to regain their respect when you return to the same group.

You may not be fulfilling your organizational responsibility

In crisis contexts you are speaking to address a pressing need. If you do not study your audience you will not be able to meet that organizational need. You will not be helping to restore the image of your organization.

WHAT ARE THE ELEMENTS OF AUDIENCE ANALYSIS?

There are three main areas of audience analysis.

- Stakeholder subject knowledge and perspectives
- Demographics
- Analysis of the physical context for the presentation.

1. *Stakeholder subject knowledge and perspectives*
   Specifically, spokespersons should attempt to gather information related to
   - Breadth and depth of knowledge about the subject
   - Attitudes toward the subject
   - Misconceptions stakeholders may have
   - Technological background
   - Familiarity with vocabulary and acronyms
   - Familiarity with spokesperson
   - Reasons for attendance

2. *Demographics*
   Spokespersons should attempt to discover how diverse the audience is in terms of the following:
   - Age
   - Education level: vocabulary, common experience, and expertise
   - Group affiliation (media, parents, citizens, public school teachers)
   - Gender
   - Ethnicity and culture
   - Income

3. *Analysis of the physical context for the presentation*
   In addition to discovering information about the people attending, a spokesperson needs to analyze the space for the presentation. Specifically
   - Physical setting (inside amphitheater, outside, auditorium, classroom)
   - Room size, seating capacity, and configuration
   - Podium, screen, and power locations
   - Windows and external noise
   - Available equipment
   - Time allotted for presentation
   - Time of day
   - Speaking sequence—if there will be several spokespersons

---

Apply the Principles

Review the "Meeting the Press" case that began this chapter.

- Which of the three categories of audience analysis would be most significant for the headmaster? Why?
- Would gender be an issue? Age of participants?
- Which audience analysis criterion would be least significant? Why?

SELECTING AN APPROPRIATE SPEAKING STYLE

The presentations you have heard in school, at work, in religious services, and in political speeches have all been delivered in one of four ways. They were either *impromptu, extemporaneous, manuscript,* or *memorized.* The decision spokespersons make regarding which of these styles to employ is very significant as it can affect the quality of the message and the ease with which stakeholders receive it. Speaker comfort levels and ease of preparation should be secondary, not primary, considerations when selecting the statement style. The primary consideration is this: does the style help the spokesperson communicate the messages to the stakeholders?

IMPROMPTU

An impromptu talk is delivered without any prior preparation. In the vernacular, impromptu is synonymous with *winging it.* Regardless of how much spokespersons know about a subject, if they do not prepare, the resulting message is impromptu. There are times when one must deliver impromptu presentations. Crisis communicators particularly may be thrust into situations where they must speak immediately and well. Therefore, it is good to be able to deliver a message without the time to prepare. On those occasions, however, when you have an opportunity to prepare, you should use that time. Impromptu messages may be disorganized, lack clarity, include words that are not quite right, and may be inappropriate for a particular group of stakeholders. When they do well, impromptu speakers may be impressive. When they are not as articulate as they otherwise could be, impromptu spokespersons risk doing damage to their organization's image.

EXTEMPORANEOUS

An extemporaneous presentation is delivered from some kind of note system. The notes can be as detailed as a formal outline presented on slides, or as brief as a few words listed on an index card. The idea behind extemporaneous speaking is that the words on the outline will trigger recollections of what the speaker wishes to say. When spokespersons glance at their notes they see the reminder. Then they speak about the subject indicated by the note.

The headmaster's presentation in the opening case could be guided by a simple outline that reads,

- Background of school
- Investigation
- Student history
- Regrets
- Ongoing policies

Extemporaneous speaking has its advantages. The main drawback is that crisis messages need to be precise and comprehensive. The theory behind extemporaneous speaking is that a word will trigger a thought and the words to express that thought. Under pressure, however, it might be difficult to remember all that you wish to say and/or locate the best words to express it.

MANUSCRIPT

A manuscript talk is delivered word for word from a text that is prepared ahead of time. Manuscript presentations should not be read as one would read aloud from a novel, but delivered with rate and volume variation, emphases on appropriate words or phrases, pauses to establish eye contact, and complementary body motion.

Manuscript presentations are either written by the speaker or ghostwritten for the speaker by associates. People who work in corporate communication departments often write presentations to be delivered by organizational executives. On occasion, the text for manuscript presentations is distributed to audience members before or after the presentation is delivered. The main advantage of manuscript talks is precision. Speakers can select the correct word when composing the message, more accurately determine the length of the talk, and even decide when to emphasize certain words, look up, and pause. The manuscript style creates a predetermined record of the message. The disadvantages are that sometimes manuscript statements are delivered without eye contact, emphasis, and/or appropriate vocal intonation.

MEMORIZED

A memorized talk is a manuscript presentation that has been committed to memory. Some people feel that they can finesse their apprehension by memorizing the talk. This might work but is unlikely to be effective. Memorized presentations can be disastrous for at least two reasons. The most obvious potential problem is that the speaker might forget which words come next. The second problem is that memorized presentations are often delivered without appropriate vocal enthusiasm and can *sound memorized and robotic.*

Evaluating options

Of the four choices, manuscript and extemporaneous options are the two better ones. As indicated previously, there are times when one may be compelled to deliver an impromptu talk. However, in many situations after the immediate surprise of a crisis, a press conference may be scheduled, for which there will be at least some time to prepare either an extemporaneous or manuscript statement. When in such a position, consider this bulleted list of advantages and disadvantages of each approach.

ADVANTAGES OF EXTEMPORANEOUS STATEMENTS

- *Eye contact*
  If all other factors are equal, an extemporaneous presentation will allow for more eye contact than a manuscript talk.

- *Content flexibility*
  The speaker has much more freedom in extemporaneous than in manuscript contexts. This flexibility allows the speaker to read audience nonverbal feedback and adapt to it with relative ease. If stakeholders appear confused, an extemporaneous speaker can review the point in order to clarify it.

- *Informality and interactivity*
  Some contexts require a degree of informality. Many require interaction. Manuscript talks do not lend themselves to either.

- *Movement*
  Extemporaneous formats do not require a speaker to stand behind the lectern. Spokespersons can move about, walk into the audience, or speak directly to an individual or small cluster of receivers.

- *Perception of confidence*
  Much success is a function of the audience members' perception of the spokesperson. An excellently delivered extemporaneous talk can suggest to audience members that the spokespersons really know the subject since, apparently, they do not need to have all the words in their messages written down in order to present what they know.[12]

ADVANTAGES OF MANUSCRIPT STATEMENTS

- *Precision of word choice*
  Many crisis presentations are simply too important to risk employing the extemporaneous format. Extemporaneous talks require that spokespersons select words to match ideas while the pressure is on. A manuscript presentation compels the team to consider the correct words beforehand and consequently reduces the chances for embarrassing errors. If journalists are listening and will subsequently report on the message to millions of readers, spokespersons will want to make sure that they do not utter an inappropriate word that will find its way into headlines.

- *Timing*
  Some sessions are designated for precise lengths of time. If spokespersons are

allotted fifteen minutes to make the pitch, they do not want to find themselves at minute fourteen having only progressed to the middle of the message. Since the manuscript format allows for total preparation and fewer interruptions, one can time the talk precisely.

- *Avoidance of speech fillers*
  Spokespersons can avoid problems with *ums, oks, you knows,* or *ers* by delivering a manuscript presentation.

- *Organization: Absence of digressions and omissions*
  Extemporaneous presentations can be flawed because spokespersons may, unintentionally, digress or leave something out of their talk.

- *Delivery*
  While the case has been made that extemporaneous messages are easier to deliver in terms of eye contact and vocal variation, manuscript formats allow the speaker the opportunity to carefully plan when to employ eye contact, emphasize key words, speed up, or slow down.

- *Ability to convey an uninterrupted message*
  Manuscript speaking is more linear than extemporaneous speaking. In a manuscript presentation spokespersons have the chance to make an uninterrupted case. This advantage comes with the inherent disadvantage that the speaker may be unable to reverse a message that he thought would be effective but that is actually ineffective as suggested by nonverbal feedback. Nevertheless, if spokespersons have identified the audience correctly, the manuscript message gives them the opportunity to speak without interference.

- *Formality*
  In the same way that an extemporaneous talk may be appropriate if the situation requires informality, a manuscript talk may be appropriate if the situation requires formality.

- *Ghostwriting*
  In business or political contexts, an advantage of a manuscript presentation is that the presenter does not have to actually construct the message. Someone in corporate communication can compose the address.

- *Consistency*
  If a person needs to deliver the same presentation to several groups of stakeholders located in different venues, then a manuscript talk guarantees that the same words will be spoken to each audience—assuming each group is composed of the same stakeholder profile. If organizations are concerned with the legal ramifications of a message, a manuscript talk will ensure that each representative delivering the message will not be deviating from what has been approved by the company lawyers.

- *Text delivery*
Some occasions require that the text of a talk be available to listeners either before, during, or immediately after the talk. This is impossible to do if the presentation is extemporaneous, and simply accomplished when using a manuscript approach.

- *Reduction of apprehension*
All things being equal, a speaker who has very high communication apprehension will be more comfortable using a manuscript and fewer things can go wrong with the content. However, many, many things can still go wrong with the delivery. For example, an extremely apprehensive speaker might decide after one fearful look at the audience, to read the rest of the message at warp speed and eschew any and all eye contact. However, all factors considered, a manuscript presentation affords the speaker a greater comfort level.

In sum, it is safer to use the manuscript format in a crisis scenario. It guarantees a degree of precision that is not possible with extemporaneous statements.

STRUCTURING THE MESSAGE

One of the easiest things spokespersons can do to enhance chances for success is to structure their talks intelligently. An old expression used in conjunction with presentations is that a speaker has three obligations: (a) tell the audience what you will tell them; (b) tell them; and (c) tell them what you have told them.

In essence, this maxim describes how to structure a crisis presentation or any presentation. The spokesperson describes the agenda topics in an *introduction;* proceeds to discuss these topics during the *body* of the statement; and finishes with a recapitulation of key points in a *conclusion.*

INTRODUCTION

Objective

In the introduction, spokespersons fundamentally establish an agreement with the audience. Implicitly or explicitly, spokespersons promise that listeners can expect to hear about certain subjects. In a crisis presentation, these subjects need to be made clear. For example, "Thank you for joining us. As you know, today is a very sad occasion. I would like to take a few minutes to discuss (a) the events that led up to the tragedy, (b) our relevant boarding school policies, (c) information the family wishes to relay to the press, and (d) our plans for ensuring that such a calamity is unlikely ever to occur again. I will be happy to take your questions when I have concluded these brief remarks."

Engagement

Typically, introductions to presentations should attempt to engage the audience, that is, hook them into being attentive. However, in crisis situations, most listeners attend because they are already engaged. Many stakeholders are actually hungry for the information that they expect to hear at the session. It is therefore not necessary to spend time "hooking them." If you believe your stakeholders are leery of your message and may be cynical, you might consider explaining why the information to be presented can be trusted and how it will benefit them to consider your message.

Speaker ethos

Ethos refers to the status attributed to a speaker by receivers. As we discussed in Chapter 4, ethos is a crucial communication factor. It has been referred to as a "dominant factor in rhetorical communication."[13] We know that audience members are more likely to listen to, and be influenced by, spokespersons with high ethos.[14]

Initial ethos. Initial ethos is a function of a number of variable factors.

- *Reputation:* What the receivers know about the speaker affects the speaker's initial ethos. Someone who is introduced as an expert, or who has earned an untarnished reputation in the community, will be attributed higher ethos than a virtual unknown.
- *Dress and physical attractiveness:* People judge others by what they wear and how they look. Several studies reported by McCroskey support this point.[15] The fact that dress and physical appearance is influential may be an unfortunate reality, but it is a reality nevertheless. Damon Runyon, the novelist who inspired the Broadway musical *Guys and Dolls,* commented that "It may be that the race is not always to the swift, nor the battle to the strong—but that is the way to bet."[16] It is quite possible that some environments will consider formal attire inappropriate and an undesirable reflection of stuffiness, but unless the pre-statement audience analysis has drawn this conclusion, dressing professionally and conservatively in business contexts is the way to bet.[17]
- *Posture:* Nonverbal behaviors that typically reflect comfort or interest are likely to have a positive effect on initial ethos.
- *Apparent preparation:* Spokespersons may increase initial ethos by appearing to be prepared. You may have noticed spokespersons who are awaiting a signal to begin their talks. Some seem orderly and ready. Others seem confused and disorganized. If spokespersons appear prepared, their initial ethos is likely to be higher than that of those who appear scattered. Other related factors reflecting preparation include the quality of handouts distributed, folders and other materials placed at audience members' desks, and the quality of graphics projected before the presentation begins. All of these can affect a speaker's initial ethos.

Intermediate (derived) ethos. Intermediate or derived ethos refers to audience perceptions of the speaker during the course of the statement. Essentially, it is the speaker's personal stock price, which fluctuates during the talk. Intermediate ethos is based on the following factors.

- *Content of the message:* If a speaker makes a comment that is factually in-accurate, intermediate ethos is likely to decrease. On the other hand, if the content makes sense or if word choice is particularly appropriate, intermediate ethos is likely to increase. Therefore, even experts on the subject matter of a topic should not deliver impromptu presentations. The perception of their expertise may be undermined by gaffes that could be construed as a reflection of ignorance.
- *Quality of delivery:* How spokespersons say what they say affects audience mem-bers' perceptions of them. A smooth delivery increases intermediate ethos. Disor-ganized, poorly worded messages that are overloaded with speech fillers decrease intermediate ethos. Mispronunciation of common words affects intermediate ethos as does the level of vocal enthusiasm.
- *Ability of the speaker to establish rapport with the audience:* In August 2003, presidential aspirant Senator John Kerry spoke at a forum sponsored by the Sheet Metal Workers International Association. Kerry was able to increase his ethos when he told the audience, "[President Bush] is so quick to give speeches about the heroes of New York City. Well, I look forward to remind-ing him that every single one of those heroes that went up those stairs and gave their lives so that someone else might live was a member of organized labor."[18]

Spokespersons can enhance their ethos by establishing rapport with their audi-ence and can erode ethos by failing to establish such rapport.

- **Terminal ethos.** The final type of ethos, terminal ethos, refers to the perception attributed to a speaker at the conclusion of the talk. Terminal ethos is especially important to crisis communicators or anyone who will return to speak to the same audience. Terminal ethos directly affects the spokesperson's initial ethos in subsequent appearances.

In the introduction to the presentation, spokespersons should do what they can—in terms of delivery and message content—to enhance the likelihood of being attributed high ethos. Appropriate dress, content accuracy, quality delivery, attractive visuals, understanding the audience—all of these factors affect your ethos and contribute to an introduction that will engage rather than disengage your audience.

Apply the Principles

In the preceding pages several points have been made about the introduction to a presentation.
From your vantage point as an audience member either in school, community, or business situations, which of the following affect your initial reaction to spokespersons and their messages?

- Handouts distributed beforehand
- Graphics displayed on the screen before the presentation begins

- Materials placed at the desk
- Clear explanation of presentation goals
- Explanation of why the talk is important
- Fluid delivery
- Vocal energy
- What the spokespersons say about their personal experiences
- Attempts to get the audience involved
- Physical appearance of speaker in terms of attire and attractiveness
- Speaker posture

BODY OF THE STATEMENT

In the body of the statement, spokespersons simply do what they have set out to do. In the introduction, spokespersons describe what they intend to discuss. In the body of the talk, they fulfill the promise. One can employ a number of methods to structure the body of a presentation.

Topical format

The topical approach is an easy and effective way to organize content. It involves dividing the talk into subtopics—and addressing each subtopic in turn.

Chronological

If the talk involves discussing the evolution of an incident, the chronological approach will be effective. The speaker simply structures the presentation in chronological order. For example, as it relates to the opening case, a chronological approach might include

- Events of Saturday night
- Discovery at Sunday morning brunch
- Details of search for missing student
- Sad discovery
- Family reactions and requests
- Meeting with all students and faculty on Sunday night
- Addition of new policies at the school, effective immediately
- Memorial service scheduled for Wednesday

THE CONCLUSION

The conclusion to the statement is crucial. At the end spokespersons should provide a sense of closure for the stakeholders. Too many important messages end with speakers scanning notes and then looking up to say, "Well, that's all I have for right now. Can I take any questions?" "That's all I have for right now," particularly if delivered after some apparent search for additional points, is not an appropriate way to conclude a statement.

A summary of the main points of the statement is essential to provide closure. It is a good idea to complement this recap with visual support.

QUESTION AND ANSWER SESSIONS

> . . . We [President Reagan's press team] would anticipate questions and answers on the subjects that . . . might come up. Then we would put together a briefing book by the Friday before a press conference for the President to take along to Camp David and study over the weekend. It would have several dozen domestic and foreign topics, with questions and answers on each topic. . . . In press conferences, out of thirty questions and follow-ups we might fail to anticipate one.[19]

Spokespersons must prepare for question and answer sessions as diligently as they prepare their statements. These sessions can erode credibility if spokespersons appear confused by simple inquiries, seem inappropriately defensive, or deliver their responses poorly. The opposite can also be true. Effective responses to questions can enhance the reputation of your organization, repair credibility, and facilitate image restoration.

RESPONDING TO QUESTIONS EFFICIENTLY—PREPARATORY STEPS

The preparatory steps to question and answer sessions include

- Anticipating probable questions
- Creating extemporaneous responses to anticipated questions
- Practicing the prepared responses in a simulated press conference format

ANTICIPATING PROBABLE QUESTIONS

The first step for spokespersons and the crisis communication team involves predicting questions. Of course, the team will not be able to anticipate all possible inquiries. There is no crystal ball and some inquiries can be unusual. However, often questions that are asked during question and answer sessions are predictable. A careful review of the audience analysis and the presentation content itself helps in identifying which points in the talk are likely to stimulate questions.

After predicting questions, spokespersons might wonder whether they should include content in the presentation that might preclude the anticipated questions. In many cases it is wise to incorporate that content. However, that may not be possible or even recommended for certain reasons. Time considerations, for example, create limitations. Spokespersons may decide to omit certain points—even relevant ones—because there is no room in the talk for this information given the time required to relay other salient points. Some anticipated questions may deal with peripheral or irrelevant issues. Spokespersons may anticipate that these peripheral concerns could arise during question and answer, but feel that such content is not sufficiently central to include in the presentations.

Creating extemporaneous responses to anticipated questions

After the team has predicted the questions that may surface, the next preparatory task is to outline responses to the anticipated questions. Impromptu statements can create excess communication noise. When you predict the question, think of how you will compose the answer ahead of time.

Practicing the prepared responses in a simulated press conference format

In the same way that the initial statement can be rehearsed if there is time, spokespersons can rehearse the question and answer session in a simulated environment. In the simulation, the crisis team pretends to be audience members and asks questions, while the spokespersons practice delivering their planned responses.

Delivering responses to questions

There is more to delivering an answer during question and answer than simply answering the question. Consider the following procedure for delivering responses.

Step 1: If necessary, repeat the essence of the question
Frequently, but not always, it is essential to repeat a question. Among several reasons why it may be necessary, a primary one is that all stakeholders in attendance may not have heard it. Also, repeating the question allows a speaker to buy time and consider how she will respond.

Step 2: After repeating the question, direct the answer to everyone
Spokespersons should not neglect the questioner but should also include the others in attendance. Answers to questions are not a two-way conversation between questioner and spokesperson.

Step 3: Get confirmation from the questioner and take another question
After responding, obtain some verbal or nonverbal feedback from the questioners indicating that their inquiries have been addressed. Asking "Have I answered your question?" can seem contrived or simply redundant if spokespersons say this after each response. Usually, some nonverbal confirmation can assure the spokesperson that the question has been addressed to the audience member's satisfaction.

Step 4: At the conclusion of the question and answer session restate your main point
There should be a designated time for questions. Even the most careful speaker will be unable to hold attention long term. Therefore, after a number of questions have been addressed, the spokesperson or another representative should indicate that one or two more will be taken, and then attempt to end the session after addressing a question comfortably.

After taking the last question, the speaker should summarize the presentation very briefly. During the question and answer session, spokespersons may have been taken hither and yon. If this is the case, and it seems necessary to bring the stakeholders back to the main point of the statement, restate the important points of the presentation before departing.

Apply the Principles

Is it unethical for spokespersons to plant easy questions?

Assume spokespersons are apprehensive about an upcoming question and answer session. In order to reduce the tension associated with the event, the spokespersons ask colleagues to sit in the audience. When the question and answer session begins, the colleagues raise their hands in order to be recognized and then pose predetermined questions. Is this unethical? Why?

Counterproductive tendencies during question and answer

During question and answer sessions, even very bright, industrious, and otherwise well-prepared spokespersons often behave in ways that negatively affect their performance. Readers might want to think about common counterproductive tendencies and be careful to avoid them.

Saying "That is a good question" after each or several questions. Sometimes people ask questions that make spokespersons, very honestly, want to comment that the question is a good one, or that they are glad that a particular point was brought up. Spokespersons who occasionally make these comments will not do irreparable damage. However, there are two potential problems with making such remarks. The first is that some spokespersons make complimentary comments after *each* inquiry. When this occurs spokespersons lose credibility as it is unlikely that every single question can or will be "a good question." Even if they are all "good questions," it sounds artificial to make similar remarks after every inquiry. The second problem is that if the congratulatory "That is a good question" is uttered sometimes and not every time, those who were not so stroked may feel tacitly insulted.

Implicitly disparaging questioners. Spokespersons will often preface the repetition of a question with the words, "If I understand you correctly." Sometimes this statement can be made harmlessly. However, often the phrase is vocally tinged, thus creating a message suggesting that the question was poorly constructed. When repeating the question, spokespersons should be careful not to be sharing a laugh at the expense of the person who had the courage to make the inquiry.

Explicitly disparaging questioners. Some stakeholders may wish to be recognized during question and answer, but then they speak aimlessly. Spokespersons occasionally deride a questioner who, without malice, is so unfocused. There is little to be gained by derisive cheap shots. We have all said things that are foolish at times and no person enjoys having his transgressions highlighted for mass ridicule.

Reflexively repeating a question. Having been coached to repeat a question, some spokespersons blurt back the repetition quickly and meaninglessly. This type of repetition defeats the purpose.

Restating the question incorrectly. It is stunning how often this occurs. Listen carefully to other students in your class as they attempt to repeat questions. Unless the questions are very clear, you will notice that several have difficulty identifying the essence of many of the questions. This may be because spokespersons become apprehensive in the speaking setting. It may also be because some questions are poorly expressed. Nevertheless, a recurring problem for beginning spokespersons relates to understanding the question.

Being apparently unprepared for very predictable questions. Many spokespersons do not spend the requisite time preparing for the question and answer period. As a result, some questions that are central to the topic can apparently stump spokespersons and leave them speechless.

Becoming defensive. It is easy to become defensive during question and answer. Spokespersons may fear that their weaknesses will be exposed by contentious listeners.

Even when spokespersons receive a confrontational question, it is best to take the high road. Consider responding with the following type of remark: "Obviously, we have differing opinions. I hear your point and respect your arguments. Perhaps we will forever disagree, but I promise to consider your position and I ask, respectfully, that you consider mine."

Speaking too long in response to a single question. Quintilian said that "If we devote too much time to the final recapitulation, the conclusion will cease to be an enumeration and will constitute something very much like a second speech."[20] Quintilian was referring to extended conclusions, but the same sentiments apply to long-winded orations in response to particular questions. One does not want the length of the question and answer session to render the presentation meaningless. Spending too much time on one answer, or with one questioner, not only makes it difficult for you to maintain audience attention but also can make the main part of your statement a footnote to the question and answer.

Frequently asked questions about question and answer

What should you do if you do not know the answer to a question? There is nothing wrong with saying "I don't know" to a question you cannot answer. Nobody, regardless of how intelligent or expert they may be, knows the answers to all questions. Pretending to know the answer can be disastrous. Bluffs can be detected as such even by stakeholders who do not know the correct answer. Those who do know the correct answer may correct you, and even if they do not, your stature in their eyes will plummet if you attempt to answer a question by winging it. Of course, if "I don't know" is the only answer spokespersons have to all questions, they will be standing on precariously fragile ground.

Can you say, "I'll get back to you later?" The same advice applies. There is no reason why spokespersons cannot make such a promise (assuming that they intend to fulfill it). Problems can occur only if spokespersons answer very basic questions in this manner or if, on a prior occasion, a speaker has made such promises and not "gotten back to" questioners.

What if someone is persistently contentious or heckles you? The counsel on querulous questioners is relatively consistent. The speaker is better off taking the high road whenever dealing with someone contentious. Establish that you disagree, but respect the position of the others. If you need to, comment that you want to move on to other questioners but are willing to discuss the issue after the presentation either in person or via e-mail.

Hecklers are in a different category. Hecklers are not interested in debate. They are interested in throwing the speaker off. If the heckler is persistent, and cannot be removed, reiterate the main points of your statement, express your regret that your message has been obstructed by the listener, explain where interested persons can obtain unobstructed communications about the crisis, and end the session.[21]

What if someone asks the same question that another person recently posed? As indicated earlier, there is fool's gold in deriding a questioner in front of others. The comment, "I guess you were not paying attention" will make some stakeholders chuckle at the expense of the questioner. There is no benefit in being so derisive. Assuming that the person's inquiry was innocently repetitive, answer it again, and give the person the respect she or he deserves for being a human who sometimes makes mistakes. Your audience members will respect you for respecting the audience member.

What if I receive a loaded question? A loaded question, as the name suggests, is one that is "loaded" with an implicit statement as well as a question, or is loaded with multiple questions. Consider this example:

> The transit strike is causing many citizens enormous discomfort. When are you going to stop harassing employees?

The way to answer a loaded question is to unload or unpack it. This question actually contains at least three parts: (a) comment on how citizens are being inconvenienced; (b) why are you harassing employees? and (c) are you going to stop?

A speaker may respond to the example in the following way:

> Well, Andy, apparently you believe that employees have been harassed. I am genuinely sorry that you feel this way. What constitutes harassment for some may be different from what constitutes harassment for others. However, I can assure you that we do not condone and will not tolerate inappropriate behavior. We will look into any and all allegations. If you or any person in attendance here today believes they have been harassed let me know

and I promise you that we will address the situation quickly, firmly, and correctly. We, like you, want the strike to be over soon. It is in our interest and everyone's for the citizens of our municipality to be able to get to work comfortably.

What if nobody asks any questions? Give the audience some time. Count to ten in your head. Restate that you would be happy to address questions that people may have. If still nobody asks a question, bring up a question that is typically asked. For example, "I'm surprised that nobody has asked me about . . . ," and then answer the question yourself.

Most often—eventually—someone will ask a question. Once the ice is broken other questions will follow.

VISUAL SUPPORT

A visual aid should be just that; a visual complement that helps improve the statement. Occasionally, spokespersons mistake esthetic appeal or sophisticated graphics for productive visual support. An academic expert has remarked, "Visual Aids not used properly could be called Visual Hindrances."[22] A practitioner comments "the sad truth is AV ruins more messages than it helps."[23] Effective spokespersons intelligently employ various types of visuals and avoid common problems that spokespersons have when using these complements.

Values of visual support

- *Visual support can increase audience understanding.* The use of a picture, computer-generated graphic, map, or chart can clarify information. If spokespersons are explaining the location of the party in relationship to the school, a map may be a better way to describe it than a verbal description alone.
- *Visual support can increase audience attention.*
- *Visual support can increase audience retention.*
- *Visual support may reduce speaker apprehension.* Earlier we discussed how preparation can reduce communication apprehension. Spokespersons may feel that some of the attention will be deflected from them when stakeholders view slides or other visual support. In and of itself, this is not a good reason to use graphics.
- *Visual support can improve organization.* Often graphics are used to outline the agenda for a talk. The act of creating these slides may help spokespersons consider how they will move through the content of their message. During a talk, the slide can facilitate the speaker's staying on the road map outlined on the visual.
- *Visual support can help audience members follow the talk.* In addition, to assisting the speaker, a visual outline can help listeners literally see where the talk is going.
- *Visual support can increase ethos.* Visuals that reflect preparation can enhance the status stakeholders attribute to the organization. In many contexts, since visual support is expected, its absence could—in and of itself—reduce ethos.

Recurring problems with visual support

The potential for visuals to actually be helpful does not guarantee that they will be helpful. If not used effectively they will have a counterproductive effect. Consider the following common problems associated with using visual support.

- *Spokespersons may tend to address a screen and not the stakeholders*
- *The graph, map, or font may be too small for all to read*
  It may surprise readers, but spokespersons frequently begin a sentence with the words, "As you can see" and then hold up a photo or graphic that cannot conceivably be seen. It does no good to ask, "Can you all see this?" What if they cannot? And why did the speaker not consider that size might matter when preparing the graphic?

- *There is too much text written on a slide*
- *The slides have too many bells and whistles. The results are not effective*
- *The visuals contain a spelling, content, or grammatical error*
- *Items are passed around*
  A difficult challenge for spokespersons involves engaging the audience. When spokespersons pass around objects they actually encourage listeners to disengage. Spokespersons are implicitly telling audience members that when the item gets to them, they should cease paying attention to the spokespersons, and focus on the object. In addition, passing objects around is problematic because the logistics of the procedure can be disconcerting.

- *Handouts can be distracting*
  Similarly, handouts—even those distributed prior to the talk—can be distracting. Audience members may be leafing through the handouts instead of being attentive to the spokespersons. If the handouts are too detailed and the spokespersons are stating precisely what is on the handouts, the audience may not pay attention assuming (correctly) that they can read the material subsequently. Handouts that are referred to by the speaker should have page numbers. Spokespersons do not want to remark, "As you can see in your handout," without identifying the location of the section they are discussing.

- *Chalkboard/flipchart writing can be indecipherable, inaccurate, and embarrassing*
  Apprehensive spokespersons may not be able to endure the added responsibility of writing clearly while speaking. Handwritten comments may be incomprehensible. Very intelligent spokespersons have spelled very simple words incorrectly when using flipcharts and chalkboards as visual aids. A six-figure executive leading a seminar on grant writing headed his flipchart with the scrawled words, "Organizational Tenants" instead of "Tenets."

- *Valuable displays are left up after they have been used*
  An attractive map becomes distracting if it remains displayed after the speaker has referred to it.

- *Apprehension levels become evident*
  As we discussed, while almost everyone has some degree of speaking apprehension, the extent of the anxiety is not always discernible. When visuals are employed it may become easier for audience members to observe anxiety. Manually describing how a product operates may be more difficult when your hand is shaking.

Suggestions for using visuals effectively

The problems identified above may seem insurmountable. However, while they recur with discouraging frequency, they can be addressed. Consider the following recommendations.

- *Follow these guidelines for slide preparation:*
  - Make sure the font is large enough for all to see.
  - Proofread each slide. Have others proofread the slides.
  - Keep them simple. Do not overwhelm the audience with too much text or too many distracting images.
  - Be able to answer this question: How will the visual help?

- *Use premade graphics.*
  Spokespersons are under enough pressure during a presentation. By creating maps, charts, outlines, and graphs ahead of time, spokespersons reduce problems related to misspellings, incomprehensible writing, and sloppy drawings.

- *When there is time, practice with the visual.*
  - Practicing without the visual aid has limited value. Spokespersons cannot predict which problems can surface unless they have attempted to integrate the aids into the presentation during rehearsal. Consider the following during rehearsal:
  - Power: Ensure that outlets exist where they will be needed.
  - Equipment: Spokespersons should be completely familiar with the computers, projectors, and control panels that will be used.
  - Eye contact: While using any equipment, the spokespersons should be able to maintain frequent and sustained eye contact with the audience. Spokespersons should practice avoiding looking at the screen or other inanimate objects while delivering the message.
  - Coordination: If assistants will be manually controlling the computer while other spokespersons address the audience, then practice should include coordinating the statement with the operation of the computer or any other equipment.
  - Pressure: It is difficult to simulate pressure. However, it is wise to conduct a dress rehearsal that is nearly as real as the actual experience will be. Under pressure, simple maneuvers can become complex.

- *During the talk:*
  - Be vigilant about looking at the audience and not the screen.
  - Replace pointers and markers when not using them.
  - Remove visual complements when not employing them so that they are not distracting to the audience.
  - Refer to graphics or relevant sections of handouts when speaking. Sometimes slides appear at the appropriate time, but there is no reference to them. The aid cannot be an aid if the audience members see no correlation between what is being said and what they are seeing.
  - Refrain from passing objects around the room.

ELEMENTS OF DELIVERY

"It's not what you say; it's how you say it."

We have all heard that expression. Professional speechwriter Burton Kaplan comments that "There is only one thing worse than saying the wrong thing and that is saying the right thing the wrong way."[24] President Ronald Reagan's press spokesperson Larry Speakes remarked that one of Reagan's predecessors, Gerald Ford, exhibited a "halting manner of speaking [that] contributed to the general impression that he was not smart, that he was unsure of himself."[25] Verbal dimensions of delivery are also important to consider. Spokespersons who cannot or do not find descriptive words for their messages will be less effective than those who strive to select the right language.

The following sections discuss nonverbal and verbal factors that affect delivery of statements made to the press and other stakeholders.

NONVERBAL FACTORS

Vocalics or paralanguage

> Herbert Hoover who carefully crafted a speech as an engineer might construct a bridge succeeded only in boring audiences with his droning voice.[26]

Paralanguage refers to how we say what we say. There are several paralingual factors that affect how stakeholders perceive spokespersons and their messages.

Rate and volume

One's performance during presentations is affected by the speed of delivery and the ability to project. You may have found it difficult to take notes when an instructor is racing through a lecture. Similarly, it is difficult to take mental notes when words are spoken too quickly. In large rooms particularly, it is important to make sure that volume is sufficient for all those assembled. It is not especially helpful to ask if all can hear you. While some who cannot may indicate their difficulty, others may be too shy to comment.

Pitch, inflection, and emphasis

Pitch refers to the tone of your voice. Listening to a person who speaks using a consistent tone can be boring. We typically refer to such a consistent speaking voice or speaker as *monotone* (literally: one tone). As often as not, when we complain about a person who speaks in monotone we really mean that she or he does not vary the rate, volume, or pitch of the voice, thus making both the sounds and rhythm predictable.

Inflection refers to pitch and volume variation within a sentence. Understanding the meaning and effects of inflection may be easier if you consider a dictionary definition of the term. "Inflection" is defined as the "act or result of curving or bending."[27] When we speak our voices tend to "curve and bend" sometimes in disconcerting ways. For example, a common problem for spokespersons is that they raise their voices at the end of declarative sentences as if the sentences are questions. You may have even asked people for their name and heard responses that sound like "Pat Wilson?" This can be confusing to listeners attending to any one sentence and very annoying if repetitive during a presentation. Another common problem occurs when a sentence is uttered in a "rhythmic" pattern. For example, "I am here to speak to you about the events of Sunday night," should not arbitrarily ascend at "here" and "to you" and then descend on "Sunday night." Over the course of even a short statement, this inflection pattern could, very literally, drive even very interested stakeholders to distraction. A third common problem related to pitch and inflection occurs when spokespersons, often very innocently, use a tone that sounds condescending or patronizing to listeners.

The words spokespersons emphasize within a sentence and at any time during a talk can affect how successful they are when they deliver a presentation. When spokespersons desire to highlight a point they should emphasize the salient words, phrase, or sentence that makes their point. Emphasizing the wrong word changes meaning.

Articulation, pronunciation, and enunciation

These three related, but different, vocal factors can strengthen or weaken the quality of a statement. Articulation means distinctly uttering the words you are saying. For example, many people say "goin'" instead of "going," "dint" instead of "didn't," or even "revelant" instead of "relevant."

Pronunciation refers to the correct way to emphasize syllables within a word. The correct pronunciation of the word syllable is (SYL la ble) not (sil LA ble). Incorrect pronunciation can damage speaker ethos as it may reflect a lack of preparation or intelligence. If you are discussing research related to tobacco consumption and cancer, you will want to pronounce *carcinogen* and *carcinogenic* correctly. Incorrect pronunciation can also affect the meaning of words. Emphasizing the wrong syllable of the word *desert* or *present,* for example, changes the meaning.

Enunciation, like pronunciation and articulation, can help your statement to be successful or a less-than-positive influence. Enunciation refers to the distinct uttering of consecutive words. In formal speaking situations, one should say "What do you think you would do if faced with a similar situation?" as opposed to "Whaddayathink you would do?"

Speech fillers

Ums and ers plague many spokespersons and the receivers who are compelled to endure them. When speech fillers are pervasive the common audience response is to marvel at their frequency and not focus on the speaker's intended message. The first step in addressing problems with speech fillers is to become aware of how often you employ them. This can be done by taping a message and counting the regularity of the interjections. Another method involves asking team members to listen to the talk. Have these colleagues raise their hands each time you say er or um. Initially, you will sense the upcoming negative reinforcement and this may cause you to deliver practice talks in a halting fashion as there will be some hesitancy each time you feel an um coming on. However, continued sensitivity and diligence will result in a relatively smooth delivery.

Apply the Principles

Several vocal factors have been discussed in the previous pages.
Which three create the most disconcerting and distracting problems for you as a listener?

- Articulation
- Emphasis
- Enunciation
- Inflection
- Pitch
- Pronunciation
- Rate and volume
- Speech fillers

What recommendations would you make to colleagues who were creating these problems for you as a listener?

Eye contact

Spokespersons need to establish eye contact with the audience. Even if spokespersons do not actually make eye contact with listeners, it is important to give receivers the impression of maintaining eye contact.[28] The best way to leave that impression is to actually have frequent and sustained contact with the audience.

There are three common problems related to eye contact. The first was discussed in a prior section: spokespersons will avoid eye contact and speak to inanimate objects in order to avoid the audience. The second is that spokespersons attempt to finesse their apprehension by gazing in the direction of the listeners, but still avoid any meaningful eye contact. The third problem is that spokespersons, having been coached to establish eye contact, glance very briefly at members of the audience. These glances are not sufficiently sustained to be meaningful. You may have seen persons lifting their heads up abruptly throughout a talk and then just as abruptly snapping their heads down. No real bond is made in this way. It appears as if the speaker intends to meet some quota of appropriate numbers of eye contacts.

Spokespersons can become aware of their counterproductive habits by watching a videotape of their behavior when speaking to the audience. A second method for improving eye contact involves observing others speak and identifying counterproductive behaviors. Subsequently, spokespersons now aware of others' annoying tendencies are more likely to avoid the behaviors themselves.

Body motion

Follow this simple rule as it relates to body motion when you speak. Your movements should be consistent with, and not a distraction from, your message.

One problem occurs when spokespersons arbitrarily but rhythmically move or shake their legs during the course of talks. Similarly, hand gestures that are unrelated to the message being uttered can cause listeners to become attentive to the odd motions instead of the content. Another problem arises when spokespersons assume a posture that appears uncomfortable or peculiar. Speakers, for example, may place their hands in front of their stomach, or on their hips, for long stretches during a talk. While that gesture does not mean anything universal, it may be distracting since it appears so unnatural. A third recurring problem is that spokespersons develop a rhythmic pacing in front of the room. Movement is not necessarily detrimental—an absence of motion can actually seem peculiar and be distracting. However, predictable pacing can make a listener dwell on the persistence and regularity of the motion as opposed to the message being relayed.

The first step toward improving any of these tendencies requires becoming aware of the behavior. Using videotape to record your presentations is an excellent vehicle. Spokespersons can witness counterproductive motions and become sensitive to the behavior.

VERBAL DIMENSIONS OF DELIVERY

> Words have a magical power. They can enable the orator to sway the audience and dictate its decisions.[29]

On October 22, 1962, President John F. Kennedy addressed the nation and the world in what has come to be known as the Cuban Missile Crisis speech. He intended to announce that the United States would prevent the Soviet Union from continuing to transport to and store missiles in Cuba. The world would be told that the United States would establish a naval blockade to halt the transfer of these missiles.

However, Kennedy never identified the action as a blockade. For days preceding the speech, members of Kennedy's staff debated the wisdom of using the word *blockade*. It was feared that the word might sound too bellicose and consequently trigger an unleashing of hostilities. The staff decided to substitute the word *quarantine* for *blockade*. The thinking was that quarantine sounded less aggressive.[30]

When spokespersons deliver their messages they must select words intelligently. Word choices may seem insignificant but subtle changes can "direct listeners to view the message in one way rather than another."[31] For this reason, the same military action may be labeled a *massacre* by some world leaders and a *preemptive strike* by others. One group's *terrorist* becomes another group's *freedom fighter.* Choice of language can affect receivers' perception of both the speaker and the presentation.

CRITERIA FOR LANGUAGE SELECTION

Clarity and accuracy

The following questions may provide helpful guidelines when considering word choice.

Does the word mean what you think it means? The words you select must mean what you think they mean and match the thought that you wish to express. Spokespersons who say *antidote* when they mean *anecdote* are using a word that does not match the thought that they wish to express. More significantly, when spokespersons substitute *antidote* for *anecdote,* their credibility suffers.

If you say *transgress* when you mean *digress,* an audience familiar with the words will know you have transgressed. If you employ *dilemma* as a synonym for *problem,* you will inform those in the know that you are not.

Manuscript speakers have more opportunity to check and be certain that the words they use do, in fact, match the ideas they wish to communicate. Extemporaneous speakers must select words as they are delivering the message. Both manuscript and extemporaneous speakers, however, can be victims of assuming that the words they use are correct when they may not be.

Is the word selected the best word to match the thought? Words that are closely aligned in meaning typically have shades of difference. Selecting one word as opposed to another can make your message more clear and accurate. Consider the following four examples

- When you were first smitten did you find your lover *nice* or *charming?*
- Can excessive alcoholic consumption have *bad* or *insidious* consequences?
- Are the conditions for the homeless *sad* or *miserable?*
- Did your partner *usurp* control or *take over* control?

Does the word have a low "level of abstraction?" Some words have very concrete meanings. If I were to tell you that I need a *pencil,* you would have a clear idea of what I mean. There are different types of pencils, of course, but what you think of when you think of pencil is likely very similar to what I think of when I say pencil. However, if I were to say that our organization strives for progress and success, the words *progress* and *success* will both have a very high level of abstraction. What you mean by *progress* and what I mean by *progress* can vary greatly. If the object of a talk is to clearly relay information, it may be necessary to either define terms with high levels of abstraction or use terms that have low levels of abstraction. Of course, as we discussed in Chapter 6, there are people who deliberately attempt to be strategically ambiguous.

Are you aware of the connotations as well as the denotation of the word? Occasionally spokespersons use a word that literally is utilized accurately, but has come to mean something quite different from its denotation. For example, referring to the headmaster as a pedagogue might seem benign and perfectly appropriate. The denotative meaning of pedagogue is teacher. However, the word *pedagogue* has come to mean someone who is rigid and condescending. Spokespersons, therefore, need to be careful when they employ words they have just learned, in order to make sure that they are not utilizing a word that is denotatively correct, but connotatively incorrect.

Appropriate language

You may have selected the best word to match your idea. You may know precisely what the word means and are able to use it correctly. However, it still may not be the best word to use in a professional presentation. Consider the following factors pertaining to the suitability of language for the audience.

- Will the receivers understand the word?
- Is the word employed simply to show off?
- Is the word likely to be offensive?

The expression *politically correct* has been used, often disparagingly, to refer to language use that meets a standard for propriety. Columnists dub the utterances of politicians on race and gender issues *politically correct,* intimating that more appropriate language would be selected had there not been a fear of the political repercussions for using the alternate terms. It is unfortunate that being sensitive to what may offend stakeholders has become ridiculed in this way. There is value, both political and common, in being sensitive to our receivers. Some men and women may feel as if there is nothing inappropriate about referring to men as "boys" but such a reference is offensive to many men and women. Being responsive to what others consider offensive is a responsibility of communicators regardless of the context.

Point/Counterpoint

In this exercise, two positions are presented. The first is consistent with a point made in the chapter. The second is a counterargument. Consider the counsel and counterargument. Then write a one-page position paper identifying your position on the issue.

Counsel—Vocal factors affect stakeholder perception of messages. A spokesperson who sounds indifferent will be perceived as uncaring. A spokesperson who sounds condescending will offend stakeholders. There is truth to the saying, "It's not what you say. It is how you say it."

Counterargument—This wisdom may be applicable to other presentation contexts but not to crisis situations. Stakeholders do not need vocal enthusiasm to be engaged. Stakeholders need the facts. They are listening for the facts, the words. Clarity of word choice, clear organization of messages, absence of bogus claims—these are key. Stakeholders could care less if a message is monotone. They are listening to the meat. There is no need for a spokesperson to be a performer. In the television series *Dragnet*, Jack Webb said, "Just the facts ma'am." The same thing applies to crisis messages and spokespersons: Just the facts.

Summary: A Toolbox

- Crisis communication plans must be implemented by skilled communicators.
- Organizational leaders are not necessarily skilled communicators.
- All persons who wish to become skilled can work to improve their communication abilities.
- Regardless of their level of skill, crisis communicators are obliged to simulate crisis situations and practice their skills prior to the need to demonstrate them.
- Speaking skill in crisis situations requires
  - Analyzing stakeholders
  - Addressing speaking anxiety
  - Selecting an appropriate style
  - Intelligently structuring the message.
  - Having the ability to respond to questions during question and answer. This involves
    - Anticipating inquiries
    - Preparing responses for anticipated questions
    - Practicing delivery of the answers.
- Awareness of the value and potential drawbacks of visual complements
- Rhetorical and paralingual sensitivity

PRACTITIONER PERSPECTIVE: STEVE FRANKEL

Steve Frankel is a partner in the firm of Joele Frank, Wilkinson Brimmer Katcher. Joele Frank, Wilkinson Brimmer Katcher is a corporate communications consulting firm. Among their services, the company helps organizations with their crisis communication needs. According to its Web site, the company provides "Assistance when unforeseen or unplanned events threaten to disrupt the public or internal perception of a business or organization."

The day after 9/11, I was retained by Sandler O'Neill & Partners, an investment bank that had offices in the World Trade Center. Sixty-six of the 171 Sandler O'Neill employees perished in the attack.

Our job was to help Sandler O'Neill communicate with families, Wall Street, and clients. Personal outreach to the families of the victims was the highest priority. Many organizations in the throes of crisis focus on external audiences. While these are important stakeholders, employees and families of employees are very important in crisis communication. After the terrorist attacks, Sandler O'Neill needed to console the families and they immediately acted to do so.

Following that, we also needed to get the message out to Wall Street that Sandler O'Neill was still in business. On September 17, the Monday the markets reopened, Jimmy Dunne, the lone surviving member of the executive committee, went on CNBC to convey that message in no uncertain terms.

Instead of just communicating to the media in general we focused on the business media. While we did have a segment on *60 Minutes,* it was publications like *Fortune,* the *Wall Street Journal,* and other media outlets with a narrower business audience where we wanted to place our message.

In most corporate crises, it is important for organizations to accept responsibility when they are responsible, and do so in a timely way. This is not always an easy sell to a client. For example, we had a client (a prominent chief executive of a large company), who was reluctant to make a statement to this effect. Eventually he did, but by waiting too long the message did not have the impact it would have had had it been sent in a timely manner. There used to be a greater tension between PR and legal counsel as it relates to this issue of accepting responsibility. Lawyers were, and to some extent still are, concerned with liabilities. But in my experience the divide has narrowed and there is a greater awareness from lawyers about the importance of transparency, and therefore the PR professional's role, in crisis communication.

Reputation is a key factor that affects crisis communication efforts. Relationships and reputation go hand in hand. Simply put, the relationships you develop with your stakeholders will affect the reputation you have. When companies have earned a positive reputation it is easier for messages to be trusted during times of crisis.

Organizations should prepare for crises. All crises are unique but there are things to do ahead of time. A good example of this occurred recently with US Airways' sudden landing in the Hudson River after its takeoff from LaGuardia. Fortunately, the expertise of the pilot saved all of the passengers and prevented any serious casualties, but significantly for crisis communication it was valuable to note how prepared the company was in dealing with the passengers immediately after. That does not just happen. They were absolutely ready to deal with the stakeholders, in this instance the passengers and their families, in case of calamity.

The success of communications during times of crisis is based on both the quality of content in the message and the skill of the communicator. There are instances when a representative was a poor speaker and could not deliver a quality message, and other instances when a good speaker, or at least an adequate one, was burdened by a superficial or inappropriate message.

Of all the factors that affect crisis communication, organizational leadership probably heads the list. Executives who can convey the message with credibility and confidence and are committed to the organization can facilitate crisis communication efforts. Conversely, when leaders are not so capable and committed, they can derail crisis communication efforts, if not undermine them altogether.

Exercises and Discussion Questions

1. Will apprehension related to crisis situations render even an eloquent speaker a weak one because of crisis pressures? If so, does training really have an effect on crisis presentations?
2. Can a team really simulate crises in a meaningful way?
3. A recommendation for crisis communicators is to anticipate questions and be prepared to respond to them. Is it inevitable that the questions that surface will be, at best, a variation of these questions and therefore render the preparation only marginally valuable?
4. Can you recall a situation when correct word choice helped you to express yourself when, had you suggested another word, you might have created or intensified a crisis? In relationships have certain words (not including slang or profanity) proved to be incendiary when you would not have predicted that to be the case?
5. If you were coaching a crisis communicator prior to a press conference what would be your top three recommendations to that person?

NOTES

1. Daniel Webster, quoted in James McCroskey, *An Introduction to Rhetorical Communication* (Needham Heights, MA: Allyn & Bacon, 2001), p. 19.

2. Deanna Sellnow, *Public Speaking: A Process Approach,* Media Edition (Belmont, CA: Wadsworth/Thomson, 2003), p. xxi.

3. Cited in Joe Ayres and Tim Hopf, *Coping With Speech Anxiety* (Norwood, NJ: Ablex, 1993), p. 49.

4. For example, Joseph DeVito, *The Communication Handbook: A Dictionary* (New York: Harper and Row, 1986), p. 209.

5. Mark Sanborn quoted in Lilly Walters, *Secrets of Successful Speakers* (New York: McGraw-Hill, 1993), p. 43.

6. Dennis Beaver, "Got Stage Fright? It's a Common Feeling, but One That Can Be Turned into Confidence More Easily Than You Realize," *ABA Banking Journal* 90, no. 2 (February 1998): 96. See also Ritch Sorenson, Grace DeBord, and Ida Ramirez, *Business and Management Communication* (Upper Saddle River, NJ: Prentice Hall, 2001), p. 224; Steven Beebe and Susan Beebe, *Public Speaking An Audience Centered Approach,* 4th ed. (Needham Heights, MA: Allyn & Bacon, 2003), p. 21; Judith McManus, *How to Write and Deliver an Effective Speech* (New York: Macmillan, 1998), p. 2.

7. Steven R. Brydon and Michael Scott, *Between One and Many,* 2d ed. (Mountain View, CA: Mayfield, 1997), p. 77.

8. Beebe and Beebe, *Public Speaking,* p. 23.

9. Dorothy Sarnoff, *Never Be Nervous Again* (New York: Crown Publishers, 1987), pp. 72–76.

10. David Zarefsky, *Public Speaking,* 3d ed. (Boston: AB Longman 2002), p. 21; Brydon and Scott, *Between One and Many,* p. 74.

11. Jack P. Friedman, *Dictionary of Business Terms,* 3d ed. (Hauppauge, NY: Barron's Educational Series, 2000), p. 528.

12. See the discussion in Albert J. Vasile, *Speak with Confidence,* 9th ed. (Needham Heights, MA: Allyn & Bacon, 2003), p. 198. See also Raymond Zeuschner, *Communicating Today: The Essentials* (Needham Heights, MA: Allyn & Bacon, 2002), p. 230, where Zueschner comments that "in virtually every situation, audiences prefer extemporaneous speeches, and they rate the speakers who give such speeches very highly." I would qualify this statement by adding the modifier, "quality" before the word "extemporaneous." Regularly, MBA students and undergraduates comment that they consider speakers who deliver extemporaneously to be more credible and more knowledgeable than those who speak from a manuscript as long as the extemporaneous speaker delivers the message effectively. A poorly delivered extemporaneous presentation is not typically rated highly.

13. James McCroskey, *An Introduction to Rhetorical Communication,* 8th ed. (Needham Heights, MA: Allyn & Bacon, 2001), p. 83. McCroskey actually uses the quote as a subtitle to the chapter on ethos.

14. Michael Osborn and Suzanne Osborn, *Public Speaking,* 3d ed. (Boston: Houghton Mifflin, 1997), p. 16.

15. McCroskey, *An Introduction to Rhetorical Communication,* pp. 89–90.

16. Damon Runyon's characters were often gamblers. Several songs from the musical Guys and Dolls—for example, "Luck Be a Lady Tonight" and "Good old Reliable Nathan"—deal with betting and bettors.

17. Several writers make this point. As it pertains to the effects of dress in the classroom, see, for example, David Roach, "Effects of Graduate Assistant Teaching Attire on Student Learning, Misbehaviors and Ratings of Instruction," *Communication Quarterly* 45, no. 3 (Summer 1997): 125–41.

18. Senator Kerry's comments were quoted in the *Boston Globe,* August 17, 2003, p. 1.

19. Larry Speakes (with Robert Pack), *Speaking Out* (New York: Avon, 1988), p. 292.

20. Quintilian, *The Education of the Orator,* Book VI, chapter 1, section 2.

21. There are varied suggestions on how to deal with hecklers, all of which revolve around this idea of taking the high road and not engaging in a battle with the combative heckler. See, for example, Richard Letteri, *A Handbook of Public Speaking* (Needham Heights, MA: Allyn & Bacon, 2002), pp. 224–26.

22. McCroskey, *An Introduction to Rhetorical Communication,* p. 185.

23. J. Detz, *It's Not What You Say, It's How You Say It* (New York: St. Martin's Press, 2000), p. 42.

24. Burton Kaplan, *The Manager's Compete Guide to Speech Writing* (New York: Free Press, 1988), p. 47.

25. Speakes, *Speaking Out,* p. 68.

26. From Halford Ryan, ed., *U.S. Presidents as Orators* (Westport, CT: Greenwood Press, 1995), p. xvi.

27. *Merriam Webster's Collegiate Dictionary,* 10th ed., p. 599.

28. George Grice and John Skinner, *Mastering Public Speaking* (Needham Heights, MA: Allyn & Bacon, 1995), p. 262.

29. Sigmund Freud, quoted in L. Perry Wilbur, *Stand Up, Speak Up, or Shut up: A Practical Guide to Public Speaking* (New York: Dembner Books, 1981), p. 13.

30. Laurence Chang and Peter Kornbluh, eds., *The Cuban Missile Crisis 1962, A National Archive Documents Reader* (New York: New Press, 1992), p. 365. See also Elie Abel, *The Missile Crisis* (Philadelphia: Lippincott, 1968), p. 115.

31. David Zarefsky, *Public Speaking,* 3d ed. (AB Longman, 2002), p. 261.

9 Where Do You Go from Here?

Chapter in a Nutshell

This chapter begins with a description of the Union Carbide Bhopal tragedy. Bhopal has been called "the worst industrial disaster in human history."[1] In this concluding chapter, we examine this case not only because it is a good case for analysis but also because, sadly, the Bhopal catastrophe is a good final review case. Students can review the principles from the text as they apply to the case and understand clearly the repercussions when so many checklist items are not met. The Bhopal crisis can also be studied within the framework of an emerging area of investigation called "risk communication." This chapter describes the relationship of risk communication to crisis communication. No organization wishes to endure a Bhopal crisis or any crisis, but there are residual benefits when an organization has survived crises and these are also addressed in the chapter. The book ends with a review of the five foundational planks of crisis communication, which are discussed in the context of organizational leadership. The final "Apply the Principles" exercise challenges readers to create a communication plan for a particular organization with which they are familiar.

Specifically, at the end of this chapter, students will be able to

- Apply the concepts discussed in the book to a particular crisis case
- Explain what is meant by risk communication
- Identify values of crises for organizations
- Identify the five foundational planks of crisis communication and the importance of leadership
- Develop a communication plan for their current school or organization

CASE 9.1: DISASTER IN BHOPAL

One of the more horrific and notorious cases of crisis in the past thirty years took place in Bhopal, India, and involved the Union Carbide Corporation [Union Carbide Corporation (UCC) is now owned by Dow Chemical]. In December 1984, a noxious gas, methyl isocyanate, escaped from a Union Carbide India plant in Bhopal. At the time, Union Carbide India, Ltd (UCIL) was owned by UCC.

Methyl isocyanate is deadly. The leak occurred after midnight on December 3, 1984, when most residents of Bhopal were asleep. Residents awakened and panicked. Their lungs seemed to be on fire as they endured the effects of the toxic air. Victims were unable to breathe. The scene was horrific, "Even more horrifying than the number of dead was the appalling nature of the dying—crowds of men, women, and children madly scurrying hurriedly in the dark, twitching and writhing."[2] The initial report was that over 2,000 people died in the tragedy. Now, nearly twenty-five years later, it is estimated that maybe nine times as many people perished either as a direct result of that night or because of related diseases. In addition to the deaths, thousands more were affected to the extent that they are now encumbered by permanent injuries.

In the past twenty-five years, Union Carbide has received a great deal of criticism for its behavior as it relates to the tragedy. Its actions or inactions have been subject to scrutiny by crisis communication scholars. The case is often identified as an example of how not to communicate during a crisis. This may be unfair because, undoubtedly, many good people tried to do the right thing at the time. It is difficult to believe that Union Carbide employees—who are routinely pilloried and identified as villains—are content with what transpired. It makes more sense that at Union Carbide, as elsewhere, some very moral people are distraught when they reflect on what occurred at Bhopal. Nevertheless, in retrospect, many of Union Carbide's crisis communication efforts were unsuccessful and failed to alleviate the situation or improve the company's image.

In terms of proactivity, it is contended that Union Carbide had no real plan in place to prevent or address such a disaster and crisis. It has been alleged that Union Carbide was aware of a variety of safety concerns in Bhopal. For example, a 1982 Union Carbide study indicated problems at the Bhopal plant that could result in a "serious accident."[3] Prior to 1984 there had also been other—far less significant—leaks from tanks in Bhopal. Given this background, critics contend the company should have been better prepared to preempt the disaster, or at least ready to communicate in the event of a "serious accident." Possibly, other organizations that have not experienced such a horrible crisis could identify similar safety problems at their plants that never resulted in a catastrophe such as Bhopal's. Nevertheless, this possibility or even likelihood does not exonerate Union Carbide. The fact that others who play Russian roulette are spared does not absolve the offending party of guilt for taking a foolish risk—especially when the potential victims of the negligence were other people.

Post crisis, the company's communication efforts were also criticized. The crisis communication strategy got off to a terrible start when CEO Warren Anderson declared that he would fly to Bhopal. This was a noble gesture. However, when he arrived in India he was arrested. Anderson was set free on bail, but the travel and his presence did little to reduce criticism or facilitate the crisis communication effort. Aside from the announcement of the executive visit, there was a lack of information in the early hours after the leak and, in this vacuum, the presence of misinformation. The lack of communication from UCC made it seem as if there was not appropriate concern for the problem. There likely was great concern, but the absence of information made it appear as if whatever concern there was, was insufficient. There are claims that UCC did not want to communicate information—they wanted to gather information. There is some sense to this. That is, it is difficult to know what to communicate unless you know what has transpired. However, in the panicky aftermath of the disaster, as people succumbed in astonishing numbers, animals were found bloated and dying if not already dead, and leaves fell off trees almost immediately, there was an urgent need for communication from UCC. As it relates to medical care, for example, Seeger,

Sellnow, and Ulmer write, "Union Carbide failed to communicate appropriate information to stakeholders about the nature of the chemicals involved, making medical treatment more difficult."[4]

One of the earliest messages the parent company relayed in 1984 was that it was a safety problem and not a structural problem. The structure of the plant was sound, they claimed, but people at Union Carbide India had not done an efficient job of monitoring and applying safety procedures. UCC explained that a number of pieces of apparatus had been neglected, were inoperable when the crisis symptoms could have been identified, and that in general safety recommendations UCC had made previously had been ignored. The company made the case that while they owned over 50 percent of UCIL, they had little control over the operations. (This claim was contested by critics who argued that UCC did in fact exercise control over UCIL.)[5] UCC argued that they could not be held accountable because by decree of the Indian government, all managerial and technical workers at UCIL had to be citizens of India.[6] It is also important to point out that Union Carbide, to this day, claims that the source of the disaster was related to negligence and sabotage. Visit their Web site in 2009—twenty-five years later—and you will be directed to a statement about the incident that continues to cite a study that supports these assertions.

To support the case that the source of the problem was safety and not structural deficiencies, Union Carbide made another serious blunder. It asserted that the Bhopal plant was every bit as structurally sound as its plant in the United States located in a town called Institute, West Virginia. This tactic did not work well. Instead of successfully displacing responsibility on UCIL and resurrecting the UCC image, the claim created new damage—it worried people in Institute, West Virginia. Apparently the people in Institute did not find the assertion that the Bhopal problem was a safety issue to be wholly comforting. If the plant in Institute was like the plant in Bhopal, there could be a leak in Institute. In fact, in 1985, just months later, there *was* a leak in the Institute plant, which made people in West Virginia very nervous despite assurances that this leak was of a different sort than the one that caused the Bhopal disaster.

Union Carbide has also been accused of attempting to stonewall the crisis as opposed to addressing it. Rene Henry reports an exchange that took place at a press conference between a reporter and UCC director of health safety and environmental affairs ten days after the tragedy.

> Reporter: I think you've said the company was not liable to the Bhopal victims.
> UCC: I didn't say that.
> Reporter: Does that mean you are liable?
> UCC: I didn't say that either.
> Reporter: Then what did you say?
> UCC: Ask me another question.[7]

In an attempt to reduce image damage, Union Carbide also used a strategy of bolstering, identifying the successes of the chemical industry and the value of chemical products to society.[8]

Questions for Analysis

- If you were a spokesperson for Union Carbide and were awakened on the morning of December 4 with the news of this tragedy, what would be the nuggets in your immediate message to the media and stakeholders?
- How do the following issues/concepts in crisis communication pertain to this case?
  - Stakeholder theory
  - Legitimacy
  - Four Rs
  - Attribution theory
  - Personal control
  - Emotional stability
  - Counterfactuals
  - Sleeper effect
  - Instructing information
  - Nuggets
  - Halo and Velcro effect
  - Supporting behavior and honoring the account
- The book has addressed several issues related to crisis communication.
  - How could UCC have proactively addressed this crisis?
  - What ethical issues did UCC have to face when it delivered its crisis messages?
  - How might a systems orientation have precluded the crisis?
  - How might cultural and critical theorists analyze this crisis?
- Identify the image restoration strategies UCC employed in this case.
  - What strategies would you have employed?
- Assume it is December 4, 1984. You are awakened by this horrible news. You gather your crisis team together to discuss how to address the crisis.
  - What primary and secondary conflicts would your team experience?
  - Would interventions work to help the team function?
- Besides the nuggets, what would be the keys to the success of any press conference statement delivered by a UCC representative on December 4, 1984?

INTRODUCTION

We have examined crisis communication from the perspective of proactivity, image restoration strategies, and ethical considerations. The Bhopal case includes elements of each. Your responses to the questions following Case 9.1 should have provided a review of many principles discussed in this text. The tragedy at Bhopal can also be studied within the framework of "risk communication," a type of crisis communication. In the next few pages we discuss risk communication and then examine an unlikely subject—the possible benefits of crisis, even a horrific one like what occurred at Bhopal.

RISK COMMUNICATION

WHAT IS RISK COMMUNICATION?

Risk communication is essentially a type of crisis communication that deals with risks, often health risks. Scholars have defined risk communication as the "exchange of information among interested parties about the nature, magnitude, significance, or control of a risk."[9]

Many of the cases we have discussed in this book—for example, Jack in the Box, Peanut Corporation of America, and Schwan—could be categorized as risk communication as well as crisis communication. Freimuth, Linnan, and Potter write that risk communication "most often is associated with the identification of risks to the public health and efforts to persuade the public to adopt more healthy less risky behaviors."[10] SARS (severe acute respiratory syndrome), the anthrax scare of 2001, spread of lyme disease, even the escape of animals from a zoo would involve risk communication. If the crisis involves a need to get information out to stakeholders about some impending or current threat, then the crisis could be labeled a risk and the communication analysis pertaining to the risk, risk communication. A review of publications such as the *Journal of Health Communication* and *Health Communication* reveals that they routinely discuss risk communication issues and cases.

Risk communication differs from crisis communication primarily in terms of the variables affecting quality and the need for image restoration. For example, emotional stability is an important factor in risk communication as is instructing information. Understanding how people in Institute, West Virginia, might react to news—even accurate news—is a challenge when health issues, in fact life and death, may seem to be in the balance. Emotional stability in such cases can, understandably, be very low, and efforts at comforting stakeholder concerns can be a challenge even if there is absolutely no reason for stakeholders to be concerned. As indicated in the description of the Union Carbide crisis, instructing information for the afflicted in Bhopal was insufficient.

In risk situations the quality, quantity, speed, and delivery method for instructing information is paramount. If you recall in the Schwan case, not only did Schwan quickly communicate instructing information to its consumers it also selected the richest medium—face-to-face communication—to do so. Interestingly, a sloppy effort at communicating instructing information may cause stakeholders to attribute responsibility for a health crisis to the very agency that is acting altruistically to supply information to stakeholders. For example, the Federal Emergency Management Agency (FEMA) has been excoriated for its reactions during Hurricane Katrina. FEMA did not cause the flood, but stakeholders (and critics) perceived their behavior in reacting to the risk as having exacerbated the crisis.

In the *Journal of Health Communication,* Reynolds and Seeger describe a model for Crisis and Emergency Risk Communication (CERC). This model appears on page 229.

Those who work for health agencies and are involved in risk communication have responsibilities that vary depending on the nature of the risks they face. Readers may

Table 3.1

Model for Crisis and Emergency Risk Communication (CERC)

I. Precrisis (Risk Messages; Warnings; Preparations)
   Communication and education campaigns targeted to both the public and the response community to facilitate:

- Monitoring and recognition of emerging risks
- General public understanding of risk
- Public preparation for the possibility of an adverse event
- Changes in behavior to reduce the likelihood of harm (self-efficacy)
- Specific warning messages regarding some eminent threat
- Alliances and cooperation with agencies, organizations, and groups
- Development of consensual recommendations by experts and first responders
- Message development and testing for subsequent stages

II. Initial Event (Uncertainty Reduction; Self-efficacy; Reassurance)
   Rapid communication to the general public and the affected groups seeking to establish:

- Empathy, reassurance, and reduction in emotional turmoil
- Designated crisis/agency spokespersons and formal channels and methods of communication
- General and broad-based understanding of the crisis circumstances, consequences, and anticipated outcomes based on available information
- Reduction of crisis-related uncertainty
- Specific understanding of emergency management and medical community responses
- Understanding of self-efficacy and personal response activities (how/where to get more information)

III. Maintenance (Ongoing Uncertainty Reduction; Self-efficacy; Reassurance)
   Communication to the general public and to affected groups seeking to facilitate:

- More accurate public understandings of ongoing risks
- Understanding of background factors and issues
- Broad-based support and cooperation with response and recovery efforts
- Feedback from affected publics and correction of any misunderstandings/rumors
- Ongoing explanation and reiteration of self-efficacy and personal response activities (how/where to get more information) begun in Stage II
- Informed decision making by the public based on understanding of risks/benefits

IV. Resolution (Updates Regarding Resolution; Discussions about Cause and New Risks/New Understandings of Risk)
   Public communication and campaigns directed toward the general public and affected groups seeking to:

- Inform and persuade about ongoing clean-up, remediation, recovery, and rebuilding efforts
- Facilitate broad-based, honest and open discussion and resolution of issues regarding cause, blame, responsibility, and adequacy of response
- Improve/create public understanding of new risks and new understandings of risk as well as new risk avoidance behaviors and response procedures
- Promote the activities and capabilities of agencies and organizations to reinforce positive corporate identity and image

V. Evaluation (Discussions of Adequacy of Response; Consensus About Lessons and New Understandings of Risks)
   Communication directed toward agencies and the response community to:

- Evaluate and assess responses, including communication effectiveness
- Document, formalize, and communicate lessons learned
- Determine specific actions to improve crisis communication and crisis response capability
- Create linkages to precrisis activities (Stage I)

find it valuable to consider some excerpts from an interview with Jason Kravitz that appears below. Kravitz is the communication director for Direct Relief International, an organization involved in communicating information to health programs in areas "affected by natural disasters, wars and famine."[11]

> *How does the relief effort start? Do you wait to hear from the*
> *affected area or self-initiate?*
>> We initiate contact immediately. Whoever hears about the emergency
>> first starts the wheels spinning for us. I think it makes sense that
>> if Santa Barbara was affected by a disaster, health professionals
>> would be scrambling already. We do the same; we call immediately.

> *Does the communication structure change when a disaster occurs?*
>> Communication structure is a work in progress. Normally, [the head]
>> lays out the assignments for everyone in the departments, like "contact
>> this person or contact Reuters," and then directors branch out . . .
>> Essentially, after you have those initial tasks allocated, everyone goes off and does his
>> or her thing. The Operation's warehouse was being renovated when Katrina hit, yet
>> they were so efficient, we shipped out over 15 tons or US$24 million
>> worth of medical products. It works out so well that once we find the
>> needs and the partner, we can move forward. . . .

> *What is the most common method of communication in an*
> *emergency?*
>> Both phone and email are the most frequently used mediums, but it
>> really depends on necessity and also on the nature of the program. It
>> has been 10 months after the tsunami in Southeast Asia, and they
>> have allocated over US$7 million in cash grants toward various
>> redevelopment projects and to create an infrastructure. Sometimes
>> these improvements aren't immediate, so phone needs aren't met.
>> You'd be surprised that they have the Internet in very rural places.
>> They may not have clean water, but they have the Net. But actually, I
>> think that the phone correspondence happens more often internationally
>> than domestically.

VALUES OF CRISIS COMMUNICATION?

Is there anything positive about what happened in Bhopal? Are there values associated with crises?

While it might seem that crises are to be avoided, and indeed, it is wise to attempt to avoid them—crises may have value that transcends the notion of a silver lining in all things. The residual effects of crisis can be very positive.

Meyers and Holusha write that as a result of crisis "Heroes are born, change is accelerated, latent problems are faced, people are changed, new strategies evolve, new warning systems are developed, [and] new competitive edges appear."[12] Nothing can ever make what happened at Bhopal positive. Organizations are far better off if they never have to deal with even relatively minor crises. However, a review of the values Meyers and Holusha identify indicates that there can be substantive advantages of crises.

HEROES ARE BORN

Crises can result in the emergence of leaders. Leaders are important for organizations and a residual effect of crises may be to identify emerging leaders who otherwise might not have been identified and promoted to important positions. Alfred Schwan and Aaron Feuerstein were already chief executives of their respective companies, but Feuerstein became a national figure because of his behavior during the Malden Mills crisis. It was almost 100 years ago, but David Sarnoff—subsequently referred to as "the General" when he led the National Broadcasting Company—rose to fame (at least according to apocrypha) because of his broadcasting heroism during the Titanic disaster of 1912. Sarnoff was working for the Marconi Wireless Telegraph Company when signals came in regarding the Titanic and, at least according to legend (some historians dispute Sarnoff's claim), worked for seventy-two consecutive hours relaying information about the tragedy.

CHANGE IS ACCELERATED

What might have taken months or years to process through a bureaucratic system can race right through the organization's sanctioning process when there is a crisis. On February 23, 2009, an economist on a National Public Radio program was discussing the world economic crisis. His comment on the value of crisis was succinct. "Crisis is an accelerant," he said.

LATENT PROBLEMS ARE FACED

Crises force an organization to address what were latent problems. In addition, crises can help an organization identify peripheral issues that might have created other disasters. This can result in actions to preempt the development of problems and preclude crises.

PEOPLE ARE CHANGED

There is no guarantee but it is possible that people will change for the better. Crises force people to find strengths in themselves that they may not have known they possessed. Crises can accelerate the process of self-actualization.

NEW STRATEGIES EVOLVE, NEW WARNING SYSTEMS ARE DEVELOPED

In the aftermath of a crisis an organization is likely to create crisis communication teams if they did not have them previously, task forces to deal with issues related to the crisis, and communication networks that could alert management of impending disasters. For example, after the Red River flood in 1997, which devastated areas of North Dakota, Minnesota, and Manitoba, a task force was created to address future natural disasters. The publication *The Next Flood: Getting Prepared* was a result of their efforts.[13]

NEW COMPETITIVE EDGES APPEAR

The result of all the activity discussed above is that the company is stronger than its rivals because of having lived through the crisis. The adage, "that which does not kill us makes us stronger" is applicable to organizations that have faced crisis.

Murphy writes that crises act as "bifurcation points that permanently redefine an organization in a new and unexpected light."[14]

It might be valuable to take a second look at the information in Chapter 3 pertaining to chaos theory, after having read this section. Some of the foundational assumptions of chaos theory are relevant to the idea that crises can have substantive value.

POLITICAL VALUES

Politicians have used crisis at times to allow them to make decisions they believe to be in the best interests of a country. Those who believe in democracy and the requirement that stakeholders be guaranteed "significant choice" to assess the responsibility of organizations and their leaders, will likely question whether the act of creating crisis for this purpose is correctly labeled a value.

Nevertheless, organizations and politicians have used crisis toward this end and to them, at least, a crisis has value. Richard Cherwitz discusses a specific incident in which President Lyndon Johnson created a crisis and used it to change the course of action in the country.[15] President Johnson had not been a proponent of escalating the Vietnam war when he ran for president in 1964—and indeed had ridiculed his Republican opponent, Barry Goldwater for supporting escalation. Yet as time went on Johnson became a believer in the need to escalate U.S. involvement in the war.

According to many historians, the 1964 Tonkin Gulf incident did not occur as described by the president.[16] Johnson used the incident to request and subsequently gain from Congress support to escalate U.S. involvement in the conflict. By describing the alleged event in a nationally televised address, Johnson persuaded the public and, significantly, Congress to pass the Tonkin Gulf Resolution, which gave the president great latitude to increase military involvement in the war.

For students of crisis communication, the Tonkin Gulf incident and resolution suggests how a politician or any leader can create a crisis to justify behaviors that otherwise would not be condoned. Johnson, ostensibly, was against escalation. How could he change his public position without appearing to equivocate? How could he—in the vernacular of political discourse—not appear to be "flip-flopping" on the issue? How could he gain voters' support for a stance that he had, only months before, ridiculed an opponent for endorsing. He could do so by fabricating or mischaracterizing an incident in the Tonkin Gulf suggesting that the United States had no recourse but to defend itself against unscrupulous actions taken by the enemy. In this way, crisis was used and could be seen as having merit because—as indicated in the title of Cherwitz's article—it allows leaders to "mask inconsistencies."[17]

LEADERSHIP AND CRISIS

President Johnson's behavior with the Tonkin Gulf Resolution and, some contend, President Bush's comments that expedited U.S. involvement in Iraq lead us to consider the power of leadership in crisis communication.

In his book, *Where Have All the Leaders Gone?* ex-Chrysler CEO Lee Iacocca rants about the sad quality of leadership as it relates to crises. Consider his remarks below.

> Am I the only guy in this country who's fed up with what's happening? Where the hell is our outrage? We should be screaming bloody murder! We've got a gang of clueless bozos steering our ship of state right over a cliff, we've got corporate gangsters stealing us blind, and we can't even clean up after a hurricane much less build a hybrid car. But instead of getting mad, everyone sits around and nods their heads when the politicians say, "Stay the course."
>
> Stay the course? You've got to be kidding. This is America, not the damned "Titanic." I'll give you a sound bite: "Throw all the bums out!"
>
> You might think I'm getting senile, that I've gone off my rocker, and maybe I have. But someone has to speak up. I hardly recognize this country anymore.
>
> The most famous business leaders are not the innovators but the guys in handcuffs. While we're fiddling in Iraq, the Middle East is burning and nobody seems to know what to do. And the press is waving "pom-poms" instead of asking hard questions. That's not the promise of the "America" my parents and yours traveled across the ocean for. I've had enough. How about you?[18]

Iacocca elaborates on nine Cs of leadership, with crisis being the first.

> The Biggest "C" is Crisis! Leaders are made, not born. Leadership is forged in times of crisis. It's easy to sit there with your feet up on the desk and talk theory. Or send someone else's kids off to war when you've never seen a battlefield yourself. It's another thing to lead when your world comes tumbling down.
>
> On September 11, 2001, we needed a strong leader more than any other time in our history. We needed a steady hand to guide us out of the ashes. A hell of a mess, so here's where we stand. We're immersed in a bloody war with no plan for winning and no plan for leaving.
>
> We're running the biggest deficit in the history of the country. We're losing the manufacturing edge to Asia, while our once-great companies are getting slaughtered by health care costs.
>
> Gas prices are skyrocketing, and nobody in power has a coherent energy policy. Our schools are in trouble. Our borders are like sieves. The middle class is being squeezed every which way. These are times that cry out for leadership. But when you look around, you've got to ask: "Where have all the leaders gone?" Where are the curious, creative communicators? Where are the people of character, courage, conviction, omnipotence, and common sense? I may be a sucker for alliteration, but I think you get the point.
>
> Name me a leader who has a better idea for homeland security than making us take off our shoes in airports and throw away our shampoo? We've spent billions of dollars build-

ing a huge new bureaucracy, and all we know how to do is react to things that have already happened.

Name me one leader who emerged from the crisis of Hurricane Katrina. . . . Everyone's hunkering down, fingers crossed, hoping it doesn't happen again. Now, that's just crazy. Storms happen. Deal with it. Make a plan. Figure out what you're going to do the next time. . . .

Name me a government leader who can articulate a plan for paying down the debt, or solving the energy crisis, or managing the health care problem. The silence is deafening. But these are the crises that are eating away at our country and milking the middle class dry.

I have news for the gang in Congress. We didn't elect you to sit on your duffs and do nothing and remain silent while our democracy is being hijacked and our greatness is being replaced with mediocrity. What is everybody so afraid of? That some bonehead on Fox News will call them a name? Give me a break. Why don't you guys show some spine for a change?

Had enough? Hey, I'm not trying to be the voice of gloom and doom here. I'm trying to light a fire. I'm speaking out because I have hope—I believe in America. In my lifetime, I've had the privilege of living through some of America's greatest moments. I've also experienced some of our worst crises: The "Great Depression," "World War II," the "Korean War," the "Kennedy assassination," the "Vietnam War," the 1970's oil crisis, and the struggles of recent years culminating with 9/11.

If I've learned one thing, it's this: "You don't get anywhere by standing on the sidelines waiting for somebody else to take action."[19]

How important is leadership in crisis situations? In the first chapter of the book, five foundational tenets of crisis communication were cited. My hope is that these will stick with readers and that the principles, theories, and cases discussed in this book have reinforced these tenets. As a review and as it relates to leadership, let us reconsider these five points.

1. Crises are inevitable. Crisis communicators can and must acknowledge the inevitability of crises and plan for them before they occur.
2. In case after case, transparent and honest communication has been proven to be a key to effective crisis communication.
3. When in doubt follow a golden-rule approach.
4. An organization's culture can determine crisis communication success.
5. Crisis communication requires training and skill sets that even bright executives may not possess.

Can a leader facilitate preparatory crisis communication activities including the skills training of organizational representatives? Can leaders be genuine champions of a culture that reveres transparency and consideration for stakeholders? Is leadership central to the crisis communication effort?

The answer to these questions is clearly yes. A good way to reinforce this point is to consider prior jobs you have had and the leaders of the organizations. Were these people capable of undermining a crisis communication effort? Were they capable of facilitating it? In the face of a Schwan crisis, would they have done the right thing, or somehow spent their time imagining how to extricate themselves from the situation?

Edgar Schein writes, "When an organization faces a crisis, the manner in which leaders and others deal with it creates new norms, values and working procedures and reveals important underlying assumptions."[18]

Lee Iacocca's rant suggests he believes that contemporary leaders' behaviors create norms and values that will undermine organizations.

Most readers of this book will likely be leaders at some point. Some of you may currently be leaders. You may not own Schwan's or be CEO of Union Carbide, but you may have your own business, manage many others, head a civic organization, and/or lead a family. Even classroom teachers are leaders of sorts within the confines of the classroom. If one point has been made clearly in these pages it is that crises are inevitable. Some have greater ramifications than others. The Peanut Corporation of America's crisis certainly affected more persons than, perhaps, a crisis you might endure when you manage a group of employees in your workplace. Yet every crisis requires effective communication and the courage to communicate in a way that is in the best interests of all. I trust these pages have made it clear that in both the long run and the short run, crisis communication requires knowledge, planning, intelligence, and courage.

Where do you go from here?

Apply the Principles

In the first chapter of the book you were asked to complete an exercise that essentially represented a crisis communication plan. Sixteen minicases were presented. You were asked to identify stakeholders, select messages to relay to the stakeholders, and identify methods used to communicate these messages.

This final "Apply the Principles" exercise, asks you to consider the information from this course and create a similar crisis communication plan. If possible in your class, this exercise should be done in teams since crisis communication activity is often done in teams.

- Identify an organization with which you are familiar.
- Describe a crisis that could affect your organization (or one that has already occurred).
- For this crisis:
  - Identify the internal and external stakeholders
  - List the nuggets that would go to these stakeholders
  - Select the best method for communicating these messages
  - Determine the sequencing for the messages.
    - For example, would external group A receive a message before internal group B?
- List what you imagine would be the responses to these messages.
- Explain how you would respond to these responses.
- Describe what you would have done proactively to
  - Reduce the likelihood this crisis would surface.
  - Be prepared to address this crisis.

Point/Counterpoint

In this exercise, two positions are presented. The first is consistent with a point made in the chapter. The second is a counterargument. Consider the counsel and counterargument. Then write a one-page position paper identifying your position on the issue.

- **Counsel**—Union Carbide was inefficient in its communication regarding Bhopal. Its leaders did not meet the golden-rule criterion.
- **Counterargument**—This is so unfair. Horrible things sometimes happen. What could they do? They are awakened in the middle of the night, told of the catastrophe, the

leader travels to India, and he is arrested. The fact is that this was a no-win situation. Nothing at all that UCC could have done would possibly have made this right. Sometimes communication is at best a palliative. In this case UCC could do absolutely nothing. Stuff happens.

Summary: A Toolbox

- Union Carbide's Bhopal tragedy was the worst crisis of its kind. Examining the case reinforces key principles in crisis communication that have been addressed in the text.
  - The significance of organizational culture in any crisis plan
  - The need to address crises proactively
  - The importance of transparency and a golden-rule compass for crisis communication efforts
  - The importance of communication skill in delivering the crisis communication effort
- Risk communication is a type of crisis communication. Key crisis communication concepts in risk communication include
  - Instructing information
  - Honoring the account
  - Emotional stability
- There can be value associated with organizational crises, including that
  - New heroes can emerge
  - Necessary change is accelerated
  - Latent problems are faced
  - People can grow qualitatively
  - New methods for preempting crises develop
  - Organizations work on crises proactively
  - New competitive edges appear
  - Some politicians have used crises to facilitate political objectives
- Most readers are likely to be leaders of organizations or units within organizations. The willingness of leaders to communicate appropriately and courageously during crises will be a large factor in the success of their organizations and the leaders themselves.

Exercises and Discussion Questions

1. Assume you are speaking to someone who has not taken this class. How would you explain why crises can be beneficial to organizations?
2. Have you ever been in a situation when risk communication efforts were particularly successful?
3. Is the quality of leadership the most significant factor in determining crisis communication success? Explain.
4. Which of the cases in this book seem most significant in terms of lessons derived from studying them? Why?
5. Assume you are applying for a job in a department of corporate communication. Assume the interviewer asks you to comment on the keys to effective crisis communication. What is your response?

NOTES

1. Steven Fink, *Crisis Management: Planning for the Inevitable* (Cincinnati, OH: Authors Guild, 2002), p. 169.

2. Ibid.

3. Ibid., p. 172.

4. Matthew Seeger, Timothy Sellnow, and Robert Ulmer, *Communication and Organizational Crisis* (Westport, CT: Praeger, 2003), p. 131.

5. Fink, *Crisis Management,* p. 174.

6. LaRue Tone Hosmer, *The Ethics of Management* (Homewood, IL: Irwin, 1987), p. 55.

7. Rene Henry, *You Better Have a Hose if You Want to Put Out the Fire* (Windsor, CA: Gollywobbler Productions, 2000), pp. 18–19.

8. Information on this case comes from several sources. See, for example, Richard Ice, "Corporate Publics and Rhetorical Strategies: The Case of Union Carbide's Bhopal Crisis," *Management Communication Quarterly* 4, no. 3 (October 1991): 341–62.

9. V.T. Covello, "Risk Communication: An Emerging Area of Health Communication Research." In *Communication Yearbook 15,* ed. S.A. Deetz, pp. 359–73 (Newbury Park, CA: Sage, 1992), p. 359.

10. V. Freimuth, H.W. Linnan, and P. Potter, "Communicating the Threat of Emerging Infections to the Public," *Emerging Infectious Diseases* 6, no. 4, http://www.cdc.gov/ncidod/eid/v016n04/pdf/freimuth.pdf, accessed July 24, 2009.

11. Gina Genova, "Crisis Communication Practices at an International Relief Agency," *Business Communication Quarterly* 69, no. 3 (September 2006): 329.

12. G.C. Meyers and J. Holusha, *When It Hits the Fan: Managing the Nine Crises of Business* (Boston: Houghton Mifflin, 1986), p. 28.

13. Timothy Sellnow and Matthew Seeger, "Exploring the Boundaries of Crisis Communication: The Case of the 1997 Red River Valley Flood," *Communication Studies* (Summer 2001): 153.

14. P. Murphy, "Chaos Theory as a Model for Managing Issues and Crises." *Public Relations Review* 22, no. 2 (1996): 95–113; here, p. 106.

15. Richard A. Cherwitz, "Masking Inconsistency: The Tonkin Gulf Crisis," *Communication Quarterly* 28, no. 2 (Spring 1980): 27–37.

16. A description of the Gulf of Tonkin incident can be found in Marilyn Young, *The Vietnam Wars 1945–1990* (New York: Harper Collins, 1991), pp. 116–21. She quotes then deputy attorney general Nicholas Katzenbach as saying that the Tonkin Gulf incident "was an absolute nothing" (p. 120).

17. Cherwitz, "Masking Inconsistency."

18. Lee Iacocca, *Where Have All the Leaders Gone?* (New York: Scribner, 2007), pp. 2–3.

19. Ibid., pp. 11–14.

20. Edgar Schein, *Organizational Culture and Leadership* (San Francisco: Jossey-Bass, 1992), p. 237.

Index

About the Author

Alan Jay Zaremba earned his PhD from the University of Buffalo and his MS and BA from the University of Albany. He has been teaching at Northeastern University in the Department of Communication Studies since 1981. From 1976 until 1981, he was on the faculty at the State University of New York College at Fredonia. Dr. Zaremba is the author of five other books, including *Organizational Communication: Foundations of Business and Collaboration* and *Speaking Professionally: A Concise Guide.* His book on fan subculture, *Madness of March: Bonding and Betting with the Boys in Las Vegas,* was recently published in March 2009. In August 2008, he was the keynote speaker at the 8th Annual International Conference on Knowledge, Culture, and Change in Organisations held at Cambridge University in the United Kingdom. Dr. Zaremba has twice earned Northeastern University's Excellence in Teaching Award, is a recipient of the State University of New York Chancellor's Award for Excellence in Teaching, and in 2001 was one of two alums who received his alma mater's excellence in education alumni award. In addition to his work in the department of Communication Studies, Dr. Zaremba is the academic coordinator for graduate and undergraduate programs in corporate and organizational communication in the University's College of Professional Studies.